THE COMPLETE BOOK OF GREED

THE
COMPLETE
BOOK
OF
GREED

M. HIRSH GOLDBERG

ILLUSTRATED BY RAY DRIVER

THE STRANGE

AND AMAZING

HISTORY OF

HUMAN EXCESS

WILLIAM MORROW AND COMPANY, INC.

NEW YORK

It is the policy of William Morrow and Company, Inc., and its imprints and affiliates, recognizing the importance of preserving what has been written, to print the books we publish on acid-free paper, and we exert our best efforts to that end.

Goldberg, M. Hirsh.
   The complete book of greed : the strange and amazing
history of human excess / M. Hirsh Goldberg.
      p. cm.
   Includes index.
   ISBN 0-688-10614-5
   1. Avarice. I. Title.
BJ1535.A8G65 1994
178—dc20   93-11254
                                                            CIP

Printed in the United States of America

First Edition

1 2 3 4 5 6 7 8 9 10

BOOK DESIGN BY PATRICE FODERO

To
my children

my daughter, Aviva
her husband, Scott
and
their children
(my grandsons, Aryeh and Aharon)

my son Stuart
his wife, Ilana

my son Seth

Each one is worth a million to me.
(Actually, they're priceless.)

CONTENTS

CONTENTS

Greed is good! Greed is right! Greed works!
Greed will save the U.S.A.!
—MICHAEL DOUGLAS,
in his Academy Award-winning
performance as Gordon Gekko in
Wall Street (1987)

Where there is too much,
something is missing.
—LEO ROSTEN, author

PROLOGUE

A teenager who was learning in school about money and ethics in the working world asked his merchant father to explain the term "business ethics."

"Well, son," said the father, "suppose a customer buys a $100 item in my store with a shiny new $100 bill. As he leaves the shop, I suddenly realize he gave me not one but two $100 bills that are stuck together.

"Now it becomes an issue of business ethics. I must ask myself, 'Should I tell my partner?'"

Money. It does strange things to us.

Among the passions, the lust for money is supreme. Unlike sexual lust, the mania for money can be constant and unending. Not even old age assuages it. Age may even increase the interest and concern about money and what it can buy.

And greed seems to be escalating in our day, with many referring to the 1980s as the Decade of Greed, although what came before and after show human nature to be little different in other times.

But what is seemingly different today is both the widespread outburst of greed—from the proliferation of $80,000 autos and $10,000 wristwatches—and the increasing reaction of horror to such needless or overdone displays of consumption.

And what is also different is the growing disparity between the haves—who have even more than before and want still more—and the have-littles and the have-nots—who have increased in numbers but little else.

What is this need fed by greed? Why are some individuals propelled to accumulate ever more money and acquire ever more possessions with that money? And although wealth is not itself a sign of greed, what is done or not done with that wealth often is. In too many instances, people seem driven to amass more money than they can ever intelligently spend—and prove it by making lavish, unintelligent expenditures. The evidence of our times is clear: It is greed at any speed.

This book explores this phenomenon of money lust and the odd ways mankind deals with dollars. It shows the unusual, fascinating, humorous, ironic, and—yes—tragic aspects about greed. Also on display is a gallery of the greedy, along with facts, stories, anecdotes, studies, statistics, and quotes about how humanity has worked for, fought over, and abused money. Here, too, are some of the more unusual psychological aspects of money mania—extending even to those who in their miserliness are unable to properly enjoy their wealth.

And though *The Complete Book of Greed** is certainly not intended to be a self-help book, it looks at some of the ways in which people can put the drive for money and possessions into perspective for a healthier lifestyle. But despite the ability of many to control this major human foible, the message is clear: with mankind, when it comes to material gain, excess marks the spot.

*A word about the title of this work. No book can ever be complete about any subject. The reference to 'complete' in the title marks the author's attempt to cover his topic extensively in a greedy pursuit of having it all—a frustrating and ultimately unachievable goal whether it's in daily living or book writing. The author, though, hopes the result is comprehensive if not complete.

THE
COMPLETE
BOOK
OF
GREED

••

IN PURSUIT OF EXCESS:

THE PLIGHT OF THE GREEDY IN HISTORY

O, Lord, the sin,

Done for the

things there's

money in.

—JOHN MASEFIELD
(1878–1967), poet
laureate of England

Eve and then Adam wanted more. Cain, their son, coveted what his brother Abel had—and got branded for life for his murderous greed. The pharaohs built massive burial crypts called pyramids and filled them with all manner of gold in hopes of literally taking it with them.

Babylonian emperors, Roman caesars, Spanish monarchs, French kings, English royalty, Russian czars, Persian shahs—they all pursued extravagant lifestyles and built costly monuments to themselves that eventually led to their demise or their country's dissolution. Gold and silver proved to be very precious metals to these leaders, but their subjects have proven to be no less enthralled. Diamonds and furs, gilded mansions and glistening pearls, sumptuous banquets and sleek yachts—all have fascinated all manner of mankind through the ages, and the lustful, mindless, often self-destructive pursuit of these luxurious items has been fueled by greed.

17

Avariciousness has been with humanity since the beginning of time. Greed is considered one of the seven deadly sins. Harvey Cox, a theologian at Harvard University, has pointed out that "virtually every religious tradition I know of agrees" that greed is to be opposed. "The Hebrew prophets were intense about it, and there's sharp expression in the Gospels."

Even so, the intriguing aspect about greed is that it fosters numerous reactions. Some religious leaders, for instance, have even found redeeming factors in the pursuit of wealth. Bishop Lawrence, the leader of the Episcopal Church at the turn of the century, proclaimed in a now famous statement: "Godliness is in league with riches; it is only to the moral man that wealth comes." Of course, at the time one of Bishop Lawrence's parishoners in his New York congregation was the wealthy financier J. P. Morgan. The early America of Puritan times was also enamored of the accumulation of worldly possessions, terming it a sign of grace. "The love of property to a certain degree seems indispensable to the existence of sound morals," declared the president of Yale in 1795. But still, greed— unbridled, covetous, grasping—has always been seen as corrupting.

Although the avaricious can be found in all periods, some ages have erupted with more widespread greed than others—such as the Gilded Age in the America of the latter part of the nineteenth century, the Roaring Twenties in the early part of this century, and the Decade of Greed, as it is now widely referred to, of the 1980s. Interestingly, with such conspicuous displays of consumption have usually come reactions in the following decades, as can be seen in the economic downturn in the America of the 1890s, the stock market crash of 1929 followed by the Depression in the 1930s, and the recession and belt-tightening of the 1990s. It is as though the excesses that fuel greed—and that in turn greed feeds—lead eventually to a shaky economic situation, which in turn creates a reaction of shame and sanity that counterbalances greediness.

We begin our excursion into how greed affects so much of our lives by looking at various occasions in history when this compulsion has been an important factor.

The Rulers Who Tried to Take It with Them:
The Pharaohs and Their Pyramid Scheme

"At first I could see nothing . . . but presently, as my eyes grew accustomed to the light, details of the room within emerged slowly from

When King Tut's 3,300-year-old tomb was discovered in 1922, it revealed a sumptuous display of gold treasures. As with the other pharaohs who tried to take it with them, King Tut had a gilt complex.

the mist, strange animals, statues and gold—everywhere the glint of gold."

This is how Howard Carter, a British archaeologist, writes about his discovery in 1922 of what has been called one of the greatest archaeological finds ever made—the 3,300-year-old tomb of a pharaoh called Tutankhamen, better known to the modern world as "King Tut."

It was on November 4, 1922, after trying since autumn of 1917 to locate the tomb of the only ruler from the great eighteenth and nineteenth Dynasties not to be identified, that Carter finally discovered Tutankhamen's tomb in Egypt's Valley of the Kings. Although he had long believed that Tutankhamen's burial place was in this vicinity, in an area between the tombs of Ramses VI and Ramses IX, Carter was running out of financial support and energy when he made a "last despairing effort" that resulted in "a discovery that far exceeded our wildest dreams."

Tutankhamen's small underground tomb had been largely untouched since it was sealed in the fourteenth century B.C. with the young leader's mummified body and possessions. When opened, his tomb was found to contain several chambers and a burial crypt filled with a stunning array of solid gold, gold-embossed, gold-sheathed, and gold-inlaid treasures. The gold coffin alone weighed 243 pounds. Other treasures included hundreds of such objects as furniture (beds, couches, chairs), art pieces, vessels, statues, vases, walking sticks, even chariots. In typically pharaoh fashion, everything had seemingly been placed with the dead ruler to accompany him on his "trip" into the next life.

The findings electrified the world at the time of discovery and have continued to fascinate ever since. Millions of people have viewed touring exhibits of the King Tut artifacts in museums around the world and have visited the Egyptian Museum in Cairo to see the Tutankhamen collection, considered among that museum's major glories.

Despite the magnificence of the treasures found to be buried with him, Tutankhamen was not a major pharaoh, as can be seen from the fact that he was not buried in an imposing tomb or pyramid, nor did he rule very long. After he came to the throne at the age of nine, he served only nine more years, dying at the age of eighteen.

The reason he has made such an impression on today's world is that his was one of the few tombs left largely intact over the centuries. Although there was evidence that King Tut's tomb had been invaded in the first few years after completion, it seems to have been overlooked and forgotten thereafter, while the pyramids and the tombs housing other pharaohs have been repeatedly plundered and vandalized by treasure hunters. If, then, we marvel at the gold and sumptuous trappings stored with King Tut, we can only guess at the fantastic treasures that had been placed with those major pharaohs buried in the pyramids or more imposing tombs.

The pyramids can be seen as monuments to the mania to have and to hold possessions forever. Although built as funeral crypts to preserve the body and prepare for an afterlife, the pyramids were also sturdy storehouses for material goods. Pharaohs wanted to make certain that the best things in this life could go with them into the next life. The means by which they hoped to accomplish this—the method by which they tried to preserve and protect their possessions—was the construction of some of the most massive structures the world has ever seen.

Indeed, the pyramids are so large that in some cases they sit astride thirteen acres of land large enough to cover ten football fields, contain as many as two million stone blocks weighing an average of 2.3 metric tons, and soar high enough to be taller than a modern forty-eight-story skyscraper. Taking as much as twenty years apiece to build, there are sixty-nine pyramids still in existence. The great pyramids at Giza are justly known as one of the Seven Wonders of the Ancient World.

The pyramids, then, are a reminder of how ancient an impulse greed is and how long we have, as human beings, wished very much not only that we could have it all in this life, but that we could even take it with us to the next.

◆◆◆

EVEN 4,400 YEARS AGO, THEY KNEW THE PROBLEM

"Beware an act of avarice; it is a bad and incurable disease."

—PTAHHOTEP
Twenty-fourth century B.C.
(from *The Literature of Ancient Egypt*)

◆◆◆

The Explorers:

Was Greed the Driving Force?

It has been called the Great Age of European Discovery. Starting in the 1400s, a burst of exploration took hold among the nations of Europe that would last two hundred years and change the course of history. So great was the drive to discover new worlds that the existing one was altered forever.

Historians have pondered why such activity on such a scale took place at that time. Some have said it was the desire to spread Christianity and convert the heathens. Others have noted that it was the ability to build larger ships that could undertake longer voyages and transport bigger loads. But the most widely accepted theory is that most of the explorations were driven by the desire to make money trading with the East or extract gold and valuables from lands encountered in the effort.

The need to find shorter or alternate routes to the East became paramount after 1453, when the Turks conquered Constantinople, thereby cutting off Europe's access to Eastern sources of spices, silks, and other valuables. Fueling this interest in the East and the desire to trade with the countries located there were such enticing reports of wealth and luxury as Marco Polo's account of his life with Kublai Khan, the Mongol emperor of China. Written a century before the 1400s began, *Description of the World* told of Polo's travels throughout China, Ceylon, India, Persia, and central Asia from 1271 to 1295. As had his father and uncle before him who had spent ten years in China, Polo amassed a huge fortune from his experience.

So while Columbus in 1492 attempted to go westward in belief that this was a shorter route to the East, Vasco da Gama in 1497 went southward and rounded Africa on his way to India. In 1519, Ferdinand Magellan, believing as Columbus that the best way to the East was west but that one had to go farther south than Columbus had, began a voyage that would take him around the tip of South America and eventually around the world. Then the race was on to explore the lands encountered by these and other adventurers. And what was propelling them was the sentiment expressed by Columbus upon his return to Spain after his first voyage: "The gate to the gold and pearls is now open."

Ironically, Columbus did not find much gold or pearls himself, though he looked for them mightily (he thought he had found them when he later encountered natives wearing gold ornaments and thereby came to call the land Costa Rica, which means "rich coast" in Spanish but the Costa Rica of then and of today is one of the poorest lands mineralwise in Latin America).

But other explorers did begin to find gold in the New World, which served to draw numerous greedy adventurers. Hernando Cortés, leading Spanish forces in search of wealth, encountered the Aztec Indians in Mexico in 1521 and soon destroyed their civilization for their gold. Francisco Pizarro, exploring the western coast of South America in the 1530s, devastated the Incas in Peru and plundered their wealth.

Soon the lure of gold was fed by legends about the existence in South America of El Dorado, Spanish for "the gilded one." This term was first applied to the king or chief priest of a South American tribe said to have such enormous wealth that he would cover himself with gold dust every morning. (Such a legend may have been based on a ceremony of the Chibcha Indians in which the chief was sprinkled with gold dust at an annual religious festival and who then threw a sacrifice of gold into a lake.) It was also applied to a legendary city (called Manoa or Omoa) and a kingdom, both of which were said to be on the Amazon River and to possess great amounts of gold and gems.

A number of Spanish explorers actually conducted expeditions to find the king, the city, or the kingdom. In 1531, Diego de Ordaz undertook one such expedition, prodded in part by his lieutenant, who claimed to have been saved from a shipwreck and taken to Omoa, where El Dorado greeted him. Other journeys were undertaken in 1540–1541 by Francisco Orellana (who went over the Andes and down the Amazon), in 1541–1545 by Philipp von Hutten, and in 1569 by Jiménez de Quesada. Even Sir Walter Raleigh, in 1595, tried to find El Dorado, and he described Manoa as a city on what he called Lake Parima in Guiana. All of these expeditions failed, including Raleigh's—who had the added problem that his lake, which was made a part of English and other maps, was later proved to be nonexistent.*

But the legend of El Dorado was not the only one enticing explorers to look for gold in the New World. Another concerned a tale of seven cities—they were called the Seven Cities of Cíbola—in what is now the southwestern United States said to possess great wealth from gold and

---

*Today the legend of El Dorado lives on in our language as "any fabulously rich place." Or, spelled as Eldorado, it serves as the name for a line of luxury Cadillac automobiles.

23

gems. In 1540, Francisco Vásquez de Coronado, the Spanish governor of Mexico, was guided by a Moorish slave named Estevánico, who had heard the stories, to look for the cities in what was to become New Mexico and Arizona. With a force of three hundred Spaniards and several hundred Indians, Coronado searched for the cities and for gold, but found only modest pueblos, herds of buffalo, and more Indians. He and a band of followers eventually covered large areas of the Southwest, reaching the Colorado River, crossing the Great Plains, and discovering parts of the Rio Grande, Kansas, and the Continental Divide. A segment of his party discovered the Grand Canyon.

While the lust for gold extended the dominion of mankind, it also left death and devastation, as in the case of the Aztecs and the Incas, in its wake. One more vivid example involves the Spanish explorer Hernando de Soto, who for four years, from 1539 to 1542, searched for gold in what is now the southeastern United States. Even though he had helped Pizarro conquer the Incas and had returned to Spain with a fortune worth more than $4 million, he became excited by reports of wealth in Florida, which had been described to him as a "land of gold." As a result he returned to the New World in 1538 as governor of Cuba and then, in 1539, with a force of 620 men, 123 horses, and four ships, began exploring Florida. In his quest for riches, he eventually pushed himself and his men through not only Florida, but what is now Georgia, South Carolina, North Carolina, Tennessee, Alabama, Mississippi, Arkansas, and Louisiana. On May 8, 1541, he became the first white man to cross the Mississippi River.

But throughout, de Soto was looking for gold and finding none along the way. Although credited as being the first to explore this area of the New World, he hardly basked in his discoveries but was left frustrated at not finding another fortune.

De Soto eventually died of fever in 1542. His men weighted his body and buried it in the Mississippi River so that his corpse could not be found and mutilated.*

---

*Today, de Soto lives on in another memory—an automobile called the DeSoto was launched in 1928 and manufactured in the United States until November 1960. Unlike the Cadillac Eldorado, it is no longer produced.

THE $2 BILLION RANSOM THAT COULD NOT SAVE THE LEADER OF THE INCAS

The greed of the explorers can best be seen in how they dealt with the Incas and their leader, Atahualpa. Under Pizarro and de Soto, the Spaniards, in trying to subdue the Incas, held Atahualpa captive for months until one day, realizing how much his captors were attracted to gold, the head of the Incas proposed to buy his freedom. He offered to have his people over the next two months fill the room in which he was being held with gold and the finest work of Inca goldsmiths. He would also have the adjoining room filled twice with silver. The deal was that he would then be freed immediately.

The Spaniards agreed. As the Incas responded to their leader and filled the room (an area 20 feet long by 17 feet wide by 9 feet high), "the metal value" of this ransom came to total 1,326,539 ounces of gold, which at today's value of approximately $380 an ounce would be worth $500 million. The silver represented close to another $2 million (at $4 an ounce). But it has been estimated that because of the many works of art fashioned out of gold that were deposited in the room, the actual commercial value of the ransom was "nearly four times as great," which means that the Incas offered a ransom of more than $2 billion to free their leader.

So much gold was delivered and so many items were smelted down into gold ingots, which were then shipped back to Spain, that the value of gold in Spain and in the other possessions in the Indies actually dropped. But once the ransom was delivered and even though Pizarro, de Soto, and their men greatly benefited, the Spaniards felt differently about the deal, concerned that a freed Atahualpa would tilt the balance of power back to the Incas. Although some among his captors argued in his behalf, Atahualpa was subsequently brought to trial, accused of various crimes, and sentenced to death by burning at the stake. He was granted one act of clemency: he could convert to Christianity and thereby could die by strangulation.

On Saturday night, August 29, 1533, after converting to Christianity only because he believed that burning would prevent his soul from going back to his Father the Sun, Atahualpa was tied to a stake and a black hood was placed over his head. An executioner, using a wooden rod, then twisted a rope around his neck until he was dead.

The Incas reacted with horror and the episode left a heritage of bad blood between Spain and the Inca descendants. Many of those who had brought about the Inca leader's death were later slain in various ways. And ever afterward, Spain and the Indians of America clashed in violence, with Spain never fully achieving the dominion in the Americas it might have had with a less destructive and avaricious approach to the New World.

Behind Many Great Revolutions Is the Issue of Greed or Taxes—or Both

The one seeming constant of history is that the origin of many revolutions has invariably been that deadliest combination of all for a ruler—his or her prolonged greed followed by the imposition of higher taxes.

From Roman times to the time of the Romanovs, leaders who have pursued lives of unbridled luxury have usually had to take more money from the populace in the form of higher taxes or outright confiscation of property to pay for their elevated lifestyles—or for errors made in greedy grabs for more power. And ironically, as was shown during the last years of czarist Russia and Iran under the shah, what usually ignites the people is not only the greed of the ruler, but any subsequent halfhearted attempt to improve his people's living conditions, since the new whiff of freedom and the possibility for improved living conditions arouses the impatient desire for more.

The American Revolution, for instance, was born not so much in the bosom of freedom-loving colonists as it was in the hearts of angry taxpayers and businesspeople, some of whom turned to smuggling to make money. After all, the American colonists had lived largely free and independent lives and been loyal subjects of the British empire for a hundred years before rumblings of revolution started. What changed all that was the British crown's need for money to pay for its role in the French and Indian War, which although a victory for England, left her deeply in debt.

When England turned to the American colonies for those funds beginning in 1765 with a Stamp Act requiring tax stamps be purchased by the colonists for use on certain business and legal documents as well as on newspapers, almanacs, and even entertainment items such as cards and dice, the native populace protested. In the face of vigorous dissent, the Stamp Act was repealed the following year, but soon the British were back with the Townshend Acts, imposing taxes on such imported goods as paints, lead, glass, paper, and tea.

Now the colonists were really miffed and the cry of "No taxation without representation!" could be heard in the land. Again, the English repealed all the import taxes except for the one on tea, but even this stuck in the craw of the colonists. Within several years, the Boston Tea Party, in which the patriots dumped the offendingly taxed tea into Boston harbor, followed by the British blockade of Boston in reprisal, led inexorably to outright warfare and the American Revolution, in which England lost not only a colony but a source of revenue for royal coffers.

And the heroes of the American Revolution turned out to be largely those who had been most upset by the British taxes and who had tried to profit from circumventing them. These were people like John Hancock, famed today for his large signature on the Declaration of Independence, but before the revolution a businessman who made his fortune by smuggling into America those foreign goods that he could bring in surreptitiously and sell without the high import taxes. It was when England finally cracked down on the increase in smuggling and strongly enforced her trade laws that John Hancock and hundreds, if not thousands, of other smugglers suffered huge losses. Those losses turned Hancock and the others into bitter revolutionaries.

In the ensuing years, as the rift with England widened and a new country was formed, the concepts of liberty and freedom were born, but "We the people," which starts off the U.S. Constitution, could well have been in those early days, "We the smugglers."

✦✦✦

POOR RICHARD'S WEALTH OF WISDOM

"Avarice and happiness never saw each other, how then should they
become acquainted."

—BENJAMIN FRANKLIN,
Poor Richard's Almanac (1734, November)

✦✦✦

The French Revolution Was a Palace Revolt—
and the Revolting Palace Was Versailles

The French Revolution is considered the great turning point in modern history. It not only brought the principles of the American Revolution to France and dramatically altered French government and society, but expanded upon those principles and spread them, inspiring other peoples with the concepts of liberty and equality and igniting widespread opposition to the absolute rule of kings. But the French Revolution, as did the American Revolution, had much of its origins in issues concerning money—in the free spending of it by some and the lack of it among many others.

Before the Revolution, France was one of the richest countries in Europe, but most of the wealth was in the hands of the king and the nobles, while the vast majority of the populace had little. This did not stop the rich from seeking ways to avoid taxes and shifting the tax burden for France's wars onto the shoulders of the poor. France's involvement in the Seven Years' War, followed by its support of the American colonists, had cost it dearly. By the late eighteenth century, France was so deeply in debt that most of its tax revenues were being used just to pay interest on the loans it had taken out, some of which ironically were to help America fight for independence from England and its royal form of government.

With its treasury depleted and more loans almost impossible to obtain, France could only turn to itself by raising revenue through higher taxes. But here, too, the way was blocked—those now paying the taxes, the middle and lower classes, could not pay more. Indeed, conditions had become so strained that bread riots were a frequent occurrence. When the king, Louis XVI, tried to tax the nobles, he was blocked by their refusal to assume more of the burden. Eventually he was forced to convene the Estates General, a body in which all the layers of French society were represented and in which the erosion of the king's powers and the privileged status of the nobles began. The march to revolution, the overthrow of the monarchy, and the beginning of the downfall of the other kings of Europe had begun. As with the American Revolution, the question of taxes had started it all.

But also fueling the discontent of the French people throughout this period was the lavish lifestyle the kings and nobility of France had adopted. The Versailles Palace, twelve miles southwest of Paris, was a vivid symbol of this. Originally a modest hunting lodge, the edifice was transformed by King Louis XIV, the great-grandfather of the king overthrown in the revolution, into one of the most ornate and ostentatious structures in history.

Beginning in 1661, Louis XIV hired the best architects, sculptors, and landscape gardeners of his day and began spending what amounted to $100 million. He extended the palace by creating enormous wings and adding hundreds of rooms, all sumptuously furnished and decorated. Outside, he constructed parks, walks, and fountains, and employed hundreds of gardeners to tend to all the trees, shrubs, plants, and flowers. Over the years, other kings added even more rooms and features until Versailles was more than half a mile long.

This kind of expenditure, as much as its wars, sapped the finances of the kingdom. And what added to the profligacy was the lifestyle at the Palace, which under Louis XVI had become even more wildly lavish. Here life was a whirl of balls and banquets, as well as entertainments and performances. The theater was made into an opera house with gilded sculptures, brocaded velvets, and crystal chandeliers holding 5,000 candles. So public was the extravagance that it led to the weekly *Grand Couvert*, in which Louis XVI, who had become gluttonous, and the rest of the royal family dined on sumptuous meals while visitors were allowed to watch.

What became especially galling to the people was Louis XVI's queen, Marie Antoinette. Her own lavish expenditures led to her being called "Madame Deficit." Every winter she would order twelve gala dresses, twelve formal dresses, and twelve simple dresses, plus linen and muslin dresses for summer, as well as a wide variety of accessories and ornaments. The gala gowns were usually embroidered with either gold or pearls at an estimated cost of 1,000 francs per gown. She also slavishly followed the creative suggestions of her milliner, who seemed to come up with a new color or idea monthly (one such idea that took hold in 1776 was a brownish-purple referred to as *couleur de puce* or "color of the flea"). Her example led women to begin buying such costly clothes that husbands of the day openly complained. She herself was astonished when she learned she had spent 87,594 livres with her favorite milliner, plus 31,000 francs with an English tailor on riding habits, in just one year (and that did not include her expenditures with the court dressmaker).

Marie Antoinette was especially infatuated with jewels. Many she bought on credit, and once, even though she had already exceeded her annual allowance by double, she purchased a pair of bracelets for 200,000 francs, then went to her husband, the king, to ask for a loan to help pay for it (he grudgingly helped her). Another time she swapped some of her diamonds to buy a pair of chandelier diamond earrings for 400,000 francs. When her own mother warned her about her buying habits, she told her not to worry, that it was just a "bagatelle."

She also helped popularize some of the extravagant styles of the day, such as a hairstyle in which the hair was piled at least a foot tall, sprinkled with a pound of powder and pomade, and topped with a coronet on which plumes of feathers, ribbons, flowers, and diamonds were further piled. Such a hairstyle did not stop her from pursuing one of her other interests—dancing—and she spent hours learning different dances and preparing for the balls. Her one guiding principle may have been her response to another caution from her mother about her actions. "I am so afraid of being bored," she explained.

Although many historians do not believe she ever responded to the Paris bread riots by remarking, "Let them eat cake," she was easily associated with that statement because of her frivolous lifestyle. Indeed, Marie Antoinette, who became Queen of France at the age of nineteen and who died on the guillotine at thirty-eight, has become the foremost symbol not only of the excesses of the royal life at Versailles, but of the excesses inherent in the royal form of government.

It was more than fitting, therefore, that it was at Versailles that the Estates General met in 1789 in a session that has come to mark the beginning of the French Revolution—and the beginning of the end for the royal form of government that so often in history was corrupted by the greedy, lavish living of a few on the backs of so many.*

---

*Versailles was also the site for another important historical event—the signing, in the palace's Hall of Mirrors in 1919, of the Treaty of Versailles between the Allies and Germany following World War I. Today Versailles is a national museum, which means that the extravagant self-indulgence and wastefulness of an earlier age is preserved. It also

◆◆

FOOL EMPLOYMENT

"If the rich could hire other people to die for them, the poor could make a wonderful living."

—YIDDISH PROVERB

◆◆

The Robber Barons and "the Gilded Age"

During the second half of the nineteenth century, America became a land of opportunity—but the opportunity was for a relatively small band of people to make a lot of money very fast, then spend it very openly. With the end of the Civil War, with the train opening up the middle and western portions of the continent, with the mining of gold, silver, and coal, with the development of oil, railroading, shipping, banking, and steel—coupled with low to nonexistent taxes and governmental restrictions—those bent on making money at any cost could find a way to do so.

The result was fabulous wealth for people like Rockefeller, Vanderbilt, Mellon, Morgan, Carnegie, Harriman, Astor, Frick, Gould, and others of lesser fame today. But the result was also such appellations for these people as "robber barons" and for the period of 1861 to 1901 to be labeled (by humorist Mark Twain, with little humor intended) as "the Gilded Age."

The greed demonstrated by the robber barons during the Gilded Age helped develop and industrialize the United States and set the stage for the country's entrance onto the world stage of the twentieth century as a superpower. But the greed also propelled these barons into wasteful displays of indulgence to satiate their boredom and created, in this professed land of equality, a moneyed class that sought for itself privilege and profligacy at the expense of others.

Consider these examples of extravagance:

means that turning the place into a tourist attraction was the only way its upkeep and heating bills could be paid.

31

- The head of the Southern Pacific railroad system poured $2 million into building a mansion at 57th Street and Fifth Avenue in New York City, then decided against living there because a rival baron, William H. Vanderbilt, had built a mansion several years before but then had died soon after moving into it.

- An owner of a mine in Nevada moved to New York, paid the most money ever for land in the city (across from St. Patrick's Cathedral on Fifth Avenue), then instructed a decorator to do whatever had to be done to make his new mansion complete. The final decorating bill: $450,000.

- Dinner receptions among New York's social elite were so lavish that during one dessert guests were given cigarettes wrapped in hundred-dollar bills for smoking. Another dinner, given in honor of the host's dog, wound up with the owner presenting the animal with a $15,000 diamond collar.

- One tycoon had a bedstead fashioned out of oak and ebony, then inlaid it with gold, all at a cost of $200,000.

- Servants were of course necessary and socially required (at least two to serve tea and three to serve dinner, dressed in livery, plus a butler), as well as a stable of horses (six to ten for such carriages as an opera bus, one-horse cabriolet, and basket phaeton for the ladies).

- The rich hosted social balls built around ever more ostentatious themes—for example, the coal and gold barons who hosted parties in simulated coal or gold mines, complete with waiters dressed like miners, or the ball held on horseback in a hotel ballroom, with guests in their riding clothes dining on champagne and truffles from a table attached to the horse.

The era was marked by booms and busts, by periods of overheated speculation in which the unscrupulous made fortunes followed by panics in which the unwary lost theirs. Even those shrewd speculators and traders who should have known better made and lost enormous fortunes. One robber baron, Jay Cooke, made so much money as head of the banking house that virtually financed the Union during the Civil War that he built a $1 million mansion in Philadelphia with fifty rooms decorated with three hundred paintings. He eventually went bankrupt in the panic of 1873 (however, a few years later, he scraped together $3,000 for a stake in a small Utah silver mine, which five years afterward he sold for almost $1 million). So much was the Gilded Age marked by greedy grabs for wealth that near the end of the nineteenth century Mark Twain remarked to his friend Joseph Twichell, "Money-lust has always existed, but not in the history of the world was it ever a craze, a madness, until your time and mine."

Who Says War Is Hell?

War has been one of history's most forceful instruments of change. With all its death and destruction, one may wonder how anybody could profit from military conflict. But through the ages, there have been those who, like vultures feeding on carrion, have made money—even fortunes—out of war.

Consider the deadliest war in United States history. During the Civil War, from 1861 to 1865, nearly 530,000 soldiers lost their lives—more Americans than have died in any other war (in comparison, 405,400 died in World War II). And yet here, too, many people profited, including some whose names are well known and admired in American history. In fact, the U.S. Civil War was marked by corruption, payoffs, rampant speculation, shoddy deals, and shoddy merchandise.

One outstandingly greedy grab involved several speculators making huge profits from the purchase and resale of a large number of used but still usable rifles owned by the Union Army. It started when Arthur Eastman paid the War Department $3.50 a rifle, then turned around and sold them for $12.50 each to a Simon Stevens, who then resold all the rifles to the Army—for $22 apiece. The profit realized by the private sector was a whopping 600 percent.

During the height of the war, both sides engaged in illicit trading with the other side. Union soldiers stationed in Memphis freely engaged in the trading of Confederate cotton, buying it from Southerners for resale to Northerners (cotton could be bought in Memphis in 1864 for 20 cents a pound and sold up north for $1.90). A War Department official, sent to investigate, reported that "every colonel, captain, or quartermaster is in secret partnership with some operator in cotton."

Notable leaders of the day were caught up in the frenzy to make money. Abraham Lincoln's first secretary of war, Simon Cameron, was eventually censured by the House of Representatives for allowing his friend, Alexander Cummings, whom he had helped to become a government purchasing agent, to arrange for the buying of unnecessary goods at high prices from business friends (among the items were straw hats and pickles). After also being found to have favored the Northern Central Railroad (controlled by his family) over the Baltimore & Ohio, Cameron was forced to leave his post as head of the War Department.

One way in which fortunes were grabbed was through the production and sale of inferior merchandise to the government. Contractors bent on making money wound up using such flimsy material in the production of uniforms that they would fall apart in the rain. In one instance, a man-ufacturer was found to have offered to the Army a boot with a sole that could not last a half hour of marching before falling off. When confronted with the evidence of his poor work, the manufacturer had an explanation: The boot was made for the cavalry.

Some of the most notable names in American mercantile history made large sums of money during the Civil War by dumping poorly made or outmoded goods on the Union. Cornelius Vanderbilt sold the army rotted transport vessels. Jim Fisk sold shoddy blankets. And J. P. Morgan foisted on the Union forces outdated carbines at exorbitant prices (when the deal was exposed, delaying his payment, Morgan demanded his money—and received it).

As a result of such merchandise rip-offs (it is estimated that one-fifth of all sales to the Army involved fraudulent materials), the New York *Herald* declared, "The world has seen its iron age, its silver age, its golden age, and its brazen age. This is the age of shoddy."

Wall Street also profited handsomely from the Civil War. In 1862, the average value of stock zoomed up 40 percent. In 1864, the dollar value of stock traded in New York climbed from $25 million daily to more than $100 million. One observer noted that speculators drawn into the market had become "frenzied by the general passion for gain."

Stock prices went up with Union victories and down with Union defeats, while the price of gold, the historic hedge against bad times, went up with Union defeats and down with Union victories. One financier noted that a long war meant the possibility of large profits for "every man in Wall Street who is not a natural idiot."

The real winners were those nonidiots in Washington and New York among the politicians and the bankers who had advance political and military information and acted on that inside knowledge. This is how Jay Gould, one of the leading robber barons, first became wealthy. John D. Rockefeller took another tack—he made his initial money from the war's inflated food prices, then took that income to build his oil business.

The profit to be gained during the Civil War can be seen by one statistic. Before the Civil War, there were three millionaires living in New York. At the height of the war, this number had increased to several hundred.

But not everybody was reaping huge or even modest rewards. The average workingman was barely keeping pace with the cost of living. A blacksmith was on the average earning $2 a day by midwar and a laborer $1.25 (both figures representing just a 25-cent increase from the beginning of the war). In contrast, someone like the New York dry goods merchant Alexander Stewart was making $4 million a year and paying just 10 percent in taxes.

Of course, the big losers were the soldiers and citizens on both the Union and Confederate sides who fought, died, or were maimed while all this was going on. After all, a total of one million people were either killed or wounded (with disease actually killing more people than combat) and countless others suffered property damage that along with the expense of waging war drove the cost of the Civil War to an estimated $15 billion (General Sherman alone estimated that on his devastating drive through Georgia he destroyed $100 million worth of property). That disparity alone—between the dead and the high living, between those who lost lives or possessions and those who made money out of the tragedy—made the Civil War era indeed a shoddy, greedy age.*

The Businessman Who Ruined Germany

Adolf Hitler ultimately rode the inflation-shattered Germany of the 1920s into power in the 1930s, attracting an ever-growing number of followers by haranguing that the ravages of that country's hyperinflation were the result of the allies' unfair punitive measures following World War I and the "stab-in-the-back" actions of the Jews for causing Germany to lose the war. And yet, as cited by a close observer of Germany during the 1920s, a German businessman did more by his greedy actions to harm Germany and his fellow Germans than anyone else.

---

*See *Twenty Million Yankees: The Northern Home Front* by Donald Dale Jackson (Civil War Services, Time-Life Books, 1985). What also contributed to the greediness of the Civil War era was that during that vicious conflict money talked as never before. A draft-age man could get an exemption from military service by providing a substitute or paying $300.

George Seldes, a noted journalist who covered Berlin at the time for American newspapers, writes in his memoirs, *Witness to a Century: Encounters with the Noted, the Notorious, and the Three SOBs* (Ballantine Books, 1987), that Hugo Stinnes, known in the early 1920s as Germany's richest person, "was then engaged in business operations that did more to ruin Germany than the actions of any other person, dead or alive." Ironically, while active in the industrial world and before Seldes returned to the United States in 1927 and started writing about him, Stinnes was considered "a symbol of a resurrected Germany."

Seldes met Stinnes when they were fellow residents at the same German hotel, the Adlon, but Stinnes kept mysteriously to himself and it was only later that Seldes was able to learn that during that period Stinnes had become "the greatest looter, the chief destroyer of the German Republic."

What Stinnes did was build a vast industrial empire and then loot it of its hard currency by shipping such sums to foreign banks at a time when inflation-ravaged Germany was desperate for hard currency. Stinnes was the sole owner of coal, iron, and steel companies and owned or had control of sixty-three newspapers. In all, he employed 600,000 people. When inflation hit Germany, he borrowed millions of dollars' worth of marks from the Reichsbank to fund his operations in Germany, then sold what was produced to other countries for dollars and other hard currencies. The money that accumulated from such sales—it reached into the billions of dollars—was then deposited in foreign banks, rather than brought back to Germany to help shore up the devalued German money. Stinnes converted just enough of the foreign money into marks to pay his workers back in Germany, but these marks were often worth half or as little as a tenth of what they were worth at the beginning of the two-week pay period.

But Stinnes did not stop there. He then used his rapidly accumulating foreign hard currency to buy numerous properties within Germany at huge savings—mines, hotels, banks, steamship companies, and real estate. He also began buying companies in Europe and South America. By the time inflation ended in 1923, Stinnes had a personal wealth of billions of dollars and owned more than two dozen coal mines, entire oil fields, refineries, three telegraph companies, more than fifty lighting and heating companies, and several large banks.

"All had been bought with depreciated paper marks—while he kept his hard money abroad," writes Seldes, who points out that what Stinnes did had another impact: "For every cent Stinnes gained this way another German had to take a loss."

And the number of Germans affected was huge. In 1924, a year after the mark was finally stabilized and inflation ended, a study presented to British Parliament estimated that not counting low- and middle-income Germans, inflation had ruined at least one million affluent Germans.

As for Stinnes, notes Seldes, the end of inflation seemed to ruin him. He died in 1924 at fifty-four. As for the vast domain he had built on the backs of his fellow Germans, with no designated or trained successor ready to take control, Stinnes's business world disintegrated within one year.

◆◆◆

TYRANTS ARE MADE BY GREED

"The greatest crimes are caused by surfeit, not by want. Men do not try to become tyrants in order that they may not suffer cold."

—ARISTOTLE,
Politics

◆◆◆

1929—When Wall Street Came Tumbling Down

Greed destroyed countless lives, threw an entire generation into despair, and shaped a decade in United States and possibly in world history when overspeculation, overuse of credit, and shady, corrupt manipulation of prices led to the stock market crash of 1929 and the Great Depression of the 1930s.

During the 1920s, especially the years of 1928 and early 1929, there was such a run-up of stocks that the atmosphere from Main Street to Wall Street amounted to almost a panic of buying. As one financier later noted in looking back at the times, the American public was "determined to speculate . . . determined that every piece of paper would be worth tomorrow twice what it was today."

The Crash of '29 was the culmination of such widespread speculation that shoeshine boys and elevator operators were giving stock tips to businesspeople, wives were pocketing house money to buy shares, corporate executives were boosting company values in questionable ways, and all levels of stock market players were borrowing to buy stocks (stocks in 1929 could be bought on 10 percent margin, unlike today when it takes at least 50 percent).

As a result, the run-up in stock prices was often dramatic. First National Bank of New York, one of the premier bank stocks, zoomed $500 in one day to a per-share price of $7,900 (giving the chairman of the bank a profit of $2 million an hour for each of the day's five hours of trading). AT&T stock rose in value by nearly $76 million in one day. RCA stock soared more than 400 points in eighteen months to reach a high of $505 a share. Montgomery Ward went up by more than three hundred points during the same period. American Tobacco surged $38 per share in one day.

But when the Crash came, it came with a resounding thud, the result in large part of an economic reality that could not sustain the greedy illusion of stock players and of overborrowing from brokers that had reached the dramatic level of $7.8 billion. The fall in stock prices actually began September 3, 1929, when the Dow Jones industrial average reached its then record height of 452. The dramatic decline started on October 24 (Black Thursday) and picked up speed on Monday, October 28, when values dropped by an estimated $14 billion on the New York Stock Exchange, but the collapse came the next day, October 29, when in five tumultuous hours of trading stock prices fell by an amount equal to what the United States had spent on World War I. Before the initial slide ended two weeks later on November 13, the New York Stock Exchange lost more than a third of its value from its high point in September ($30 billion out of $80 billion) and losses on all U.S. exchanges totaled nearly $50 billion.

The severity of the drop in the market and in the value of people's fortunes can be seen in the following statistics:

- RCA stock eventually dropped from 505 to 28
- General Electric lost 128 points from its high
- AT&T plunged 106 points from its earlier peak of 310
- Blue Ridge Corporation, an investment trust that had opened at 100 in August, sank to 3 (it eventually went to 63 cents)
- General Motors eventually went to 8
- Chrysler stock tumbled 90 points
- U.S. Steel dropped 240 points

And the market just kept on sliding downward, not reaching its low until July 8, 1932, when the Dow Jones industrial average was just 58. Along the way, the Crash wiped out fortunes and left millions homeless and destitute. Initially the poor were hurt as they lost jobs as servants to the now formerly wealthy, then workers were hurt as companies cut back or closed down in the face of reduced demand. Since so many of the shares on Wall Street had been bought on margin, the drop in stock values wiped out many of the overly extended wealthy and the middle class yearning to be wealthy. Homes, furnishings, autos, and luxury items purchased on credit on the expectation that rising stock values or profits would take care of future payments were now unaffordable and a drain on the populace's ability to purchase newly produced goods. With less revenues from taxpaying citizens, governments across the country cut staffs and their own spending, contributing further to job losses.

The result was an economy that spiraled downward, not only in the United States but in Europe, causing in the wake of its misery the conditions that contributed to the rise of Nazism and the coming of another world war. Between 1929 and the end of 1931, more than 4,000 U.S. banks failed. The production of factories eventually fell by half, automobile manufacturing by 80 percent, and national income by more than 50 percent.

By 1933, the unemployment rate reached 25 percent (which meant that nearly 13 million people could not find work—one million in New York City alone) and those who could find work found that the average worker's weekly paycheck, which had been $25.03 in 1929, had shriveled to $16.73.

In many ways, the nation continued to suffer the economic damage from the excesses of the 1920s until war loomed on the horizon and America had to put its people back to work to wage and win World War II. Not until the early '40s did the United States finally emerge from the Great Depression, although many of the generation who lived through its worst times would years later still remember and be affected by the belt-tightening and job insecurity of those days.

But a new generation of Americans would grow up largely ignorant or indifferent about that era of stock market greed until they themselves encountered their own record-setting 500-point stock market drop in October 1987, followed by a severe recession as the Decade of Greed of the 1980s ended.*

---

*Two of the best books on the Crash of 1929 and a resource for some of the statistics and incidents of greed cited here are *1929: The Year of the Great Crash* by William K. Klin-

Max Heiliger and the Holocaust of Greed

The Nazis said they did not want to associate with anything Jewish, but somehow the Nazis did not mind taking and using Jewish possessions. While the Holocaust was an example of racial and religious hatred gone wild, it was also a witness to greed on an obscene scale.

The extermination camps were not only a way to facilitate the killing of Jews; they were also a way to strip Jews of their money and valuables. Cash, jewelry, watches, clothing, furs—they were all systematically taken from the doomed victims either before they entered the gas chambers or afterward. What more vivid a symbol of the Holocaust is there than the Nazis' extraction of gold from the teeth of gassed Jews while their bodies were still warm?

The process of stealing money and valuables from the Jews began soon after Hitler took power in 1933. Those Jews who tried to leave Germany at that time found they had to sell homes and property at far less than market value, but by 1935 even this prospect was denied them. The Nazis moved at that time to prevent emigrating Jews from taking substantial sums of cash with them. Eventually it was decreed that any Jew leaving the country could only take ten German marks—a sum equivalent to $2.50.

As for those who stayed in Germany until the outbreak of war trapped them, they soon faced deprivation and poverty as the Nazis forced them out of their professions, the arts, and the commercial life of Germany while Aryanizing the ownership of their property for little if any remuneration. Boycotts were instituted as early as April 1933 to keep Germans from buying from Jewish merchants and using Jewish doctors and lawyers. In November 1938, following the "Crystal Night" nationwide pogrom, decrees were issued eliminating German Jews from the economy and assessing the Jewish community with a collective fine of one billion marks. And by the end of 1938, 80 percent of the 39,000 Jewish-owned businesses had been "Aryanized."

With the start of World War II, robbing the Jews escalated as the

gaman (New York: Harper & Row, 1989) and *The Day the Bubble Burst: A Social History of the Wall Street Crash of 1929* by Gordon Thomas and Max Morgan-Witts (Garden City, N.Y.: Doubleday, 1979).

Nazis launched their Final Solution and the Holocaust spun into its frightful madness. Now the object was both the physical and economic destruction of Jewry, not just in Germany, but throughout Europe.

That's when Max Heiliger was created.

Max Heiliger was the name the Nazis gave to a bank account to which they funneled the monies and valuables taken from the Jews sent to the concentration camps. These camps were a Nazi invention not only for killing large numbers of people, but also for enslaving them as free labor and vacuuming from them whatever possessions they still had. After all, Max Heiliger was waiting.

The first step in the scheme was to encourage Jews to bring all their valuables with them for what the Germans promised would be "resettlement." So when the Jews arrived at their deadly destinations they were carrying what was left of their money and valuables, instead of having hidden them, given them away, or spent them in an effort to escape. It was a simple matter for the Nazis to complete the process and plunder their doomed victims soon after arrival.

The extraction of gold from the mouths of the dead was initially begun at the Chelmno death camp and, proven feasible, was then instituted as the first step in body salvage actions at all other camps. At Auschwitz, the SS set up a gold-melting room and, using blowtorches, had the gold melted into molds. As much as 110 pounds of usable gold a day was produced in this way.*

Once the money was collected, the valuables sorted out, and the gold melted down, it was all shipped to the Reichsbank where, under a secret agreement between the SS Commander Heinrich Himmler and the bank's president, Dr. Walther Funk, the booty was deposited to the credit of the SS in the account of "Max Heiliger."

The Reichsbank and Max Heiliger were soon being drowned in a sea of gold watches, gold earrings, diamond wedding rings, silver pocket watches, necklaces, bracelets, pins, even silverware and eyeglass frames. As early as 1942, the bank's directors—always conscious of the profit

*In 1925, a renowned German doctor wrote an article entitled "The Gold of the Dead" in which he advocated the removal of dental gold from corpses, saying it was a waste to let it be buried with the deceased. To the objection that medical personnel would shrink from doing such extractions, he noted that postmortem dissections were accepted. Besides, the easiest way to recover the gold, he wrote, "would be to cremate all corpses." The proposal received much attention in German circles when it first appeared. (The German doctor's proposal for extracting the dental gold of corpses can be found in *Hitler's Death Camps: The Sanity of Madness* by Konnilyn G. Feig [New York: Holmes & Meier, 1979].)

motive—decided to turn the booty into cash by—yes—pawning them at Berlin pawnshops. But by 1944, the pawnshops became overwhelmed by the flood of goods stolen from Jews, and pawnshop owners told the Reichsbank officials they could accept no more items.

What then happened? At the end of the war, the Allies discovered in abandoned mines in Germany some of the Nazis' plunder—an overflow from Max Heiliger's account that could have filled three large vaults in the Frankfurt branch of the Reichsbank.*

Not surprisingly, the Nazis were intent on taking this stolen wealth with them. Evidence exists that in the closing days of the war, in 1945, Martin Bormann, Hitler's deputy, utilized a German submarine operation to transport booty taken at the death camps to Argentina. The Nazis' own records reveal that six U-boats carried across the Atlantic 550,000 ounces of gold, 3,500 ounces of platinum, and 4,638 carats of diamonds, plus gold marks, pounds, dollars, and Swiss francs amounting to millions of dollars, not to mention hundreds of works of fine art.

And this was just part of the hoard. Jewish homes, businesses, and institutions across Europe had been looted throughout the war by advancing German armies. And those who made use of these stolen goods ranged from the common soldier to the führer himself. One example: Hitler's Reich Chancellory used dinnerware taken from a Jew.

The Holocaust has been called a study in tyranny. It is also a study in murderous greed.[†]

---

*A discussion of the "Max Heiliger" bank account can be found in The Rise and Fall of the Third Reich: A History of Nazi Germany by William L. Shirer (New York: Simon and Schuster, 1960).

[†]How much did the Nazis steal from European Jews? In discussions about German reparations following the war, it was estimated that Jewish economic losses totaled $12 billion (in values at that time). West Germany agreed in the 1950s to reimburse the new State of Israel an average of $3,000 per person for the rehabilitation and absorption of 500,000 Jewish victims of Nazi Germany—a sum of $1.5 billion. By December 31, 1968, West Germany had paid out $6 billion to Israel and to survivors and their families as restitution for injuries, loss of property confiscated by the Nazis, and rebuilding of Jewish communal life. Not until the breakup of the Soviet Union did East Germany agree to work out some compensation for property seized in its area. Note that the losses suffered by European Jews were not only those of millions of individuals, but also those of thousands of communities in which synagogues, schools, buildings, libraries, and their contents were either destroyed or taken and utilized by the Germans.

Communism: A Failure in Greed Control

During the twentieth century, an entire political movement, which transformed the face of much of the world and affected the lives of hundreds of millions of people, was based on the concept that the controlled distribution of money and possessions and the end of class differences would promote equality and economic security for all. It was a noble idea, but in actual practice this economic system proved to be a failure on a grand scale.

That system is Communism and at its height it ruled fourteen nations, including one with the largest land area—the Soviet Union—and another with the largest population—China. A third of the world's people lived in countries with a Communist government—a population that exceeded one billion. Even most non-Communist countries have Communist parties, including the United States. But strangely enough, even within Communist countries, only a small proportion of the populace are members of the party—usually no more than 8 percent.

The yearning of a populace to end the great disparity in wealth between the few haves and the many have-nots usually aided a Communist takeover. This was the case in Russia after years under Czarist rule. But even with the leveling of pay and possessions, many people in Communist countries found themselves with less—less freedom and fewer possessions, while their leaders and a privileged few seemed to create their own worlds of more.

The downfall of Communism in the Soviet Union as the 1990s began may be partly due to the inefficiency of Communist government and its failure to provide its people with a modicum of goods and the good life. But also feeding the frustration was the fact that many Communist leaders showed more of a "capitalist" bent for themselves. Indeed, while Communism was supposed to stamp out greed by fostering a classless society in which materialism would be a thing of the past (certainly not like the "money-mad capitalist societies" that were decried as not caring for the worker), the reality was far from this selfless picture.

To see how the great social effort to conquer greed had its own downfall within Communism, consider the case of the longest ruling Communist leader in history.

His name was Enver Hoxha. He ruled Albania, Europe's poorest country, for forty-one years, until his death in 1985. He was a strong supporter of Soviet dictator Joseph Stalin and guided Albania along strict Communist lines.

It was all the more revealing, then, that when in 1991 Hoxha's widow wrote that the family had always lived a simple life, the newspaper *Zëri i Popullit* ("Voice of the People") published a scathing response, reporting that the former Albanian dictator lived in a house with twenty-eight color televisions and twenty-five refrigerators. He also had nineteen telephone lines and ran up telephone bills of hundreds of thousands of dollars—a strange situation in itself since Albania has only a rudimentary domestic phone system and is virtually isolated from the rest of the world.

The Albanian newspaper published the story under the biting headline: "The Hoxha family does not like luxury."

With leaders like that, is it any wonder that Communism, the great experiment to stamp out greed, failed within the same century it was founded?

◆◆

WAS MOSCOW IN THE SPRINGTIME HIS SECOND LOVE?

"Money is my first, last and only love."

—ARMAND HAMMER,

U.S. oil tycoon who was friendly with both American and Soviet leaders during the height of Communist rule and once remarked he preferred Russia to America

◆◆

"Nine Out of Ten Got Screwed in the 1980s":
The Decade When the Rich Got Richer and
the Poor Got More Numerous

More than any other decade of the twentieth century, the 1980s seem to be firmly associated now in the public consciousness with the avaricious pursuit of wealth. After all, this was the ten-year span when Wall Street ran up some of its most dramatic gains (and, if you remember October

1987, most dramatic losses; but in the five years from 1982 to 1987, the Dow Jones index zoomed up 230 percent). It was a decade in which excess marked too many spots—in which paintings were bought for $40 million, in which far too many savings-and-loan executives turned out to be using other people's savings for loans to their own friends and families, in which salaries in frivolous pursuits such as sports escalated to ridiculous heights, in which graft, corruption, and fraud seemed rampant on and off Wall Street, in which the most famous statement of the decade appeared to be the one proclaimed by the stock market manipulator Gordon Gekko character in the movie *Wall Street*: "Greed is good!"

Anthony Sampson in *The Midas Touch: Understanding the Dynamic New Money Societies Around Us* (New York: Dutton, 1990) terms the 1980s "a decade of individual money-making and shifts in the balance of values unprecedented since the nineteenth century." Indeed, the 1980s marked not only the growing wealth of many but the increasing poverty of others. While the top 10 percent increased their incomes by 7 percent, the real incomes of the poorest 40 percent of the U.S. population fell by 3 percent between 1980 and 1984, according to the U.S. census. By the end of the decade the disparity had increased. In early 1991, the Census Bureau reported that the wealth of affluent people grew substantially while other Americans barely kept pace with inflation. From 1984 to 1988, in fact, wealth rose by 14 percent for the nation's most affluent 20 percent of all households (after adjustment for inflation). For others, there was barely any change.

Consider these other statistics collected by the Congressional Budget Office, the Internal Revenue Service, the Tax Foundation, and others:

- The average income of the richest 1 percent of the U.S. shot up from $280,000 in 1980 to $560,000 in 1989.
- While this was going on, the average working family in America saw their annual income fall by as much as $2,000.
- The pay of executives in America's major corporations went up by 149 percent after inflation (the average zoomed from $116,000 to $289,000), while hourly wages in America's major corporations actually decreased by 5 percent after inflation.

As Richard Reeves, the national columnist, noted in commenting on these statistics, "Nine out of 10 people . . . got screwed during the 1980s. The richest 10 percent of the nation got richer and paid fewer taxes. The middle class made less money and paid more taxes. The poor got poorer and there were more of them."

The culprit in all this was seen to be the tax policies and "trickle down" economic theories of President Ronald Reagan. When the studies were done of the 1980s, it was found that Reaganomics had caused a dramatic redistribution of wealth in the United States during the 1980s— a redistribution from the bottom and the middle to the top, according to Reeves. "The money was trickling up, not down. What was trickling down was the lifeblood of Americans who worked with their hands or had to be at their desks at 8 a.m. or 9 a.m. five days a week."

Because of Reagan tax policies, in which rates were cut to stimulate the economy, the richest 1 percent of Americans wound up with their income tax rates lowered by 25 percent. By the end of the decade, on the average, they were paying $40,000 less in income taxes than at the beginning of the decade. However, the median American family was actually paying $400 more in taxes than if there had been no tax reform during those ten years.

Paul Taylor of *The Washington Post* put the situation into perspective when in an article in 1991 he compared what a $1,000 raise would mean to various levels of people in the U.S. in income taxes because of the new tax laws that went into effect during the 1980s.

- An investment banker with $200,000 income: $180 in extra taxes.
- An auto mechanic with $27,000 income: $356.50 in more taxes.
- A self-employed plumber with working wife and joint income of $86,000: $483 in additional taxes.

Because of this redistribution of wealth, as well as the greater ease with which the Decade of Greed enabled the wealthy to get even wealthier, the census was showing that by 1988 there were over a million millionaires in the United States and more than 20,000 households were worth $10 million or more. But the gap between the have-a-lots and others has only widened.

According to surveys undertaken by the Federal Reserve Board, 1 percent of the households in America now hold 33 percent of all personal wealth in the nation.*

The New York Times reported on the widening shift of wealth in the United States in a front-page article on March 5, 1992 ("Even Among the Well Off, the Richest Get Richer/ Data Show the Top 1% Got 60% of the Gain in the 80's Boom").

Indeed, the definition of *rich* is also going up. Lewis Lapham and Michael Thomas, who track such things, now say that to be described as rich today one needs to have assets of at least $20 million. That's the minimum. Anything less just won't do, thanks in large part to the Decade of Greed.

••

A SIGN OF THE TIMES

The degree that is viewed by many college students as the key to opening doors to the business world and the lucrative executive suite is the MBA—Master of Business Administration. With the average starting salary for an MBA graduate reaching $34,000 in the early 1990s, the MBA program is now among the most popular graduate school courses in the country. It was, however, during the 1980s that interest in the degree soared. In fact, approximately half of all the MBA degrees awarded in the history of higher education in America were given out during the decade of the '80s. (Ironically, because so many MBAs were awarded in the 1980s, it was later reported that among employers the degree began losing its luster in the 1990s.)

••

The Decade of Greed Was Also the Decade of Giving

The decade of the 1980s may have been marked by greed, but ironically it seems to have also exhibited an unusual level of charitable giving.

This is the finding of Richard B. McKenzie, who in 1991, while an economics professor at the University of Mississippi, studied how greedy the 1980s really were, since he felt "greed has been around a long time" and could not believe any one decade could lay any more claim to the greed label than any other.

What he found, he said, after looking at the data, was evidence of widespread and record levels of charity that astounded him. In a research paper he prepared for the Center for the Study of American Business, a nonpartisan research institute at Washington University in St. Louis, he revealed:

- People increased their donations to charity at a greater rate than they increased their outstanding consumer credit, which often is used for material purchases.
- Individuals also increased their giving at a greater rate than they increased their spending for such luxury goods and services as jewelry, watches, beauty parlors, and health clubs.
- Private charitable contributions by individuals actually went up at a faster pace in the 1980s (5.2 percent a year) than in the previous two and a half decades (3.1 percent a year between 1955 and 1980).
- Even after figuring in inflation, the total amount of contributions by individuals, corporations, and foundations reached record amounts in the 1980s.

The question then arises as to whether such charity was a guilty response to the greed that was erupting all around. In any event, the professor's findings are fascinating for what they say about the many-sided human psyche and the prevalence of good along with greed in many people.

AN EXAMPLE OF DEEP(-FRIED) THINKING

"There's no reason to be the richest man in the cemetery; you can't do any business from there."

—COLONEL HARLAN D. SANDERS,
founder of Kentucky Fried Chicken

•••

MONEY TALKS:

A LOOK AT OUR FUNNY MONEY

The Buck

Starts Here

—SIGN AT THE ENTRANCE TO
THE VISITORS' GALLERY OF
THE BUREAU OF PRINTING
AND ENGRAVING IN
WASHINGTON, D.C.

Greed can be expressed for many things—for mansions, for jewelry, for minks, for cars. But of course to gain these possessions, one must have money. In and of itself, money is inert. While gold shines and diamonds sparkle and minks warm and autos transport (in more ways than one), money does nothing, yet is the tool to snare all the rest. Money is also a way for the avaricious to keep score, to know who is ahead and who is behind in the pursuit of excess.

It is also the multifaceted answer to the riddle with which Guy de Rothschild, a member of the wealthy Rothschild family, opens his memoirs:

Everyone has some; no one has enough. People despise it when they lack it, yet they welcome it with open arms. Reluctant to discuss it, they think about it constantly. Lifeblood of the economy, source of all activity, key to success, symbol of strength, it is the essence of power.

49

It cures, it destroys, it saves, it kills, it is ideal, it circulates, it fertilizes, it vanishes, it corrupts, it grows, it changes hands. It is fairly—or unjustly— earned. It is used, dreamed of, hidden, shown off, squandered, scorned, worshipped. Hoarded, it is a treasure—only to become sterile. It is reviled, repudiated, coveted. People invest it with their own intimate feelings: their rivalries, triumphs, frustrations, ambitions, resentments. At night it grows into something living, overpowering, enlightening, protective, crushing. It is a phantasmagorical god whom we both pray to and dread. It is the scapegoat for our misfortunes. Created as a convenience, it is burdened with our emotions; it is a means, but it has become an end.*

As Rothschild would indicate, throughout history mankind has shown a strange, ambivalent attitude toward money and riches. On the one hand, everyone obviously wishes to be wealthy rather than poor, and invariably the wealthy person is honored in his or her community while the poverty-stricken are at best tolerated and at worst looked at with pity, if not contempt.

Yet there is much in literature and religious teachings that shows an inherent disdain for the pursuit of riches. One of the most vivid sayings in Christianity is that "It is easier for a camel to go through the eye of a needle than for a rich man to enter into the Kingdom of God." And Paul counseled that "the love of money is the root of all evil" (I Timothy 6:10).

Interestingly, Paul's famous saying is usually misquoted as condemning money itself—rather than the love of it—as the root of all evil. The fact, however, that this misunderstanding has entered the public consciousness offers evidence of the guilt with which most people view this commodity.

A possible insight into humanity's strange attitude toward money can be found in the writings of Sigmund Freud. The father of psychoanalysis notes in his essay "Character and Anal Erotism" that there is for many people a connection between money and defecation, that those who hoard their money or show an undue interest in amassing money are those who are anal neurotics. Writes Freud: "In reality, wherever archaic modes of thought have predominated or persist—in the ancient civilizations, in myths, fairy tales and superstitions, in unconscious thinking, in dreams

---

The Whims of Fortune: The Memoirs of Guy de Rothschild (New York: Random House, 1985).

and in neuroses—money is brought into the most intimate relationship with dirt."

Freud cites the fact that in mythology "the gold which the devil gives his paramours turns into excrement after his departure, and the devil is certainly nothing else than the personification of the repressed unconscious instinctual life." He also makes reference to the superstition "which connects the finding of treasure with defecation." Furthermore, ancient Babylonian doctrine, as well as Oriental mythology and from it popular legends and fairy tales, held that gold is "the feces of Hell." Even Mammon, the god of riches, is in Babylonian another name for Nergal, the god of the underworld.

But the child who is fascinated with his bowels and has an erotic interest in defecation often extinguishes this interest as he matures. In place of the anal erotism, according to Freud, there later develops an interest in money.

Although Freud's views are subject to debate (he himself colors his insights with the phrase "unless I am much mistaken"), it is still fascinating to realize that our present-day language has such expressions as "dirty money" and "filthy lucre." And don't we refer to the wealthy—especially those who display greed and an ostentatious lifestyle—as "the filthy rich"?*

Then, too, the human being has shown an attitude toward money that could be said to be more warped than his or her views about sex. Research has shown that people are far less willing to discuss their financial situation than they are their family or sex lives. "Often people are as secretive about their money as Victorian ladies were about their sexuality," writes Dr. James A. Knight in *For the Love of Money* (Philadelphia: J. B. Lippincott Co., 1968). His experience is that patients "show far less resistance in relating hatred for their parents or in disclosing sexual perversities than in discussing their money status or transactions. It is as if they equated money with their inmost being."

Here are some of the peculiar ways people have viewed, thought about, and dealt with money.

---

*Freud's essay, "Character and Anal Erotism," can be found in the *Standard Edition of the Complete Psychological Works of Sigmund Freud*, Volume 9 (London: Hogarth Press, 1959)

A Penny for Our Thoughts: A Sampling of Words for Money

Our fascination with money can be seen in the many names we have for the stuff.

Here are some often-used slang words for money:

bread
buck
cabbage
dinero
do-re-mi
dough
dust
fin
gelt
greenback
jack
kale
mazuma
moolah
rhino
sawbuck
shekel
simoleon
wampum.

Some of these slang expressions, as well as other colorful words for money, have interesting origins:

buck The slang word for dollar comes from the shortened version of buckskin, a unit of trade with the American Indian.

cash Derived from the Old French word *casse*, meaning "money box."

doit Anything of trifling value; based upon the former small Dutch coin worth ¼ cent.

dollar	Originating from the German word *taler*, a large coin first minted in Bohemia in 1519.
gelt	The Yiddish word for money.
lucre	Money, profits; from the Latin *lucrum*, meaning "gain" or "profit" (the word "lucrative" is based on this).
filthy lucre	Tainted money or profits.
peag	North American Indian money.
mazuma	The slang word for cash, from the Yiddish *mezumen*, "ready," as in "ready cash."
rouleau	French for a small roll of coins wrapped in paper.
shekel	Slang for a coin, cash or money; derives from the Hebrew meaning "to weigh," the word for a Hebrew unit equal to half an ounce.
specie	Money in coin.
wampum	Based on the North American name of *wampumpeage* for the white string of beads used as money.

A Wealth of Expressions

Rich as Croesus	Based on Croesus, last king of Lydia (560–546 B.C.), who had great wealth. He was killed by the Persians under Cyrus.
Wealthy as a nabob	A nabob was a viceroy in India during British rule or a Mogul Empire provincial governor—all of whom acquired wealth.
A Mississippi bubble	A financial scheme that proves to be fantasy that eventually collapses, leaving many people with losses. John Law, a Scotsman living in Paris, devised a scheme to colonize the land along the Mississippi River and spread fantastic stories about gold being in the area. He sold shares in his development company, which were widely bought, but eventually the scam was found out and the value of the shares plummeted.

53

To find a Golconda	To uncover great wealth. Golconda, a city in India, was noted for having riches.
An El Dorado	An area of fabulous wealth. El Dorado, Spanish for "the gilded one," was, according to legend, a rich South American king or a kingdom or city in the Amazon in which huge amounts of gold were located (see Chapter One).
To play ducks and drakes	To squander something, especially money. Ducks and drakes is a sport in which flat stones are thrown to skim along the top of water.
Born to the purple	To be born into great wealth (or position). In Roman times, the dye for purple came from small amounts of a fish found in the Mediterranean. Items dyed purple were therefore more expensive and the color was associated with royalty.
To yearn for the flesh pots	To want the material aspects of life. In the Bible, after the exodus, the children of Israel were said at one point during their hardship in the desert to have regretted leaving Egypt, where they had "sat by the flesh pots" and "did eat bread to the full."
Mammon	The false god of riches and avarice; also signifying riches being regarded as objects of worship.

IT'S THE PRINCIPLE *AND* THE INTEREST

"When a fellow says, 'It ain't the money, but the principle of the thing,' it's the money."

—KEN HUBBARD

"The Midas Touch" Is Not the Thing to Have

We speak of a person who acquires wealth easily as someone with "the Midas Touch." The expression is derived from the fabled King Midas, who, according to legend, was granted the power of turning to gold all that he touched. This power led to the death of his beloved daughter—the result usually forgotten when people today speak of the Midas Touch. Indeed, the story of the Midas Touch is really a story of the tragedy that can befall the greedy.

According to Greek mythology, Midas was a king who was poor like his subjects. But when he befriended a stranger, Silenus, who was the foster father of Dionysus, the god of wine (he was called Bacchus by the Romans), Dionysus offered to repay Midas for his kindness by granting him one wish. Midas, who yearned to be wealthy, asked that everything he touched be turned to gold.

When Midas's wish was granted, he soon found that when he tried to eat, all his food turned to gold. When he held his daughter, she was transformed into gold. Distraught, the king pleaded to be free of this fatal touch. He was then told by Dionysus to wash himself in the Pactolus River. When he entered the waters, the magical powers of the king disappeared and in its place the sandy beaches of the river turned to gold.

Interestingly, this tale of the wages of greed has some basis in fact. Although originally thought to be a mythical figure, it is now known that there was not only one but several King Midases. In fact, there was a Midas dynasty that controlled the land of Phrygia, an ancient country in west-central Asia Minor settled by people from the Balkans in the thirteenth century B.C. Now what is central Turkey, Phrygia was a poor country, but then gold was discovered in the Pactolus River in the eighth century B.C., and the people became wealthy. Phrygia then became a dominant force in the region for several centuries—until its neighbors to the north, the Lydians, also rich with gold, descended on it and brought it under their rule.

To Be "Rich as Croesus" Is to Be Richer Than Midas

The expression "to be rich as Croesus" is based on a real person who is actually linked to the fate of the Midas dynasty.

Croesus was the last king of Lydia, the nation that eventually took over Phrygia, ruled by the Midas dynasty. Lydia, located in what is now northwest Turkey, also had substantial deposits of gold, much of it controlled by the royalty. Croesus, who ruled from 560 B.C. to 546 B.C., became a symbol of great wealth not only because of the gold he had amassed, but also because he ruled over a country that became the first to standardize coinage that used gold as a medium of exchange. It was Croesus, however, who took much of the confusion and risk out of coinage, which then often had variance in gold content and a mixture with other metals. He minted coins with a standard purity of metals. The Croesus stader, which was oval shaped with the picture of a bull and lion imprinted on it, is considered the first coin to be accepted throughout the world.

Croesus's creation eventually led such nations as Greece and Persia to create their own official coins. But the allure of Croesus's wealth and that of Lydia's proved too enticing to the Persians, who in 546 B.C. under Cyrus invaded Lydia, killed Croesus, and annexed his gold-laden land to the Persian empire.

So much for wealth being a protection. It is as often in history a magnet for trouble borne of greater greed.

◆◆

A CHINESE VIEW FROM 2,500 YEARS AGO

"There is no calamity greater than lavish desires. There is no greater guilt than discontentment. And there is no greater disaster than greed."

—LAO-TZU (604–531) B.C.,
Chinese philosopher and founder of Taoism

◆◆

The Folklore About Getting Rich

Harvard's Widener Library is the repository of a large collection of folklore, much of it amassed by scholars who interviewed people from different states and backgrounds about their native insights about life. Much of the folk beliefs that have emerged deal with wealth—how to be born wealthy, how to get rich, how to marry money, even how to get money while eating, sleeping, and dressing.

Among some of the more picturesque beliefs recounted from this collection in the 1992 edition of *The Old Farmer's Almanac:*

- Give a newborn baby a penny. If she clutches it tightly, she will be rich. (Kansas)
- Dream of snakes, money will arrive the next day. (Nebraska)
- Eat cabbage on New Year's Day, and money will flow your way all year. (North Carolina)
- A piece of money tied to or around your ankle prevents poverty. (African American)
- If a bluebird flies into your house, it brings wealth with it. (Georgia)
- When you see a shooting star, say "Money, money, money" before the star goes out. Riches follow. (Alabama)
- Turn your money over when you see the new moon, and it will double in value. (North Carolina)
- When you see a white horse, put your little finger under your lips and spit over it to attract money. (Maine)

Certain bodily features are said to foretell fortune, such as a mole on the neck (means money by the peck) or a mole on the back (means money by the sack). Eyebrows that meet in the middle mean a destiny for riches, a mole on the nose means business success, the letter M on the palm will bring wealth, an itching palm portends the coming of money, and a baby whose initials spell a word will become rich.

What all this seems to underscore is that the human yearning for riches is not only widespread but is accompanied by a desire that the coming of wealth be quick and easy. And with that kind of wisdom, easy come is often accompanied by easy go.

••

WOULD YOU BUY A CAR FROM A MONEYGRUBBER?

"God, was I greedy! My generation wasn't looking for 'quality of life'; we were money-grubbers. I really wanted to make money fast."
—LEE IACOCCA, chairman of Chrysler Corp.,
interview with Gail Sheehy in *Esquire* (August 15, 1978)

••

Gresham's Law Is One Law That's Never Broken

Gresham's Law is the economic principle that "bad money drives good money out of circulation." An example of Gresham's Law in action occurred following World War I, when so much paper money flooded Europe that people began hoarding metal coins for their intrinsic metallic worth and as insurance against a drop in value of paper money. As a result, coins—the "good money"—virtually disappeared. Another instance: In 1896, Americans began hoarding gold coins when it appeared that the government might begin making silver coins legally equal in value to gold coins.

This observation about human nature—and the nature of money—is named after the English financier Sir Thomas Gresham (1519–1579). A founder of the Royal Exchange in London, he observed that people would hold on to heavier-weight coins and pass on the lighter-weight ones. This was because dealers would often shave the sides of coins and the public would keep as long as possible the unshaved ones, which were heavier and seemed to have more intrinsic value, while spending the shaved, lighter ones. He was not the first to notice this behavior, but he was one of the first to articulate it.

Here, then, is the language of Gresham's Law:

Where by legal enactment a government assigns the same nominal value to two or more forms of circulatory medium whose intrinsic values differ, payments will always, as far as possible, be made in that medium of which the cost of production is least, the more valuable medium tending to disappear from circulation.

In other words, watch what you spend.

••

"Money doesn't talk, it swears."
—BOB DYLAN

••

Germany's Hyperinflation and the "Disaster of Prosperity"

History's most astonishing example of a country's money losing its value with sickening speed—Germany's hyperinflation during 1922 and 1923—was preceded by a period of prosperity marked by widespread speculation, enormous spending, accumulation of riches, and an inflationary atmosphere that went unchecked as all manner of excess gripped the nation. Historians trace the ultimate collapse in the mid-1920s back to the summer of 1914, just before the beginning of war, when Germany abandoned its gold standard and began to spend more money than it really had, thereby going into debt and leading the government to expand the supply of money. Until the ultimate collapse on November 15, 1923, Germany followed a course that initially led to a boom at home even after the war, while the victors suffered a correcting recession.

How bad was the nightmare in Germany during 1922 to 1923? Consider the following:

- At one point, interest rates reached 22 percent—a day.
- Patrons ordering dinner in a restaurant might find that the cost of the meal had gone up 20 percent by the time they got around to paying.
- Prices in 1923, near the conclusion of the disaster, were quadrupling weekly.
- German money, the reichsmark, deteriorated so much that reichsmarks totaling in the trillions had to be printed, but the govern-

59

ment's printing industry, with 30 paper mills and 133 printing plants, could not keep up with demand.

- A worker would be paid in bales of German money, but he would have to immediately purchase something tangible or watch its value dissipate totally (one of the most memorable sights from this time is of people pushing wheelbarrows filled with money to go buy bread).

- The price of a newspaper eventually became 200 billion marks.

- In July 1922, the total German money supply was 190 billion marks; by the end of the hyperinflationary period in 1923, 190 billion marks was worth less than 5 cents.

What eventually pulled Germany out of this catastrophe was the wrenching decision to stop printing more reichsmarks, to issue a new form of paper money with the proviso that no more would be printed by the government so that its value would be constant, and to insist the government and the people begin living within their means. Thus, the false boom led to an agonizing bust that, before the correction took over and normal life resumed, caused soaring unemployment (400,000 government workers were let go), a severe drop in government spending, the end of many businesses as credit virtually disappeared, and the financial collapse of the German middle class, who lost the value of their savings and pensions.

And of course Germany—and the world—eventually got Adolf Hitler, whose party picked up strength in the elections of May 1924 and who was finally elected in 1933 after another period of economic chaos had set in.*

*The theory that the cost of war reparations imposed on Germany after World War I had led to the nation's economic woes is disputed by the fact that Germany never paid anywhere near the full amount of the reparations. The allies had presented a claim for 132 billion gold marks in May 1921, but from the end of the war until the hyperinflation ended, Germany paid out 2.4 billion gold marks, which represented only about 5 percent of one year's national product. Also, the inflation in Germany meant that foreigners lost money on the billions of worthless marks they had—a figure that has been calculated at a loss six or seven times more than Germany paid in reparations (see *Dying of Money: Lessons of the Great German and American Inflations* by Jens O. Parsson [Lincoln, Mass.: Wellspring Press, 1974]).

•••

CURRENCY QUICKIES

- The average $1 bill wears out in eighteen months.
- "In God We Trust" was first placed on U.S. coins in 1864 during the Civil War, when religious fervor was high, but it took nearly a hundred years—until 1955—until a law was passed making it mandatory on coins and money. (Perhaps this solidifies the American concept of the Almighty Dollar.)
- Silver may be worth something as a treasured substance second only to gold, but it is also the best conductor of heat and electricity among the metals.
- Money at compound interest builds incredibly over time. If the American Indians had taken the $24 for which they sold Manhattan in 1626 and invested it at 8 percent daily compound interest, their $24 would today be worth $30 trillion.

•••

Want to Double Your Money?

Here's the Formula

Money may not grow on trees, but it does grow and grow—thanks to the fact it can draw interest.

For those who want to double their money, there is in fact a formula that, based upon the interest rate, will tell you how long it takes for money to double.

This rule-of-thumb states that the length of time for doubling money can be determined by dividing the annual interest rate into 72. Thus, if money is drawing interest at 8 percent a year, it will double in nine years. If the interest rate is 6 percent, it takes twelve years. An interest rate of 10 means your money will double in 7.2 years.

The growth rate feeds itself at an astonishing rate after a while. At 8 percent interest, money doubles in nine years, then quadruples after eighteen years. In twenty-seven years it will grow to eight times its original size.

It Takes Money to Make Money

One of the axioms about making money is that it takes some of it to make more of it. Let's not forget that it also literally costs money to make money. Here are the metal fabrication and manufacturing costs involved in the U.S. mint producing the following coins:

Penny—0.77 cents
Nickel—3.42 cents
Dime—1.71 cents
Quarter—3.82 cents
Half-dollar—7.29 cents

Interestingly, based upon percentages, a penny is the costliest coin to produce. It takes nearly 77 percent of its face value for a penny to be made. The cheapest coin? A dime, taking only 17 percent of its value to mint.

IN A GODDESS WE TRUST?

"The word 'money' is said to be derived from the Latin *moneta*, meaning 'mint.' *Moneta* itself comes from the place where the Romans housed their mint."

—INSCRIPTION FROM THE TEMPLE OF THE GODDESS JUNO MONETA

Some People Are Allergic to Money

People have different reactions to money, but some people are literally allergic to the stuff.

The reason is nickel. Not only coins, but most paper money actually has some traces of nickel. That small amount can cause people allergic to nickel to experience stubborn hand rashes from handling money.

The August 1991 issue of the *Journal of the American Academy of Dermatology* reported on this phenomenon. And the two researchers who wrote the report, Dr. Rainer Gollhausen and Dr. J. Ring, noted that people who become allergic to money may owe their allergy to pierced ears.

The reason for this is that jewelry, especially earrings for pierced ears that contain nickel, can cause an allergic reaction through repeated exposure to the metal. The researchers reported that this presensitizing to nickel can result in such symptoms as rashes when money touches their body.

These people manage to get by, however, by using credit cards (plastic) and checks (paper).

••

"The lack of money is the root of all evil."
—GEORGE BERNARD SHAW

••

Groucho Marx on Money

Groucho Marx was notorious for rapier responses. This was especially true when it came to money matters. Leo Rosten, in *People I Have Loved, Known, or Admired* (New York: McGraw-Hill, 1970), relates two such stories about Groucho. Once, when a bank official wrote to him, "If we can ever be of assistance, please let us know," Groucho wrote back: "Frankly, the best assistance you can give me is to steal some money from the account of one of your richer clients and credit it to mine."

When *Variety*, the newspaper of the show business industry, published the observation that the Marx Brothers, who had split up, would make $20,000 a week if only they would get together again, Groucho sent a letter to the editor:

Dear Sir:

Apparently you are under the impression that the only thing that matters in this world is money. This is quite true.

GROUCHO MARX

Pass Go and Collect Your Dough:

The Most Successful Board Game Is Based on Greed

Is it more than coincidence that the best-selling board game of all time is Monopoly? After all, this is a game built on a megalomaniacal fantasy—accumulating so much money and property that you drive your opponents into bankruptcy.

Monopoly's evolution over the past one hundred years paralleled the growth of capitalism. Games based upon real estate rents were played in England in the nineteenth century. And in 1885 a game also based on money and bankruptcy was put on the market in the United States. Its name: The Monopolist.

The first to patent a Monopoly-like game was a woman, Elizabeth Magie Phillips. A game called Finance also began taking hold during the early days of the Depression. And an unemployed inventor, Charles B. Darrow, came forward in the 1930s with the board game we know now as Monopoly. After first rejecting his creation as having "52 fundamental errors" that would prevent it from being successful, Parker Brothers in 1935 bought the rights not only to Darrow's game, but to Phillips's game and to Finance.

With this monopoly on games based on monopoly, Parker Brothers has had huge success. Since 1935, more than ninety million sets of Monopoly have been sold in thirty-three countries—some in such odd formats as a set in chocolate and a $495 edition with twenty-four-karat-gold and silver accents.

The game is now played by more than 250 million people of all ages—from those too young to know what a mortgaged property is to those old enough to know too well. Indeed, so successful has Monopoly been that Parker Brothers is actually a bigger printer of money than the United States government. Those ninety million sets have contained more money (albeit Monopoly money) than all the real money currently in circulation in the United States.

The example of Monopoly's wide and continued appeal shows, if nothing else, that success awaits those who know how to tap into the human tendency to delight in playing with money.

●●●

BRAINS AND MONEY — DO THEY GO TOGETHER?

Are the money-hungry smarter or dumber than you and I?

It could be that the brainier you are, the less interested in money you may be. Mensa is an organization of people with IQs in the top 20 percent of those who have taken IQ tests. But in a survey of Mensa members it was found that they rank only at median levels when it comes to financial well-being.

In an interview with *Money* magazine, the executive director of Mensa explained this fact about his members by noting: "They could probably make more, but they tend to work at what they like, not what pays best."

●●●

How to Handle Jealous Greed

One characteristic of the greedy person is coveting other people's possessions or monetary successes. How can you make the best of this negative human trait? Sholem Aleichem, the great Yiddish writer and humorist (he has been called the Jewish Mark Twain and his character, Tevye, is the central figure in the Broadway play, *Fiddler on the Roof*), once wrote of how one can adroitly forestall jealousy in others.

Says a Sholem Aleichem character on how he handles his return from a business fair: "(I)f I went to the fair . . . and did well, my heart bursting with joy, I never failed to tell my neighbors that I had lost every kopeck and was a ruined man. Thus I was happy, and my neighbors were happy.

"But if, on the contrary, I had really been cleaned out at the fair and brought home with me a bitter heart and a bellyful of green gall, I made sure to tell my neighbors that never since God made fairs, had there been a better one. You get my point? For thus I was miserable and my neighbors were miserable with me."

A Person in Greed Is a Person in Need

Greed can be a powerful motivator, as seen in the following true story. Bennett Cerf, the former head of Random House and a prolific editor of collections of stories, recounts in *The Life of the Party* (Garden City, N.Y.: Doubleday, 1956) how the owner of a little industrial plant in Panama had trouble getting his staff of twenty women to keep working once they had earned enough to meet their needs for several months. Even inducements of higher wages and shorter hours didn't change their attitude—they had earned all they needed for now, at least, so why work anymore?

Distraught, the boss finally hit on a solution. He collected copies of a 1,000-page Chicago mail-order catalog and sent them to all the women.

Wrote Cerf: "They were back at their places—every last one of them—the following Monday."

Is Life Worth Living—

Especially If There Is Life Insurance Money?

One of the thoughts supposedly faced by those who have suffered total financial ruin is whether to go on living, especially if there is life insurance on them that would benefit their families. An incisive answer to this question can be found in a story involving the noted American rabbi Stephen Wise and a distraught congregant who came to him following the stock market crash of 1929.

The man, who had lost everything in the crash, said that he was thinking of committing suicide so his family could at least have the insurance money. What did the rabbi suggest he do?

His response offers one way to deal with the greedy. The rabbi replied that the man should call his wife and children together and pose the question to them. Their response would give him the obvious answer.

"If they dissuade you from taking this step, there is no reason why you should destroy yourself, seeing that they would rather have you than your insurance," said the rabbi. "If, on the other hand, they approve of your design, I would go on living just to spite them. Surely you wouldn't want to sacrifice your life for such a family."

Money-Can't-Buy-Happiness Department:

The Case of Zero Mostel's Bankbook (at Least It Had More Than His First Name)

Zero Mostel, the Broadway star, said he was considered by his mother the "bum" of the family as a youngster. "My brother Aaron was so-and-so, and Milton was so-and-so, but I was definitely the BUM. She used to say, 'I'll be happy when you show me a bankbook with 10,000 dollars in it.' "

So when Mostel became a success, he showed his mother his bank-book with $10,000. Her response?

"She said, 'You call that a lot of money?' "

••

Money Talks

Richard Armour wrote that he knows money talks because he once heard it say, "Good-bye."

••

FROM TULIP BULBS TO GOLD BARS:

THE AGE-OLD MANIA FOR MORE

With money in your pocket, you are wise and you are handsome and you sing well, too.

—YIDDISH PROVERB

While the relentless pursuit of money can be a sign of greed, greediness finds its fullest flower in what people do with money to make more money. When done in a prudent way, this is an activity usually called "investing." But when taken to its outer limits, this is not investing but "grabbing"—an attempt to buy things so that they can soon be sold for more money, which can then be used to purchase more things that will grow even more in value so they can then be sold for more money that can then be used to buy . . . well, you get the idea.

This aspect of greed can be seen in the purchase of such items as gold, silver, oil, diamonds, pearls, and art. But it can also be seen in the acquisition of even such unusual sources of speculation as tulip bulbs, comic books, baseball cards, and toys. Sometimes the rush to corner markets in these commodities can lead to widespread speculative manias to get in on a good thing and later, in the aftermath of collapsing markets, panics to get out of a now-not-so-good thing.

The value of some of these commodities usually has a basis in intrinsic worth—oil, after all, is a vital energy source for the modern world. But others, such as tulip bulbs, assume a value more in the minds of the get-rich-quick than in the real world. Here are some of the major and some of the minor, if not weird, materials that have attracted the interest of those bent on making more money with their money. It is a demonstration that the mania for more has been with us throughout recorded history—and undoubtedly before.

Gold —
The One Sign of Wealth Throughout the Ages

The pursuit of wealth finds its earliest and most prolonged expression in the form of gold. Possessing it has been a sign of wealth for thousands of years. The early cave man knew about gold. Cups and jewelry fashioned out of gold have been found in Mesopotamia dating from nearly 5,500 years ago. Ancient Egyptians so prized it that, as previously shown, they placed items containing gold in their tombs, and they learned how to hammer gold so thin that a one-inch-high pile could contain 367,000 flattened leaves. During the Middle Ages, a whole science, alchemy, grew up around man's attempt to make gold out of lesser materials.

While alchemy has been derided for centuries now (although one practitioner was Isaac Newton), strangely enough, some of the alchemist's desires have come true today through the miracle of modern technology. Scientists now *can* make gold out of lesser or other materials and extract it from a new "mine." For instance, the atom smasher can make gold from lead and mercury; it can also be used to make an unstable form of gold out of platinum and iridium, although separately each is more costly than gold. Gold can also be extracted from lowly seawater, for each metric ton of seawater contains one grain of gold.

Contrary to popular belief, the rush to extract gold in America did not begin in California in 1849. That distinction belongs back east, in Georgia, where gold fever struck and America's first gold rush occurred twenty-one years before, in 1828.

Important goldfields have been found in every continent and in many countries. Gold is also found, although in minute quantities, in virtually all rock. In fact, gold is literally everywhere, not only in seawater, but also in all copper and lead ores and even in vegetation. And gold has been discovered as gold dust and gold nuggets, with the largest pure nugget ever found dubbed the "Welcome Nugget Stranger." Discovered in 1869 in Australia in a rut made by a wagon just inches below the surface, the nugget yielded 2,248 troy ounces of pure gold (69 kilograms). (With gold now valued at around $380 a troy ounce, that one nugget would today be worth about $867,000.)

Most of the world's currencies have at times been backed by gold, known as the gold standard. Money, whether paper or coin, was in the past considered of value because a nation had gold reserves that could be called on to redeem the money with the more stable and lasting value of gold. National presidential campaigns were fought over whether to stay on or go off the gold standard. By 1933, the United States went off the gold standard and paper money could no longer be redeemed for a stated amount of gold. However, gold, which can be found in coins dating back to King Croesus of Lydia about 550 B.C., continues to be worth hundreds of dollars an ounce.

Indeed, all the gold ever dug out of the ground—whether now in gold bars, dental work, machinery, or jewelry—is worth about 1.3 trillion.*

◆◆◆

"He who loves gold is a fool; he who fears it, is a slave; he who adores it, an idolator; he who hoards it up, a dunce; he who uses it, is the wise man."

—THE OLD FARMER'S ALMANAC, 1840

◆◆◆

The Search for Gold May Have Led to Modern Science

Modern science, especially chemistry, is said by some to have emanated from alchemy. Although many alchemists were fakes, others were

---

*Note that the author of this book finds gold even in his name. Nearly 30,000 families in America are named Goldberg. Where did the name come from? Goldberg is the name of a small town in the Silesia area of what was then Germany, said to owe its origin and name to a gold mine in the neighborhood. According to the *Encyclopaedia Britannica*, however, the mine has been abandoned since the Hussite wars. Maybe that's why so many of us Goldbergs have gold only in our name.

dedicated scholars who believed that matter was a balance of elements and that if this balance were properly altered one substance could be changed into another. The pursuit of gold was undertaken not only because it was highly valued, but also because its lasting quality made many believe that it held the secret of long life (the Chinese believed that eating from dishes made from gold added years to one's life).

The experimentation with chemicals and various metals and other substances thereby paved the way for today's science of chemistry. The serious alchemists "did more than anyone else to overcome scientific ignorance and advance our knowledge of the world," says one history of man's infatuation with gold. "Without them, we would still be living in the Dark Ages."

Interestingly, modern science has done what the ancient alchemists could not—actually make gold. Laboratory gold was first produced in 1936. Scientists at the University of California in Berkeley sent an electrical charge of 38 million volts through a combination of iridium and platinum. The gold that was created, however, soon decayed into base metals over a period of hours. But scientists at Columbia University in New York later used another method to produce a gold that decayed at a much less rapid rate.

Laboratory gold is now used in the radiation treatment of such diseases as cancer and arthritis. With cancer, the gold is placed in the diseased tissue so that the radiation emitted by the gold attacks only the bad tissue and not the good.

Gold is also used in the treatment of rheumatoid arthritis. Originally given by injection and now available orally, drugs with compounds containing 30 to 50 percent gold can slow the progress of the disease or even lead to a total remission in some cases. Half of those taking the gold treatment experience significant improvement. Twenty percent find they get relief for two or more years. But the process can be slow—it can take three to six months before results are seen—and side effects can occur in up to half of patients (in addition to skin rashes and possible kidney damage, one understandable side effect is a metallic taste in the mouth). The final surprise about treating rheumatoid arthritis with gold is that medical science does not really know how it works.

There's Gold in Them Thar Vaults

Although the United States dollar is no longer backed by gold reserves, the U.S. government continues to possess the most gold in the world, stored in the vaults at Fort Knox, near Louisville, Kentucky. According to the International Monetary Fund, as of December 1990 the U.S. had 262 million ounces of gold. The country with the second most gold is Germany (95.18 million ounces), followed by Switzerland, France, Italy, Netherlands, Belgium, Japan, Austria, and the United Kingdom, to round out the top ten. The country that leads the world in mining gold—South Africa—is not even on the list.

Actually, many gold coins are worth more than the gold in them or behind them. The United States issued gold coins until 1933, when the country went off the gold standard. Until then, gold coins were issued in $1, $10, and $20 amounts. But there were also $2.50 coins (20 million of these, called quarter eagles, were issued), and in 1879 and 1880 just a few of a $4 gold coin, called stellas, were minted. Today these $4 coins are considered among the rarest of U.S. coins.

The world record price paid for a single coin was established in 1990 for a high-relief double eagle $20 gold piece dated 1907. President Theodore Roosevelt, believing that the nation's coins should also be art objects, approved a design by Augustus Saint-Gaudens that led to what was considered the most beautiful gold coin ever struck. But only twenty were made, because bankers fussed that the design prevented the coins from being neatly stacked. As a result, eighty-three years later one of these coins was sold by MTB Banking Corporation to a private investor for $1,500,000—quite an increase from the coin's original $20 value.*

••

WHERE GOLD MEDALS ARE SILVER

Olympic gold medals are actually silver. There are 92.6 grams of silver in each medal and only 6 grams of gold.

••

*The highest price paid at auction for a single coin previously was for a silver one—a U.S. silver dollar in mint condition. On July 7, 1989, it was sold for $990,000.

ARMAND HAMMER'S GOLDEN RULE

"He who hath the gold maketh the rule."
—A PLAQUE WITH THIS INSCRIPTION WAS KEPT BY MULTIMILLION-
AIRE INDUSTRIALIST ARMAND HAMMER IN HIS BEDROOM

The Black Gold: Oil

While gold has fascinated humanity since time immemorial, the fastest way to immense wealth in today's world has been oil. Although the oozing black substance has been put to various productive uses since ancient times, it was not until 1859 that the first oil well was struck—not in the Middle East or the state of Texas, but in Pennsylvania.

Since then, enormous fortunes have been made in oil. The biggest fortune in the United States in the nineteenth and early twentieth centuries was amassed by John D. Rockefeller, who got his start on accumulating a billion dollars by cornering the market on this energy source. Others who prospered in oil in later years were people like Getty, Blaustein, Sinclair, Hammer, Hunt—not to mention people whose names were preceded by the word *sheik*.

Despite new inventions and discoveries, oil continues to provide the basis for unparalleled wealth. Seven of the twenty biggest companies listed on the Fortune 500 list at the beginning of the 1990s were oil companies. And among the world's billionaires, four of those who made their money from oil were said to be worth a total of $59 billion. One of them is the world's richest person—the Sultan of Brunei, said to be worth $31 billion in 1991 (up from $25 billion the year before). King Fahd of Saudi Arabia was third on the list with $18 billion (among the interesting things he is said to have built with his money is a palace in Spain that is a larger version of the White House).

Obviously, there has been incredible profit to be made in oil. Up through the 1960s, the cost of purchasing oil was less than $2 per barrel. But then in October 1973 the Arabs mounted an oil embargo on the Western world that rapidly drove the price of oil up to $32 a barrel. Since there are 42 gallons in a barrel, what had previously been costing dealers

73

4 cents a gallon was now costing about 80 cents—an increase of 1,500 percent.

This shift of wealth soon began draining Western treasuries and plunging countries into recession while it gladdened Middle Eastern hearts. Consider the case of the Saud family, which rules Saudi Arabia, the world's largest oil producer. When oil reached $32 a barrel in 1981, the Saudis were selling the world 10 million barrels a day. This meant a gross income of $320 million—every day. Since at the time oil cost "at the most 50 cents per barrel to extract, process, and market—$5 million in all . . . that leaves the Kingdom with a daily balance in its favour of $315 million," writes Robert Lacey in *The Kingdom* (New York: Harcourt Brace Jovanovich, 1982), a history of Saudi Arabia and the Saud family.

To get a sense of what the purchasing power of this sum was like at the time, Lacey further notes: "At its current rate of income the Kingdom could acquire all the stocks listed on U.S. stock exchanges in 12 years 7 months and 8 days; it could buy General Motors in 1 month 12 days 4 hours and 48 minutes, Bankamerica in 12 days 7 hours 36 minutes, all the professional football teams in the USA in 2 days 14 hours and 24 minutes—and Tiffany's in just 7 hours 55 minutes."

Although the Saudis did not carry out these possibilities, they did, as did other members of the oil fraternity, go on a spending spree with their newfound wealth from the Arab oil embargo. However, such greed met with a surprising result when OPEC countries first bought wildly after the initial run-up of prices.

In *The Prize: The Epic Quest for Oil, Money, and Power* (New York: Simon and Schuster, 1991), author Daniel Yergin tells what happened when the OPEC countries went on a massive buying spree in a "post-1973 cornucopia, which included everything from consumer goods to entire telephone systems," not to mention elaborate weapons systems. The massive expenditures resulted in overheating the economies of these countries, which led to escalating inflation, which "ensured that their financial surpluses would soon disappear."

And, as Yergin points out, the OPEC surpluses did disappear at the time—completely.

"In 1974, OPEC had a $67 billion surplus in its balance of payments on goods, services and such 'invisibles' as investment income," writes Yergin. "By 1978, the surplus had turned into a $2 billion deficit."

Oh, the wages of greed.

The Oil Rush of Pithole

One of the most dramatic cases of overspeculation and the stampede to make a fortune out of oil occurred in Pithole, Pennsylvania, in the early days of the boom in oil.

In 1865, with the Civil War coming to an end, thousands of war veterans rushed to Pennsylvania to seek their fortunes in the burgeoning oil fields there. Oil had zoomed to $13.75 a barrel and one oil well alone had generated a return of $15,000 for each dollar of investment. In the small town of Pithole, just fifteen miles from Titusville, where the first oil well had gushed forth in 1859, a well was struck in January 1865, followed by several more within months. By June, four wells were producing 2,000 barrels a day, representing a third of the total output for the oil region. The rush to acquire land in Pithole was on.

In July a farm in the area was sold for $1.3 million. By September, the same farm was resold for $2 million. Also in September, oil production in the Pithole area climbed to 6,000 barrels daily—which now represented two thirds of all the oil flowing from the region.

As a result, the population of Pithole zoomed to 15,000. And Pithole was also host now to banks, boardinghouses, a variety of businesses, and more than fifty hotels.

Within months, however, the oil suddenly began drying up in Pithole. While production of oil actually increased dramatically elsewhere in the area, in Pithole it dropped to a trickle by the end of 1865. To the horror of the townspeople, the boom was now a bust of epic proportions. Speculators abandoned the town with such speed that by the beginning of 1866, just twelve months from the time oil had first been discovered there, Pithole had become a ghost town.

The reversal of fortune caused major losses for land speculators. The farm land in Pithole that had been bought for $2 million was finally auctioned off in 1878—for $4.37.

The early days of oil were marked by similar wild speculative swings between success and failure. A popular ditty of the time was "Oil on the Brain," which talked of how the substance could "set the people crazy."

Indeed, the lust for riches led to chaotic scenes and situations. Hotels within the oil regions were populated with as many as six guests in one room, all sleeping on straw mattresses. Ramshackle wooden buildings

75

were quickly erected, the air became fouled with the smell of petroleum, and the land, stripped of trees, was a sea of mud whenever it rained.

And still the people came in a frantic race for riches. The editor of a local newspaper wrote in 1865 about how oil had caused "a sort of epidemic" that infected men of all classes, ages, and economic conditions. As a result, he pointed out, the community had been transformed:

> The court is at a standstill; the bar is demoralized; the social circle is broken; the sanctuary is forsaken; and all our habits, and notions and associations for half a century are turned topsy-turvy in the headlong rush for riches. Some poor men become rich; some rich men become richer; some poor men and rich men lose all they invest. So we go.

The editor concluded that "the big bubble will burst sooner or later." It did. Not only in Pithole, but in the entire industry as the price of oil plummeted to as little as $2.40 a barrel in 1866 and 1867.

One reason for the drop in price was the oversupply of oil for its only major use at the time: kerosene for lighting purposes. With the advent of electricity and the lightbulb, the oil business was in trouble. What rescued it was the invention of the automobile. The oil business eventually rebounded and fortunes were made, but not before other fortunes were lost and other hearts broken. Even today, oil exploration remains a huge risk and the potential for periodic oversupply—and with it falling prices—ever present.

In the world of greed, there are no sure things.*

Tulipmania: The Craze over a Flower

It may have been the strangest speculative craze of all time.

Between 1634 and 1637 in Holland, people began investing so heavily in tulip bulbs—almost as though, in today's world, it would be oil or uranium—that the price of single bulbs shot up to incredible heights.

How incredible? As much as 6,000 florins a bulb. (In comparison, the weekly wage of a skilled worker then was 2.8 florins and a small house cost 300 florins.) In fact, at the height of the craze, it was not unusual for

---

*The story of the Pithole oil rush and its aftermath can be found in *The Prize: The Epic Quest for Oil, Money, and Power* by Daniel Yergin (New York: Simon and Schuster, 1991).

One of the strangest speculations in history was the mania over tulips that occurred in Holland in the 1600s. At its height, a tulip bulb was being bought for twenty times the price of a house—until the Crash of '37.

trades for bulbs to involve the swap of homes, gold, silver, furniture, and land.

What caused such a fury of speculation in a country noted for its levelheaded citizens?

The tulip was first brought to Europe in the 1500s from Turkey (the name *tulip* is from the New Latin *tulipa* originally from the Turkish for turban [*tülbent*], which is what the blossoms of the delicate tulip look like). During the following decades, the rare, delicately beautiful tulip became a very fashionable flower in Holland, England, France, and Germany, so much so that by the 1600s people began investing and then speculating in the bulbs that could reproduce and thereby create even more of the stylish exotic flower. Growers then began experimenting with additional varieties, varying the colors and shapes of petals. This brought the tulip—originally available only to the connoisseur—to the general public, and with it came an increasing demand.

A number of other factors also fueled the speculation. Since tulips were available only during the June to October growing season, growers were tempted to take orders in the winter for the future sale of bulbs. Around 1634, the practice developed to purchase "future" bulbs, with buyers further tempted to sell to other buyers the tulips that had yet to be delivered—or even seen. These other buyers in turn offered their purchases to other buyers. Thus with spring months away, a trade in tulip futures was generated. This continued each year until in 1637, as the mania reached dizzying heights, the trading in tulip bulbs was more a trading in paper with a delivery date on it. The problem was that as the date of delivery on the paper neared, the seller was faced with having to actually settle with a grower to accept the actual tulips. Prices then began to rise daily—even hourly.

Adding to the mania was the existence of numerous varieties of tulips, each part of a ranking indicating value. The most admired were the flamed and irregularly striped varieties. They were formed into three groups, based on color: the roses, the violets, and *bizarden* (yellow with red or violet). The rarest were the red flames on white called the Semper Augustus and a clone, the Parem Augustus. Others were called either Viceroys or, in the Netherlands, where royalty was frowned upon, Admirals and Generals.

The many types and sizes of tulips—not to mention the wide range of prices—created the basis for increasing interest in the flower. Soon growers hired salesmen to travel to village fairs and markets far from the nurseries and shops that had been selling tulips. By 1635, tulips were being bought by all types of people and strata of society—from workers to shopkeepers to aristocrats.

The tulip growers eventually succeeded in creating an explosive demand. Their deliberate market innovations and production of cheaper varieties of tulips fanned a popularization of the tulip and with it the need by many to own and display this delicate flower. The result: a surge in demand—and ever higher prices. Costs were further pushed upward by the lack of tulip growing in the winter seasons and the strain on the growers to meet the increasing demand. By 1636, prices had tripled for many varieties. The rarer ones experienced even more dramatic escalation. One variety went from 40 to 350 florins over a few months. Another went from 800 to 2,200 florins in just weeks. The most prized variety of tulip—the Semper Augustus—went for 6,000 florins a bulb as the frenzy neared its peak.

The bubble began to burst when greed rushed in. With prices beginning to double and triple weekly or daily, speculators began buying paper delivery obligations and then selling them quickly to realize a profit, while others held on to theirs for later sale at even greater profit. Many of these buyers tried to delay payment so that they were selling a product they did not really own for a price that they hoped to get.

And then, on February 2 or 3, 1637, when concerned governmental officials finally moved to regulate the trade in bulbs, panic selling replaced panic buying. Prices, which had been rising by the day, began dropping by the hour. Tulip futures became worthless, and other contracts for purchases were called into question. By the end of one week, much of the existing tulip stock was unsalable and many people lost fortunes in the tulip market.

In the aftermath of the tulip mania, Dutch authorities sought to educate the public about their folly. Of special concern was the feeling that the Dutch values of moderation and prudence, and the connection between honest labor and just reward, should not be subverted by the lure of quick and easy profits and the wickedness of speculation. But even with all the prints, satires, pamphlets, and paintings that ensued with warnings, one painting of two decades before had probably the most apt and prophetic message of all. Painted in 1614, *Sinnepoppen* (*Dolls for the Spirit*) by Roemer Visscher used the tulip to indicate the foolishness of man, showing this flower with the motto: "A fool and his money are soon parted."*

*See *The Embarrassment of Riches: An Interpretation of Dutch Culture in the Golden Age* by Simon Schama (New York: Knopf, 1987). The tulip frenzy is also discussed in the classic

◆◆◆

EVEN A NEWTON CAN BE FOOLED

It obviously does not take a genius to lose money in a speculative mania. But what about a real genius? How does he or she handle such situations?

Not so well, to view the case of Sir Isaac Newton.

The great scientist and verifiable genius (his intelligence is said to have been one of the highest in history) was also supposedly something of a financial whiz, serving as England's Master of the Mint during his lifetime. In the spring of 1720, while speculative frenzy raged over the prospects of the South Sea Company, Newton decided to sell shares he had purchased and thereby gained a 100 percent profit. He had seemingly realized that things had gotten out of hand. At the time, he stated, "I can calculate the motions of the heavenly bodies, but not the madness of people." And so, on April 20, 1720, he got out of his position in South Sea at a handsome profit of £17,000.

But then something happened. Weeks later, as the frenzy continued and shares kept being bid up during the spring and summer, Newton went back into the market and bought further shares—this time for a larger amount than he had spent before. But this time his foray came at what proved to be the top of the market. When the bubble burst on the stock of the South Sea Company, Newton found himself losing £120,000.

It is said that the experience so unnerved him that for the rest of his life Newton could not bear to hear the words *South Sea*.

◆◆◆

Why Diamonds Are Forever Expensive

Among the other possessions lusted after are gems, and the gem valued above all others over the centuries has been the diamond.

on human folly and mass hysteria, *Extraordinary Popular Delusions and the Madness of Crowds* by Charles Mackay. First published in England in 1841, it can be found in an illustrated edition published by Harmony Books in 1980.

In modern times diamonds seem not only to hold their value but to increase in worth over the years. Why?

This situation is no accident.

For centuries diamonds had value and use only as jewelry until an industrial role as the bit in drilling equipment was discovered in the 1860s. Today the price of diamonds is artificially maintained by a diamond cartel called the Central Selling Organization (CSO), a group controlled by De Beers Consolidated Mines Ltd., a South African diamond mining company. De Beers is known to many consumers outside South Africa by the lush ads that tout how "diamonds are forever"—and so, it seems, is De Beers's plan on maintaining a high and steady price for diamonds.

The artificially high price is maintained by controlling the flow of diamonds to reach the marketplace and by curtailing competitive selling. De Beers and its affiliates represent approximately half of the production in the world of diamonds for use in jewelry and industry. Of the diamond production not emanating from De Beers, half is bought up by CSO, thereby maintaining the price and restricting the availability of the gems.

The system is not foolproof. In 1980, a 1-carat flawless polished diamond sold for $65,000. Within two years, the price had fallen to $19,000. Since that recessionary time, prices have rebounded. One reason is that still in place is the monopolistic hold of the Central Selling Organization.

In short, De Beers remains a diamond's best friend.

••

IS THIS WHAT THEY MEAN BY YOUR DEBT TO SOCIETY?

If you want people to remember you after you die, don't pay your debts.

—SIGN SEEN BY AUTHOR IN
WINDOW OF OFFICE SUPPLY STORE

••

For the Hunts, There Is No Silver Lining to This Story

(or How to Lose $7 Billion)

After gold, the most precious metal is silver. The lust after silver has no more an incredible story than the attempt in recent years by two of the sons of an oil tycoon to corner the world's silver market.

The Hunts of Texas must be one of the strangest families of wealth. The father, H. L. Hunt, who built Hunt Oil company into the nation's largest independent oil producer, kept three families going at one time—complete with three wives, fifteen children, and three separate residences. But it was two of those children who engaged in one of the most audacious acts of greed ever and wound up losing $1.5 billion from one venture and a total of $7.15 billion in all.

It all started in 1970, when the rotund Hunt boys, Herbert and Bunker, became interested in silver. Then selling at a historic low of $1.50 an ounce, silver doubled in price, and the brothers made a nice profit. But then they got an idea: since silver was used in manufacturing and since inflation was beginning to climb (it eventually soared into the double digits), silver would be a good prospect to continue to increase in price as both inflation and the need for the metal increased, not to mention the fact that silver could be a hedge against economic hard times as well. So by 1973, Herbert and Bunker took delivery of 55 million ounces of silver. Its worth: $160 million.

But then the Hunts devised another idea. They would corner the silver market and really see their profits zoom. By the end of the 1970s, with Arab money behind them, they purchased 130 million ounces of silver and had contracts for another 90 million. Their goal was 200 million ounces, a sum that it was said would give them world control of a metal that actually has a wider use (such as in photography) than gold.

With such buying by the Hunts going on, the price of silver began soaring. By the beginning of 1980, the cost of silver stood at $50 an ounce. The value of the Hunt holdings was almost $4.5 billion. Their profit, on paper, was $3.5 billion.

But instead of reaping the reward from their strategy and selling some or much of their hoard, they held on to their silver. It was then that the United States regulators, fearing continued run-ups in the price of silver and wishing to stabilize the market for the metal, put a limit to futures buying in silver. The action soon had its intended effect and the price of silver began to fall. By March 1980, the price was $21—less than half its level as recently as January.

Now the Hunt brothers were faced with meeting margin calls of $10 million dollars a day, a feat they became unable to do. The United States government now faced a problem of the Hunts' making. To ensure that the market did not collapse, the Federal Reserve chairman approved a loan to the Hunts to bail them out. The size of the loan needed? $1.1 billion.

This meant that Herbert and Bunker Hunt, who once had $4 billion worth of silver, were now more than $1 billion in debt. By 1985, with the last sale of their remaining silver, the Hunt brothers were out of the silver market—and out $1.5 billion for their attempt to corner that market. Bunker Hunt later tried to put a happier perspective on the experience. "A billion dollars," he said, "isn't what it used to be."

But the Hunt family troubles were not over. They still had to pay off their loans, and a later drop in oil prices soon brought their oil company to the brink of bankruptcy because of souring speculative oil leases and a drop in value of offshore oil rigs. In fact, by the spring of 1986, the Hunts had to seek protection under Chapter 11. Their oil business losses totaled almost another $6 billion.

Herbert and Bunker were eventually forced to sell even personal assets valued at $250 million to satisfy creditors, so that by 1990, while other Hunt family members who had stayed out of the silver market still had intact personal fortunes valued at billions, the two silver bugs were worth only about $1.5 million each—probably one-tenth of 1 percent of what they were worth when they first dreamed of riding silver to a golden fortune.

••

WHAT'S A FORMER BILLIONAIRE WORTH?

When a U.S. Senate committee member asked Bunker Hunt how much he was worth, he retorted, "Hell, if I knew that, I wouldn't be worth very much."

Of course, he said that before his net worth plummeted in the face of his disastrous attempt to corner the silver market. Then he knew only too well what he wasn't worth anymore.

••

With Land, the Sky's the Limit

Real estate is often said to be a sure way to wealth—at least it was until land, like much else, fell in value following the Greed Decade. But consider what happened in Japan to the price of an acre of land before the downturn in prices in the 1990s.

In 1991, for instance, Japan's National Tax Agency assessed land in the Ginza shopping district, a prestigious area of Tokyo, at $252,000 a square yard. This represented a 17.5 percent increase from the previous year.

The lowest assessment for a square yard in all of Japan was in Yamaguchi, which is 480 miles west of Tokyo. Here a square yard was valued at $1,700, but even this value had risen 9.5 percent in one year.

Overall, as of 1991, real estate continued to rise in land-restricted Japan. The national average was a 38.1 percent increase in land values, the largest since a 40.2 percent rise in assessed value occurred in 1962.

By the way, since there are 4,840 square yards in an acre, the cheapest acre in Japan was assessed at $8.2 million. The most expensive real estate in Japan was assessed at $1.2 billion an acre.

Going, Going, van Gogh: Art for Money's Sake

Another way to amass wealth is to buy art—and pray for the artist's early demise. Consider van Gogh.

As everyone knows, Vincent van Gogh was a troubled artist, possibly suffering from insanity, who sold only one painting during his lifetime. Now, a hundred years after his death at thirty-seven, his paintings sell for astronomical amounts. On November 11, 1987, a 28- by 37-inch van Gogh painting entitled *Irises* was put on the auction block by its owner, the wealthy John Whitney Payson, because it had grown too valuable even for him (he couldn't insure it and because of tax reasons could not even give it away).

After spirited bidding, a Japanese businessman bought the painting for $42 million—the highest amount until that time ever paid for a painting. It was a sum that could have purchased a skyscraper office building in almost any major city.

When a van Gogh painting fetched $82.5 million in 1990, the cartoonist for the Baltimore *Sun* drew the Dutch artist reading a newspaper with the news of the multimillion-dollar sale as the major headline. Van Gogh is shown thinking to himself: "And they thought I was insane."*

Oh, What an Impression

On May 9, 1989, Sotheby's conducted a record-breaking auction of Impressionist and modern paintings that netted $205 million, with no fewer than forty-four individual items garnering more than $1 million prices each. Slightly more than one hundred years before—on April 10, 1886—the American Art Association of the City of New York held the first showing of French Impressionist painting in the United States. The show was lambasted by critics ("Is this art?" asked *The New York Times* critic). A total of 289 works were exhibited that day, but only fifteen were purchased. The top price paid was just several hundred dollars.

••

GO INVEST, YOUNG MAN

"Buy old masters. They fetch a much better price than old mistresses."

—LORD BEAVERBROOK
(1879–1964), British newspaper publisher and public official

••

---

*Van Gogh's nephew, Vincent Willem, the son of the painter's brother, Theo, found himself years later with a number of his uncle's works (van Gogh had painted more than five hundred while alive). An engineer by profession, he lived modestly, but because he owned so many van Gogh paintings he eventually became on paper (or in oils, if you will) the wealthiest person in Holland.

So What's the Best Way to Invest?

The age-old question—or at least the question most often asked when one gets to the right age—is, What *is* the best investment? The problem with getting a right answer is that often it depends on whom you talk to—the stockbroker always seems to answer stocks; the mutual fund salesperson, mutual funds; the real estate agent, real estate; the jeweler, diamonds, and so on.

In *The Ultimate* (Garden City, N.Y.: Doubleday, 1990), William Poundstone, an author with no ax to grind except to make his book interesting and convincing, set out to discover "The Most Profitable Investment."

To accomplish this, various standard investments were surveyed over the six-decade period of 1926 to 1987 (the 1926–1987 span was used because it predates the Great Depression and thereby provides "a decent indication of the historic record").

Here is what was found: Money invested in twenty-year treasury bonds grew at an annual rate of 4.27 percent, not adjusted for inflation. A dollar invested in the Standard & Poors 500 Index in 1926 would have shown a 9.90 percent annual return at the end of 1987. Diamonds went in value from $157 for a 1-karat white flawless gem in 1926 to $15,000 in the mid 1980s—an 8.17 percent return. Gold coins rose from $20 (for United States eagles in fine condition) to $384—a 5.15 percent return. Silver moved from 50 cents an ounce to $5.23 an ounce—a 3.92 percent return. In other measures, fine art showed an 11.70 percent return; rare stamps, 11.16 percent; and real estate (using the measure of Beverly Hills property), 9.51 percent.

Even Mickey Mouse toys were surveyed. A $1 Mickey Mouse Fun-E-Flex toy purchased in 1931 was worth $125 in 1988—an 8.84 percent return.

The winner? Stocks purchased not in the Standard & Poors 500 Index (where stock prices of larger, more mature companies reflect less future growth), but stocks of a representative selection of smaller companies on the New York and American stock exchanges in the over-the-counter market. According to *Stocks, Bonds, Bills, and Inflation: Historical Returns (1926–1987)* (Homewood Ill.: Dow Jones-Irwin, 1989) by Roger G. Ibbotson, one dollar invested in 1926 in small-company stocks would have grown to $1,202.97 by 1987. That increase equals a 12.12 percent annual return.

Except for specialized and highly speculative investments over a brief time—where the risks far outweigh the slim chances of reward—no regular investment was determined over the past six decades to return more than the 12 percent returned by the stock in small capitalized companies.

There was, however, one source that did show an astonishing return over that long period. That was rare comic books. The key word here is *rare*. *Detective 27*, published in 1939, and *Marvel Comics No. 1*, also of that era, each now command prices of more than $35,000 for an initial purchase of 5 cents. The reason is that Batman and Superman, respectively, were first unveiled in these comic books. But other comic books of those or other eras do not command anywhere near those prices—or that return of 30 percent over a fifty-year period.

●●●

IT'S THEIR BLOOD, SWEAT, TEARS, AND MONEY

"Saving is a very fine thing. Especially when your parents have done it for you."

—WINSTON CHURCHILL

●●●

◆◆◆

MILLIONAIRES, BILLIONAIRES, AND OTHER POOR PEOPLE:

WEALTH AND INCOME ON AN UNGRAND SCALE

Billionaires? I wouldn't want the hassle. Give me a measly million and I'll be satisfied.

—MYRON, age eight, in David Heller's *Growing Up Isn't Hard to Do if You Start Out as a Kid*

What are the superwealthy like? Are their abilities that much better than yours or mine to merit so much money? Do they enjoy their riches?

In his famed book *The Robber Barons: The Great American Capitalists, 1861–1901* (New York: Harcourt, Brace, 1934), Matthew Josephson writes that the American tycoons of the turn of the century were typically "great silent men" who did not talk about much beyond their business dealings. They proved to be poor parents, "scarcely fit to bring up their own children." They either overindulged their sons and daughters or focused them on the pursuit of more (said one of the greatest business geniuses to his son, "I will be perfectly satisfied with you if you will only always go to bed at night worth more than when you got up this morning.")

Their single-minded focus on money and the accumulation of wealth can be seen in steel magnate Andrew Carnegie's reaction to the answer he got when he asked publisher Frank Doubleday how much money he had made the previous month. On being told that in publishing it was impossible to learn such a result but once a year, Carnegie, the sponsor of free libraries across America, is reputed to have snapped his advice to Doubleday about publishing books: "I'd get out of it!"

Henry Adams, the noted American philosopher who generally respected the landed gentry, found that the very rich led lives "no more worth living than those of their cooks." His brother Charles Francis Adams, who had twenty-five years of business dealings with such robber barons as Jay Gould, Pierpont Morgan, and James Hill, wrote in his autobiography that "a less interesting crowd I do not care to encounter. Not one that I have ever known would I care to meet again either in this world or the next; nor is one associated in my mind with the idea of humor, thought or refinement. A set of mere money-getters and traders, they were essentially unattractive." He said he was generally puzzled by the business successes he had seen, calling this "money-getting" to come "from rather a low instinct."

Theodore Roosevelt, himself a descendant of New York Knickerbockers, found it intensely boring to be with the titans of business, noting that he was "simply unable to make myself take the attitude of respect toward the very wealthy."

For all their wealth, the robber barons did not appear to know how to enjoy themselves. James Stillman, a leading figure in the banking industry and a friend of William Rockefeller, complained during his retirement years that "I have never in all my life done anything I wanted, and cannot now."

Here is a look at the superwealthy—from millionaires to zillionaires: who they are, how they make their money, and what they think about their lives of affluence.

The First Billionaire Nickeled and Dimed His Opposition

John D. Rockefeller's name has become synonymous with vast wealth. A coffee company once ran an ad campaign that announced that a better coffee "Rockefeller's money can't buy."* The allusion was less than apt, for John D. Rockefeller (1839–1937) was history's first billionaire.

---

*The ad campaign by Chock Full O' Nuts drew the ire of the Rockefeller family. The phrase was later modified to "better coffee a millionaire's money can't buy."

But not only was he history's first billionaire (which he achieved by 1913 when he was seventy-four—he would live another twenty-four years), his wealth was for its era far above that of any other private individual's. With at one time major investments in sixty-seven companies outside the oil-related industry, he was making money and watching his assets grow at a prodigious rate during his entire adult life.

To comprehend how vast his wealth was for his time, one need only note that at their peak the fortunes of John Jacob Astor amounted to $50 million; Commodore Vanderbilt, $100 million; and Andrew Carnegie, $450 million. One could add in even the fortunes of banker J. P. Morgan and rival railroad magnate E. H. Harriman. The combined wealth of all these multimillionaires would still not equal the wealth of Rockefeller.

With all this wealth, however, also came a negative image of the ruthless business tycoon. To turn around such an image, a simple dime was used. At the advice of Ivy Lee, a former journalist and the first public relations adviser to an American company, John D. Rockefeller began giving out at first nickels, then nickels to children and dimes to adults. During his later years, Rockefeller placed into enthusiastic hands an estimated 30,000 new dimes.

Rockefeller seemed to enjoy the coin giveaway, but he always kept in mind the value of even the smallest sum of money and the need to save. To an aide who had told him he need not return a nickel borrowed for a phone call, Rockefeller pointed out that a nickel had special worth: "This is a whole year's interest on a dollar."

Another practice that helped change the image of the world's first billionaire was philanthropy on a vast scale. A number of charities were set up and funded by Rockefeller's great wealth and the benefactions flowed while he was still alive. In fact, by the time of his death, he had given away $500 million, making John D. Rockefeller the world's first half-billionaire philanthropist.

What Does It Take to Be a Billionaire?

John D. Rockefeller did not come by his billion dollars by whim or chance. He had a highly disciplined mind and iron will that he directed in his singular pursuit of business and wealth. For instance, he often followed a schedule so rigid that it became almost a ritual. Even when he was in the last decades of his long life (he lived to be ninety-eight), he adhered to a set program. Here is his daily schedule late in life as contained in an itinerary given to reporters on one of his birthdays:

6:30 A.M.	Gets up
7:00 to 8:00 A.M.	Reads daily papers
8:00 to 8:30 A.M.	Breakfasts
8:30 to 8:45 A.M.	Chats
8:45 to 10:00 A.M.	Attends to business affairs
10:00 to 12 NOON	Nine holes of golf
12:00 to 1:15 P.M.	Takes bath and rests
1:15 to 3:00 P.M.	Lunches, plays Numerica
3:00 to 5:00 P.M.	Takes an auto ride
5:00 to 7:00 P.M.	Rests, is read to
7:00 P.M.	Dines
8:00 to 10:00 P.M.	Plays Numerica, listens to music played by valet
10:00 P.M.	Retires

Why a Billion Dollars Is Much More Than That

A billion dollars is not just a billion dollars. It also generates enormous sums in interest. Invested in government bonds at 9 percent, a billion dollars will put in its owner's pockets a quarter of a million dollars a day and add another $91.2 million a year. At this rate, a billionaire becomes a millionaire every four days (which means that when billionaire Ross Perot ran for president and spent $70 million of his own money, he used little more than the interest on one of his billions).

••

A DOLLAR JUST ISN'T WORTH AS MUCH — EXHIBIT I

The word *millionaire* was coined in 1740. *Billionaire*, though, wasn't invented until 1861. In 1990, *Spy* magazine referred to the coming of the *zillionaire*.

••

The Billion-Dollar Quiz

Question: Which three countries have the most billionaires today?

Hint: Two of them lost a major world war not too long ago.

Answer: (In order beginning with the country with the most billionaires):
United States
Japan
Germany

Question: Which area of the world is the leading breeding ground for billionaires today?

Hint: We used to think it was just a breeding ground for poverty.

Answer: Latin America. The area went from eight billionaires in 1991 to twenty-one in 1992, according to *Forbes* magazine. Mexico alone had seven new billionaires, with five in Brazil, three in Chile, three in Colombia, two in Argentina, and one in Venezuela. (The reason given for the rapid growth: a surge in private enterprise and foreign investment.)

Where the Wealth Is in America

One percent of the populace of the United States now has approximately 33 percent of the personal wealth—and this includes half of all the individually owned stocks and bonds. According to one research study of the rich in America,* most of this wealth is held by those in just several hundred families.

The truly large fortunes in America most often derived from original holdings in the stock of a single corporation, which usually began as a family business. The growth of a highly successful corporation can result in a huge economic success. In 1939, William R. Hewlett and David Packard formed an electronic instruments company with just $538. By 1979, just four decades later, their stock in Hewlett-Packard was valued at more than $3 billion.

The Founding Fortunes: A New Anatomy of the Super-Rich Families in America by Michael Patrick Allen (New York: E. P. Dutton, 1987).

Yet for all the bountiful possibilities of corporate America, of a system that C. Wright Mills termed "a machine for producing millionaires," the stark truth is that the majority of new businesses fold within the first year. And while many American families can be said to be affluent to a degree, few fulfill the definition of being truly rich—being able to live in luxury off of investment income. In other words, few people in America live without working.

BILLIONS: THE VIEW FROM THE SENATE

"A billion here, a billion there and pretty soon you're talking about real money."

—U.S. SENATOR EVERETT MCKINLEY DIRKSEN
(1896–1969)

The British Rich:
Are They Like You and Me?

While *Forbes* magazine has its list of the four hundred richest people in the United States, in 1989 the *Sunday Times* of London published the first real guide to England's wealthiest. The next year the list was expanded by seventy names and the minimum amount of wealth required for inclusion was raised to £50 million. Then, in December 1990, staff members of the *Sunday Times* and Philip Beresford updated and refined the list once again for a book that then listed Britain's richest four hundred people and families. Their wealth totaled £54.3 billion.*

The picture that emerges of the British 400 is awesome. Their land holdings amount to 4.4 million acres—which is nearly 10 percent of the total land area of the United Kingdom. Twenty-three of them are women, including the Queen of England, who is considered the wealthiest woman in the world. The top ten of the wealthiest have over 40 percent of the

---

*See *The Book of the British Rich* by Philip Beresford (New York: St. Martin's Press, 1990) and the *Sunday Times* of London. (Note: At the beginning of 1994, a pound was worth $1.48.)

wealth of the 400. Fifty percent of the wealth represents inherited wealth (162 of the 400).

But although Britain is still an aristocracy,* the list of British rich shows not only business executives, real estate developers, and industrialists, but also eleven rock stars (including one of the Beatles), actors, novelists (including Joan and Jackie Collins), auto dealers, brewers, and even two involved with pornography.

Twenty-five had no formal high school education. Of the top 200, almost half—98—represent what is called the New Rich. Twenty-one are Asian immigrants and 239 of the 400 built their fortunes in one generation. And the wealth of just these 400 people represents the same amount as the domestic product of the Republic of Ireland.

How Rich Is the Queen of England?

The Queen of England, according to *The Book of the British Rich*, is worth £6,700 million. This comes from not one but two fortunes: One fortune is that of the Crown Estates, the other is strictly her own.

The queen is actually the custodian and not the owner of the Crown Estates, which comprise most of the 267,000 acres she is said to own. This includes 350 acres of highly prized land in the middle of London. All the coastal land around England between high and low water marks is said to be hers. Such assets as these were valued at £2,100 million in 1987.

Counted as her own possessions are an art collection, royal antiques, stamp collection, jewel collection, racing stables, stud farms, 70,000 acres of British property, properties in Europe, properties in America, stocks and shares in equity portfolio.

The art collection has several hundred Leonardo da Vinci drawings, as well as works by Dutch and Italian masters. The royal antiques are so numerous that seventy-five volumes are needed to catalog them. More than 330 albums hold the royal stamp collection. The land portfolio represents almost £3 billion. The stock portfolio was valued at more than £2 billion in 1990.

Of course, all of this does not include what is owned by her son Prince

---

*As of 1990, Britain actually had more millionaires than aristocrats—20,000. In contrast, the United States has more than a million millionaires.

Charles, heir apparent to the throne. With vast estates totaling 140,000 choice acres, Charles is said to be worth £200 million.

Salaries in the Age of Greed

The word *salary* comes from the Latin *salarius,* meaning "of salt," and *salarium,* which the *American Heritage Dictionary of the English Language* notes meant originally "money given to Roman soldiers to buy salt." Undoubtedly the expression that someone is "worth his salt" has its origins in this period of history.

It has taken several thousand years since Roman times for salaries to have reached today's truly Olympian heights. From the corporate suite to the sports stadium, salaries for the top performers have escalated to where there seems little rhyme or reason—or, even more important, any relationship to the modest, earthbound salaries being earned by the man and woman in the street.

As the decade of the 1990s began, for instance, the salaries of some corporate heads reached such astronomical levels that Steven J. Ross, the head of Time Warner who died of cancer in 1992, received executive compensation—salary, bonus, stock options, and other benefits—that amounted to $78 million in 1990. This made him the best paid chief executive that year.

Here, according to *Forbes* magazine (May 27, 1991), is a list of the top ten best paid chief executives in the United States at the start of the 1990s:

1. Steven J. Ross, Time Warner, $78.1 million [now deceased]
2. Stephen M. Wolf, UAL, $18.3 million
3. John Sculley, Apple Computer, $16.7 million
4. Paul B. Fireman, Reebok, $14.8 million
5. Dean L. Buntrock, Waste Management, $12.5 million
6. Israel Cohen, Giant Food, $11.5 million
7. Martin S. Davis, Paramount, $11.3 million
8. Michael D. Eisner, Walt Disney, $11.2 million
9. G. Kirk Raab, Genentech, $9.2 million
10. Joseph Williams, Warner-Lambert, $8.8 million

With such lofty pay, the question could well be asked if these figures are out of line, if anybody is worth such compensation. *Forbes* asked that question with the answer on its cover: "It doesn't make sense."

And in that same issue *Forbes* reported that "there is soul-searching going on in the corporate and academic worlds about the fairness and effectiveness of existing systems of executive compensation." It was noted, for instance, that in the year Steven Ross took home $78 million his company was "struggling in the red to work off a debt of $10 billion in a merger that may or may not work out well."

In the recent past, compensation in many corporations has been dependent on personal performance, the concept being that managers would produce more if their pay were at risk. But this is now being seen more and more to result in self-serving actions that do not benefit the company as a whole. Asked *Forbes*, "Has the system of incentive pay for chief executives turned into a giant pork barrel? In many cases the answer is clearly yes." Although *Forbes* noted that in other cases the answer is no, the fact is that the current system, which pays some executives tens of millions of dollars even when their companies are showing mediocre results, "encourages little except cynicism . . . among investors, among workers, among the general public."

In other words, greed should no longer be the great motivating factor in the business world.

Greed, however, may still be the great motivating factor in the world of sports, where salaries have continued to escalate.

When the 1991 season started, baseball experienced its first $5 million man—Roger Clemens, a twenty-eight-year-old pitcher for the Boston Red Sox. A two-time winner of the American League Cy Young Award as his division's best pitcher, Clemens agreed to a four-year extension of his existing contract that would pay him a total of $21.5 million, for an annual average of $5,380,250. The salary would go to $4.4 million in 1992, $4.5 million in 1993, $5 million in 1994, and $5.5 million in 1995. The Red Sox took an option for a fifth year at $5.5 million with a $1.5 million buyout (Clemens got another $621,000 as a bonus for agreeing to the extension). Clemens at the time was finishing up a three-year, $7.5 million contract.

While Clemens was alone at the time with a $5 million average annual salary, he was soon superseded by a number of other players as the 1992 and then the 1993 seasons started. Indeed, within two years after Clemens broke the $5 million barrier, Barry Bonds, outfielder for the San

Francisco Giants, wound up with a multiyear contract that averaged close to 50 percent above Clemens's annual average figures. For the years 1993 to 1998, Bonds was to be paid at a rate that gave him $7,291,667 a year. And he was just one of four players that soon wound up being paid more than $7 million annually, with several others at more than $6 million.

Here as of the end of the 1993 season were the richest baseball contracts in terms of average annual salaries:

Player, Club	Seasons	Average Salary
Barry Bonds, Giants	'93–'98	$7,291,667
Frank Thomas, White Sox	'95–'98	$7,250,000
Cecil Fielder, Tigers	'93–'97	$7,200,000
Ryne Sandberg, Cubs	'93–'96	$7,100,000
Joe Carter, Blue Jays	'93–'95	$6,500,000
Cal Ripken, Orioles	'93–'97	$6,500,000

And these figures do not include income from potential incentive bonuses clubs may be offering their players, so these players could earn even more.

Plus there are endorsement contracts, which is another, often more lucrative story. Michael Jordan, the former Chicago Bulls basketball guard, was paid $3.5 million to play in 1992 but another $32 million for endorsements. Tennis player Jennifer Capriati secured $5.6 million in endorsement contracts as of the end of 1990. She was only fourteen years old at the time.

What do former players think of these salaries?

Jim Palmer, a pitcher with the Baltimore Orioles who is now in the Hall of Fame, once told a reporter: "Big salaries inflate bank accounts, but they don't accomplish much else." He pointed out that the inflated figures put great pressure on players already under enormous pressure. He termed baseball a game of negatives, with pressure possibly being the biggest negative of all.

"A .300 hitter makes an out seven out of ten times at bat," Palmer said. "That's a 70 percent failure rate."

As for the teams agreeing to offer such contracts, Palmer said, "Look, if owners are silly enough to pay those salaries, players are going to sign. But money shouldn't be the only motivation [for a ball player]."

It's a far cry from the hoopla when Mickey Mantle of the New York

Yankees became the first baseball player to be paid over $100,000 in a season. Or when Babe Ruth signed to play for the magnificent sum of $80,000, a figure that prompted a reporter to ask him how it felt to be paid more than the president of the United States, Herbert Hoover.

"Hell," replied Ruth. "I had a better year than he did."

••

SALARY NEGOTIATING, MUSICIAN-STYLE

Arthur Rubinstein, the famed pianist, charged huge fees whenever he was called by Hollywood to dub piano music for a movie. For three days of work on the 1946 movie *I've Always Loved You,* he said, his fee was $85,000. He admitted, out of the hearing of movie moguls, that such unreasonable charges were necessary to convince them that he was the greatest pianist they could hire.

••

Jock Greed

Perhaps the supreme demonstration of what Roger Lipsyte, New York Times sports columnist, has called "jock greed" came from Jack Morris. In December 1991, Morris, who was the pitching hero of the 1991 World Series when he powered the Minnesota Twins to a world championship, who is from St. Paul, Minnesota, and who has repeatedly said, "I love Minnesota," turned down a Twins offer of $5.375 million a year and instead signed with the Toronto Blue Jays of the same league for $5.425 million per year. In other words, for just $50,000 out of nearly $5.5 million—or about a 1 percent difference—Morris turned his back on his teammates, fans, and home city, and went to a rival team.

THE BASEBALL PLAYER WITH THE MODEST SALARY

"People think we make $3 million and $4 million a year. They don't realize that most of us make only $500,000."
—PETE INCAVIGLIA,
former Texas Ranger outfielder in *Sports Illustrated* (1991)

Does Jock Greed Pay Off?

The important question is, Do such salaries pay off for the teams and their fans?

From a look at what happened during the 1991 major league baseball season, the answer is no.

The two teams that spent the most on salaries were the Oakland Athletics with an average per player of $1.4 million and the Los Angeles Dodgers with a $1.3 million average salary. But neither made the World Series.

The two teams that competed in the World Series that year were the American League champions, Minnesota Twins, and the Atlanta Braves, the National League champions. The Twins, who became world champions, spent only an average of $921,000 a player, which was 11th on the list of 26 baseball teams. The Braves, who spent $679,000, were 18th in average salaries.

And then, too, there were individual cases in which teams got back very little value in return. The Chicago Cubs, for instance, spent $4.5 million on pitchers Danny Jackson and Dave Smith. With Smith winding up on the disabled list, the two pitchers between them won only one game (and lost 11) during the season.

Another was Keith Hernandez of the Cleveland Indians. He was paid $1.75 million, but became disabled and played no games. Over two years, he was paid $3.5 million and wound up playing only 43 games.

In contrast, some teams got great value from players with relatively low salaries. The Chicago White Sox paid pitcher Jack McDowell $175,000 and he won 17 games. They paid Frank Thomas $175,000 and

99

he hit 32 home runs, drove in 109 RBIs, and hit for one of the league's top averages with .318.

Who Are the Highest-Paid Athletes?

The highest-paid athlete in the world in one year was not a baseball, basketball, or football player. It was a boxer.

In 1991, heavyweight champion Evander Holyfield earned $60.5 million. He displaced the former champ, Mike Tyson, who still earned enough to come in second with $31.5 million.

In fact, heavyweight boxers held four of the top seven money spots that year. George Foreman was fourth, with $14.5 million. Razor Ruddock earned $10.2 million to place seventh.

Fighters, unlike other top-earning sports figures, have little endorsement money, making theirs mostly in salaries or earnings. Tyson, with $1.5 million in endorsements in 1991 before his conviction for rape, was at that time the only boxer with more than a million dollars in endorsements.

Interestingly, the next year, 1992, Michael Jordan, the basketball superstar, became that year's highest paid athlete with $35.9 million, of which $32 million was in product endorsements, according to *Forbes* magazine.

◆◆

COLORFUL LANGUAGE

"Don King looks black, lives white and thinks green."
> —LARRY HOLMES,
> former heavyweight boxing champ,
> about black fight promoter Don King

◆◆

"The Hollywood Effect":

One Reason Why Superstars Make So Much—and Others So Little

At the beginning of the 1992 baseball season, 273 players out of 650 on the major league rosters were being paid more than $1 million in annual salary. However, at the same time, in the minor leagues, thousands of players were paid hardly enough to make a living, even though many of them were almost as good as big-leaguers.

This situation can be seen in other pursuits. Artists, musicians, writers, performers, lawyers, corporate executives—all such areas exhibit a growing phenomenon: a "winner-take-all" situation in which the top few are paid the most money while many others in such fields, even those nearly as good, make far less.

This phenomenon has been labeled the "Hollywood Effect," since the movie world has been the most obvious in which such a syndrome has existed. A few stars make megabucks, while supporting actors and actresses and the extras make little in comparison. But why is this so? And will this inequity lessen or will it become worse?

One study of this situation was made in 1981 by a University of Chicago economist. In an analysis entitled "The Economics of Superstars," Sherwin Rosen determined that big markets produced big rewards that greatly favored the few top people in that industry. He found that among recording artists, the few most popular ones made far more money than those in the second rank, even though, he noted, few of the listening public could really tell the difference. He also noted that no more than two hundred comedians could make a living full-time as performers, fewer than could do so on the old vaudeville circuit, and yet the demand for comic performers was the same if not more.

Another study, a decade later, found that the winner-take-all situation had grown even more pronounced. Robert Frank of Cornell University and Philip J. Cook of Duke University pointed out that what had hitherto been largely found in sports, Hollywood, and other forms of entertainment was now occuring in investment banking, the field of law, and the corporate world. But they also discovered a new wrinkle—that the prevalence of the Hollywood Effect and winner-take-all markets was adversely affecting markets in general by drawing more people into those markets with the superstar pay and away from others where they might have been more suitable. The individual who wants to be a journalist but goes into law because he or she is attracted by the talk of much higher income, the natural-born teacher or scientist who opts instead for a chance at the megabucks of investment banking—these are just some of the results now being seen because of the skewing of income levels in favor of the few in certain industries. In other words, the Hollywood Effect arouses greed in too many people.

Some economists believe that a more progressive income tax will help alleviate such a situation. They assert that progressive taxes make possible a better distribution of wealth and make lesser paying careers more attractive, since the top earners in a market would not keep as much of their pay.

But something more clearly effective needs to be done about the growing disparity in income. As the Congressional Budget Office reported in a 1992 study, the top 1 percent of American families had 7 percent of all after-tax income in 1977, but this figure had climbed to 12 percent in 1989. In other words, in little more than a decade, the distribution of income had opened a further gap by more than 50 percent. The rich are not only getting richer, they're getting a lot richer.

THE HISTORY OF TOP FEDERAL SALARIES

The history of salaries and raises for top federal officials, always seemingly thought to be too high by the general public, show that government service is poorly paid when viewed against what has been occurring in business and sports.

George Washington and Abraham Lincoln, for instance, were both paid the same salary as President of the United States. In fact, the presidents from 1789 through 1873, a nearly one hundred-year span, were paid the same amount—$25,000 annually.

The presidential salary was finally raised to $50,000 with the presidency of Ulysses S. Grant in 1873. It was subsequently increased to $75,000 in 1909, and to $100,000 (plus $50,000 expense allowances) in 1949. Today's presidential salary of $200,000 (plus $50,000 expense allowances) has not been raised since 1969.

During the history of the United States, the salary of the vice president has gone from $5,000 in 1789 to the present $166,200. And pay for cabinet officers has increased from $3,500 to $143,800.

Congress has actually reduced some official salaries twice in U.S. history. Public outrage at raises as high as 50 percent that Congress approved in 1873 were rolled back in 1874. Three decades passed before federal pay increases were instituted again. Another reduction occurred during the early days of the Depression, when token pay cuts were made to show sympathy with the general public's declining economic situation.

Although all salaries of the federal government, except the president's, were higher in the 1990s when compared with the 1980s, nothing compares with what business and sports figures have been reaping since the Decade of Greed.

As the country slid into a severe recession in 1992, the same call for a cutback could be heard—even as the salaries for athletes and business executives continued to climb. Indeed, members of the United States Congress in 1992 were paid $129,500 a year—little more than the $100,000 minimum salary paid to a second-string baseball player in the major leagues.

The $2 Million Man: Life After the Presidency

In all the talk of million-dollar salaries, little if any of these pay scales compares to what Ronald Reagan was paid for one week's worth of work as a former President of the United States. In 1988, soon after leaving the White House at the end of his second term, Reagan traveled to Japan at the invitation of the Fujisankei Communications Group to give two speeches and attend a business event as master of ceremonies. For this work, he was paid $2 million—more than he had earned in eight years as President of the United States.

Actually, Reagan, who railed against big government and big spenders during his years in Washington, profited handsomely from the presidency. Before leaving the White House, he signed a multimillion-dollar book deal to publish his memoirs and a collection of his speeches. He also later signed up with a lecture bureau to make speeches for $50,000 each (his fee was twice that amount outside the United States, except of course in his Fujisankei appearance, which was for forty times as much). The $50,000 fee made him among the highest paid speakers in the country and meant that he could earn a million dollars a year just by giving an average of two speeches a month.

Reagan was at the same time also drawing on other sources of income and expense accounts as a former president. He receives a pension of $99,500 annually for life (he also gets a $30,800 annual pension from his two terms as governor of California), his office suite in a new California skyscraper was being paid for by the government at the rate of $173,000 a year, and he was getting another $150,000 yearly for office staff (this figure did not include his Secret Service protection, which in 1988 was then the largest in history—forty agents at a cost to the government of $10 million a year).

Let us not forget that Nancy Reagan was also earning money at the same time. She had signed her own $2 million book contract upon leaving the White House and had joined the same lecture bureau as her husband.

With Nancy working, could it be that, like most American families, the Reagans had found it necessary to become a two-income family?

◆◆◆

THE BROTHER-IN-LAW TEST

How does one determine who has wealth? H. L. Mencken, the acerbic observer of human behavior and social commentator on America during the first half of the twentieth century, once offered his sure test of wealth. It is, he wrote, "any income that is at least $100 more a year than the income of one's sister's husband."

◆◆◆

Legal Greed

Another area where incomes have mushroomed in recent years is in the legal field. This has led to significant changes for lawyers and for society.

The shift seems to have started with the Supreme Court ruling in 1977 that lawyers could advertise. Ever since, it seems that the airwaves have become filled with attorneys with one basic message—sue. As a result, court dockets are becoming ever more crowded as America becomes the land of the lawsuit.

The United States has far and away more lawyers per square foot of courtroom than any other country, and, with the lure of big money in salaries and settlements, tens of thousands of American youth have been rushing into law school. The result has been so much of an overabundance of lawyers that law school graduates began discovering it increasingly difficult in the 1990s to find jobs, let alone the hefty incomes that had enticed so many of them into law school.

How lucrative have lawsuits become?

Consider the following:

According to *The Lawyer's Almanac*, between 1962 and 1989 nearly 3,000 awards of $1 million or more in personal injury cases were made in just the top ten states. Eight states had 100 or more $1 million-and-up awards, with New York experiencing the most with 707 such cases in which plaintiffs won amounts in at least seven figures. Next was California with 540, Florida with 504, Texas with 320, Illinois with 216, Michigan with 202, Pennsylvania with 177, and Ohio with 100. Rounding out the top ten were Missouri with 96 and New Jersey 86.

The implications of this are fascinating. In just these ten states, at least 2,948 plaintiffs became millionaires from lawsuits—although it must be recognized that since these were personal injury cases some of these sums obviously went to pay off medical bills and help care for the injured in future years. The real winners, though, were the lawyers in these cases. For of the sums awarded by the courts—a staggering $2.9 billion in just these top ten states—attorneys probably received anywhere from 25 percent to 40 percent of the judgments as their industry-accepted fees (once in a celebrated case in Baltimore it was found that an attorney representing firemen injured in the line of duty tried to receive 60 percent of their award as his fee).

With attorneys reaping $1 billion in legal fees from just the $1 million cases in ten states, the advice to "Sue the bastards!" has now become one of the clarion calls of greed.

●●

HOW TO RETIRE AS A MILLIONAIRE

You don't have to lie, cheat, steal—or even work hard—to become a millionaire.

Beginning at eighteen years of age, if a person could invest just $50 a month in a stock tax-deferred retirement account compounding at 12 percent annually, such a savings program would total $1.3 million by one's sixty-fifth birthday.

●●

Is the World Mean to Millionaires?

(or, the Woes of Wealth)

But do the wealthy live easy, unfettered lives? Consider what may be one of the strangest magazine articles ever written. It surely had one of the oddest titles: "The World Is Mean to Millionaires."

The author was multimillionaire J. Paul Getty, writing the "Speaking Out" column in the *Saturday Evening Post* of May 22, 1965. The *Post* described him then as "the richest living American and probably the richest man in the world." Getty's major point is stated in the very opening of his essay: "Never have the burdens of wealth been greater than they are today, and never have its rewards been slimmer." In other words, the penalties of being rich!

What are the problems that the wealthy must endure?

For one, "rich people once lived in a world apart," Getty declares, but "today almost the only difference between the multimillionaire and the reasonably well-to-do man . . . is that the millionaire works harder, relaxes less, is burdened with greater responsibilities and is exposed to the constant glare of publicity."

It is the exposure to publicity that Getty finds the greatest trial. He relates that he usually gets at least fifty letters a day, but once his article appears he knows from experience this will zoom to three hundred or four hundred or even a thousand letters a day from strangers who nonetheless will address the letter "Dear Paul" and ask for either financial assistance for themselves or their families. Or the letters will be from "well-to-do people who wish me to contribute to their pet charities." Based upon his past experience, some requests will be from outright cranks and religious fanatics urging Getty to give away his riches for the good of his soul. A few, he predicts, might be like the one he had recently received; it demanded "one million dollars by return mail since you have so much of the stuff."

For this reason, writes Getty, he cannot respond to such requests. He points out that based upon an average request of $500 in an average of two hundred letters day, he would be giving away $100,000 daily, which he says would bankrupt him very quickly (although Getty forgets to note that the $1 to $2 billion he was then said to be worth generates $108,000 to $216,000 a day at just 4 percent interest).

All of this attention, writes Getty, does not leave him indifferent. In fact, "it often annoys me," he says candidly. Why? Because the solicitors for charities do not seem to understand the "basic financial facts of life, which is almost touching." And that fact is everyone assumes that Getty has a lot of cash around, ready for distribution. "It never occurs to them that, as an active businessman, I invest my money . . . no successful corporation, to my knowledge, has ever had a surplus of liquid cash. Why should these people assume that I do?"

Terming them the penalties of being rich, Getty says that he first learned of such problems when his father died. At that time, when Getty himself was thirty-seven, the first-time publicity of his father's wealth generated hundreds of proposals of marriage for his widowed mother from total strangers around the world. His mother was then seventy-eight years of age.

Getty himself then found people taking a different view of him, "a sinister glint that hadn't been there before." And soon he became wary of the "old friend" who calls up to renew acquaintances, only soon to make obvious why he did call up—for a loan.

To Getty, even giving away 99.5 percent of his wealth to charity would not make a real contribution to solving world poverty. He believes the best form of charity is the act of meeting a payroll, of giving people work rather than promoting passiveness caused by receiving charity.

Furthermore, to Getty, writing in 1965, the rich are no longer different from the average working person. They drive the same cars, wear the same kinds of clothes, live in much the same style, according to Getty. Indeed, for him "multimillionaires have been stripped of so many status symbols." The limousine is no longer the great elevating symbol of special wealth, nor are yachts, planes, or world tours because the nonmillionaire can have access to them too these days (besides, the huge steam yacht Getty once had gave him too much trouble and scheduled airliners are "as comfortable as—and a good deal safer than—the most expensive private planes").

No, according to Getty, most of the millionaires he knows live frugally, spending not much more on groceries than does the average working person.

And yet, finds Getty from personal experience, the rich person is often charged more by a doctor for visits and treatments, charged more by hotels for rooms, and expected to tip bigger. (Tipping seems to really bother Getty, who notes, "It's rude and inconsiderate to overtip. It only makes it more difficult—and embarrassing—for people who are not as rich as I am.")

This litany of hardships leads Getty to ask: Can really rich people live completely normal lives? Answers Getty: "It isn't easy."

With all these problems, asks Getty, why bother to become a millionaire in the first place? His answer: He has inherited wealth and is intent on using it constructively, taking special pride in running a corporation as successfully as others, if not more so.

"I could have turned all my assets into liquid cash, instead of working at the drilling business as I do, an average of 12 hours a day—longer hours, incidentally, than your average-income business executive or salary earner," but that to Getty would have been admitting he could not handle the responsibilities of running a business.

He ultimately posits that if all his money were taken away, "it wouldn't make all that much difference to me."

Concludes Getty: "At least I wouldn't be getting all those letters."

◆◆◆

WHAT PRICE HAPPINESS?

"I never enjoyed making money, never started out to make a lot of it. Money doesn't necessarily have any connection with happiness. Maybe with unhappiness."

—J. PAUL GETTY

◆◆◆

••

THOSE WITH A GILT COMPLEX:

LIFESTYLES OF THE RICH AND GREEDY

Whatever you

have, spend less.

—SAMUEL JOHNSON
(1709–1784),
English author

The lifestyles of those who overdo it have always fascinated others—as can be seen in all the gossip about the living and spending of kings and queens, rock stars and movie idols, tycoons and tyrants. What intrigues us is usually greed writ large—not just an occasional display, but routine lavish exhibits of what money should not necessarily buy.

Such opulent lifestyles have received even more exposure and a major boost in recent times through the medium of television. This is due in large part to a program that, week in and week out, celebrated conspicuous displays of consumption by those far from inconspicuous.

The TV show most unabashedly devoted to high living and spending has been *Lifestyles of the Rich and Famous*, hosted and produced by Robin Leach. A former newspaper journalist, Leach turned video chronicler of a subject he himself terms "what dreams money can buy." First aired in August 1983 (appropriately

109

enough the fourth year of the Greed Decade), the program went on to become one of the most successful nationally syndicated weekly shows in the history of television.

Lifestyles of the Rich and Famous seemed to be as marked by Leach's own high-pitched fawning over and celebration of his gaudy subject mat-ter—"the excitement of the twenty-four-karat corridors of success" as he has put it—as by "the celebrities and mega-millionaires, the sumptuous mansions and exotic hideaways" that he and his camera crew captured on tape. After all, the huge ratings success of *Lifestyles* (it led to such other Leachian TV productions as *The Start of Something Big* and *Runaway with the Rich and Famous*) is undoubtedly based on the human tendency to be attracted to and awed by what money cannot only buy, but what it can overbuy.

Leach was born in Harrow, England, a small town near London. In 1958, he started as a reporter with the Harrow *Observer*, then after three years moved to London's *Daily Mail*. By 1963, he had gone to the United States and begun a successful career as a freelance show business reporter, eventually becoming one of the world's most widely read celebrity col-umnists. He began appearing on TV with regular appearances on *A.M. Los Angeles* and *Good Morning, New York*, then joined the staff of Cable News Network for two years. He subsequently served as a roving reporter for three years on the TV show *Entertainment Tonight*.

In 1983, Leach finally launched his own series. *Lifestyles of the Rich and Famous* appeared initially as a two-hour special that scored a number one rating for an off-network show. After that auspicious debut, the pro-gram began airing regularly, bringing into homes and into countless minds each week the Leach message that "you too can be rich and famous and live life to the hilt, fulfilling your champagne wishes and caviar dreams."

Here is a look at some of the ways in which the rich and greedy spend their money as they pursue their champagne and caviar lifestyles.

The Rolls-Royce Mystique:
The Greed Factor on Wheels

What is it about the automobile that brings out the greed? Basically just a form of transportation, this invention of the twentieth century has become a prime status symbol. Maybe it is because one can easily parade

The Rolls-Royce has long had a mystique among automobiles. To own one was to have arrived—in very obvious style. Among some of the owners of Rolls-Royces have been not only sheiks, maharajahs, and shahs, but Elvis, Muhammad Ali, and those foes of capitalism—Stalin and Lenin.

it and oneself in front of others; maybe because next to a house and possibly a college education for one's child, a car is the largest investment many will make.

Autos costing $30,000 or $40,000 and up are becoming commonplace. The Cadillac, seen for so long as the top of the line in the United States, is now almost passé as the luxury models from Germany and Japan supplant it. But one automobile has throughout this century stood so far above the fray that it is the ultimate status symbol. That auto is the Rolls-Royce motor car.

The Rolls-Royce bears the names of its original developers—the Honorable Charles Stewart Rolls and Sir Frederick Henry Royce. Royce was an engineer whose pursuit of perfection had led him to start producing what was possibly the best car of his era. Rolls was an aristocrat who raced and sold cars, and he was looking for an upscale British car to sell. Brought together in 1904 by a mutual acquaintance, the two formed Rolls-Royce Limited in 1906. It was an early dramatic achievement for their car—successfully completing a 14,000-mile nonstop test—that put the Rolls-Royce ahead of the competition.

From the start, Rolls and Royce made certain their automotive product went its own superior way—with handcrafted interiors, painstaking attention to detail, relatively few changes over the years, and small numbers produced each year (2,000 Rolls-Royces are now made annually; General Motors in one week produces more cars than all the Rolls-Royces ever made—300,000 versus 95,000).*

The scarcity and the craftsmanship, combined with the high price and the seeming search for excellence, have led to what has been called the Rolls-Royce mystique. Such an appeal has attracted as owners royalty, heads of state, Eastern potentates, maharajahs, sheiks, financiers, and motion picture stars—which has fueled the Rolls-Royce mystique even more. Its long-established slogan, "The Best Car in the World," has also fed the snobbish, upper-crust aura surrounding the vehicle—a reminder that the nonroyalty, nonsheik owner has the wealth to own and maintain such a chic class of car.

The Rolls-Royce snob appeal has also been fed by doing things differently—such as rarely advertising and then when doing so embarking on the famed Ogilvy campaign with the headline: "At 60 miles an hour

---

*The Rolls-Royce people produce another car, the Bentley, which is a Rolls-Royce with just a different radiator grille and hood ornament. The Bentley usually sells for $500 less than the Rolls-Royce and has its own devotees.

the loudest noise in this new Rolls-Royce comes from the electric clock."

Over the years, a number of owners have ordered special, ultracostly customizing that transformed the interiors of Rolls-Royces from deluxe to bizarre. For example, the maharajah who had the steering wheel in his Rolls-Royce made entirely out of elephant tusks, the controls carved out of ivory, and a throne covered in damask silk in the back. Or the dealer in rare period furnishings who had his car's interior upholstered with a special tapestry costing in 1927 more than $3,000 and requiring nine months to make (not to mention the ceiling, which was painted by a French artist brought specially to England to work on the decoration). Or the person who had a car outfitted with a gold and emerald built-in vanity by Cartier for $10,000.

Then there are the Rolls-Royces converted by their owners after they took delivery. Such as the Maharajah of Nabha, who wanted his Rolls to be in the shape of a swan—and got it, with the exhaust discharged through what looked like the beak of the bird. Or the Maharajah of Patiala, who wanted his 1911 Rolls-Royce upholstered in salmon-pink silk, the bodywork painted in matching color, and the dashboard studded with diamonds.

Indeed, Rolls-Royces have found special favor with the maharajahs of India. The Maharajah of Patiala, who passed away in 1928, had 38 of them; the Maharajah of Mysore bought 35 Rolls-Royces and 9 Bentleys.

But there is one Rolls-Royce modification that must have left Mr. Rolls and Mr. Royce spinning in their graves. The Maharajah of Alwar, angered after an argument with Rolls-Royce about modifying his cars, had all six of them converted into garbage trucks.

Rolls-Royce Trivia

Some surprising people have owned Rolls-Royces:

• Vladimir Ilyich Lenin, the father of the Russian Revolution and foe of capitalism, ordered nine Rolls-Royces while head of the Soviet Union. To travel in snowy Russia, he ordered an absolute rarity—the only Rolls-Royce built to convert its back wheels to half-tracks for going through the snow. Three of those nine Rolls-Royces are said to still exist, including the one with half-tracks. Another of his Rolls-Royces is on display in the Lenin Museum in Moscow—a 1919 Silver Ghost with chassis number 16X.

- Soviet dictator Joseph Stalin also owned a Rolls-Royce.
- So, too, did the Soviet leader, Leonid Brezhnev. In fact, during his 1979 meetings with United States President Jimmy Carter in Vienna, Brezhnev had his Rolls-Royce shipped to him to use in between their talks.
- Even Henry Ford owned a Rolls-Royce. His was a Silver Ghost that he bought in 1924. The man behind the Model T and the mass-produced auto had a ready explanation for his use of a Rolls-Royce. Driving over to see a friend, he explained: "My Ford was being serviced so I drove over in the next best thing!"
- Elvis Presley, known for buying people Cadillacs as gifts—he bought his mother a pink one—bought himself a Rolls-Royce.
- Bhagwan Shree Rajneesh, the guru who headed a sect with a large following, especially women, and who lived in an Oregon retreat before he was deported back to India, had a love affair with Rolls-Royce cars. He had forty-seven—all bought for him by his followers. At one point, they were buying him a Rolls-Royce at an average rate of one a month. "He likes to go for a drive," explained a sect member. Said Bhagwan: "There is nothing holy about being poor."
- Jack Dempsey, the heavyweight boxing champ, bought a Rolls-Royce after he beat Luis Firpo for the title. Dempsey wound up buying six during his lifetime—one for each successful title fight.
- Monaco, the country ruled by Prince Rainier, has the distinction of having the highest per capita ownership of Rolls-Royces—one per 65.1 people.
- The former shah of Iran may have held the distinction of being the most comprehensive owner of Rolls-Royces. He purchased nearly every model that Rolls-Royce ever made up until his time. His collection included a Silver Ghost, Silver Shadow, Phantoms I, II, III, IV, V, VI, a Twenty, a 20/25, a 25/30, a Camargue, and a Corniche.
- Ernest Hemingway owned one.
- So did President Woodrow Wilson.
- As did Muhammad Ali.

But my favorite is Reverend Ike, the leader of the United Christian Evangelistic Association of America. His real name was Dr. Frederick J.

Eikenrenkoetter II, and he openly displayed his Rolls-Royce while teaching love and charity. Explaining the presence of such a sumptuous car with such a message, Reverend Ike told a reporter: "In my church we don't teach poverty. We teach aiming for riches. These damn cars are the nearest thing I've come across to the chariots of the Lord."*

The Rolls-Royce—
A Dissenting Opinion

Not everyone is enamored of the Rolls-Royce motor car.

Alexander Karas is the owner of a Rolls-Royce limousine service in Baltimore with six to his name. He is also a customizer of luxury cars, restoring not only Rolls-Royces but Jaguars, Cadillacs, Lincolns, and Mercedes-Benzes. So he knows something about Rolls-Royces and luxury cars. His opinion of the Rolls-Royce?

"It's a piece of crap," he says.

He points out that the Rolls-Royce breaks down so much "you almost need a mechanic with you in the trunk.

"We're always having to oil them. And they're always having to be fixed," he moans from experience. "At least one of ours would break down every weekend."

Karas says that until the mid 1950s, the Rolls-Royce was ahead of its time, but then American car manufacturers took over, coming up with sensible engines for their luxury cars. Rolls-Royce, however, continued using their engines from before World War II, according to Karas.

"They've never been able to build their own automatic transmission. From 1955 to 1965, they used the General Motors hydromatic that was being used in Buicks, Oldsmobiles and Cadillacs. In 1966, they went with the Chrysler Torque-Flight transmission, which is still being used," says Karas.

"They also haven't been able to build their own air conditioner. They get theirs from General Motors' Frigidaire Division. And the shocks come from a company in France. But they didn't really do anything about the ride until the late '60s," Karas says.

Also, according to Karas, Rolls-Royce originally would build the chassis but a coach builder would build the body for them.

*See *Rolls-Royce: The Complete Works: The Best 599 Stories About the World's Best Car* by Mike Fox and Steve Smith (London: Faber and Faber, 1984).

115

"There's so much myth, fallacy and legend about this automobile that for some people these facts don't matter. Some owners are faithful to the creed. The egomaniacs who buy them pay an exorbitant amount because the rest of the world knows the car costs $100,000. These owners accept the problems because of the image of the car."

To Karas, the Rolls-Royce mystique is not based on reality.

"It's really the biggest marketing scam in history. There's no Blue Book listing values of the Rolls-Royce. Lots of them are just investments, like art, and they do seem to appreciate faster in value than most other investments. But how can a car really be worth over $100,000? The new ones are not hand built—they're spot welded. And the drive train they now use is the same one that Disney uses in the antique cars in the Magic Kingdom. It's a marketing con job, but Rolls-Royce has a name and they're riding on it."

Karas is not alone in some of his views about the Rolls-Royce. Rocky H. Aoki, the head of the Benihana chain of Japanese stock houses and at one time the owner of eight of the motor cars, was once quoted as saying about the Rolls: "Very unreliable car. Very costly to maintain. One time I buy car from Sheik of Bahrain. Engine blew up."

But still he and others buy Rolls-Royces. Why?

"I like style of Rolls. I don't care about engine," Aoki also said. "Big car really eye-catching."

Selling the Highest-Priced Rolls-Royce:
A Prime Example of "Conspicuous Language Consumption"

It is an axiom of economics that the more money a person has, the more likely it is he or she will display openly the purchasing power of that money. The concept is called "conspicuous consumption." In other words, people who have money to burn will burn it—publicly.

Well, I hereby offer a corollary of that axiom: namely, that those who try to sell a luxury-priced item to the rich will invariably discuss the item in ways that will unnecessarily expend language, as though to match in words what the wealthy will spend in money. I call it "conspicuous language consumption."

I have long treasured a full-page ad that Rolls-Royce ran in such publications as *The Wall Street Journal* in 1976 to introduce its then highest priced model—the Camargue. At the time, the two-door hardtop sold for $90,000.*

"Introducing a masterpiece," reads the advertisement's headline beneath a picture of the masterpiece parked in front of the Metropolitan Opera House in New York City (parked by the way, right on the sidewalk, possibly to imply another Rolls-Royce benefit: The rich never get parking tickets).

"Several years ago, the restless minds that run Rolls-Royce Motors had a dream," begins the ad's excursion into Conspicuous Language Consumption. And what was that dream? "The dream was an island on wheels."

"The inspiration," we soon discover, "was the white and wild horses of La Camargue." La Camargue, it turns out, is "the all but untamed island off southern France that prizes its freedom above all else." (I would also add that Camargue is not only an untamed island but, for me at least, an unpronounceable island as well.)

For $90,000, a product must be provided with overtones of history and undertones of imagery in addition to an unpronounceable name. Here an expensive car is compared to a horse—a true irony, since for centuries mankind tried to improve upon the horse, and when it finally succeeded, the first name it gave the invention was "horseless carriage." I guess it takes a purchase price of $90,000 to get a person back to basics.

The Camargue was not a car or an automobile, but a "motor car"— in fact, "the motor car of a lifetime" that was built "one at a time by hand" (oh, the evils of mass production).

But don't think you could get your Camargue just like that. In addition to the $90,000, it would have cost you something even more precious—time. "If you decide to purchase one of the very few Camargues that will be available this year, please bear with us. It took us several years to build our very first Camargue. It will take us several months to build your very own Camargue."

See, Mother was right. To be beautiful is painful. Everything has its price—even being the first on your block to drive a Camargue.

Believe it or not, the ad begins its discussion of the basics about this "timeless pleasure" this "priceless asset" by getting its fingers dirty with talk of engines, brakes, and shock absorbers.

But then begins the waving of adjectives, proper names, and snooty

*When discontinued in the mid 1980s for a four-door model, the Camargue was priced at $175,000, many consider it the best riding car Rolls-Royce ever made.

117

materials that is supposed to feed the flames of Conspicuous Language Consumption.

"Her all but silent air-conditioning system" is said to have taken eight years to perfect, but don't worry about the results of such dull and lethargic engineers; this is an air conditioner that "will purify the air you'll breathe in any climate at two levels of the interior, automatically." Does this need for two levels of purification mean that we are right to refer to the rich as "filthy rich"?

But these were only part of "other minor miracles." Why, the very controls for the "gear selector, the seats, the doors, the windows and the luggage compartment are"—now get this—"electrical." Amazing!

But if you would like to hear more Conspicuous Language Consumption, the ad invites you to call a long-distance number to find out where your neighborhood Rolls-Royce dealer resides. That number is, interestingly, not a toll-free number. But that's part of the pose. Only those who really work for their money would be enticed by a toll-free number. The Rolls-Royce people can get away with being cheap precisely because their customers do not wish to appear cheap themselves. More conspicuous consumption.

The saving grace in all this for you and me is that we can take comfort in remembering that an automaker for the masses like Ford never went bankrupt. Rolls-Royce Motors, Inc., did, bailed out only by the British government.

Which should tell you something about what happens to people who burn money and language in public.

KEEPING SCORE: THE SIGN OF THE SECOND CAR

George Papadopoulos has been termed one of the most successful accountants in the Midwest, with thirty accountants on his staff and a suite of offices in Chicago's most glamorous office building. Said to be "acutely concerned with his image," he is quoted in the book *Warm Hearts and Cold Cash* by Marsha Millman with having some interesting observations about money and the trappings of wealth. Among his most trenchant, however, is his view of the significance of a person's second car.

"In the suburbs, you know how you can tell a successful person?

Not by the car he drives, but by the *second* car. That's the clue. If you live in an affluent community everyone has a Cadillac or a Mercedes. What the hell's the difference? But—the truly affluent guy is the one who has two Mercedes or a Mercedes and a Cadillac or a Mercedes and a Corvette," Papadopoulos says. "Think about it. It's the second car that controls, not the first."

Now, all you have to do is look into a family's two-car garage to see how well the family is doing. You don't even have to look at the garage or the house.

The Status of Status Symbols:
The Shrinking of the Stretch Limo

The status symbol of the limousine underwent a transformation in the Greed Decade of the '80s. The Cadillac limousine, popular in the '60s and '70s, grew longer and longer in the 1980s, with windows tinted ever darker for ultimate privacy. Thus was born the stretch limo.

While these extra-long limousines usually have Cadillac bodies, what most people don't seem to know is that Cadillac does not and never has made a stretch limo. These are made by custom body shops or coach builders who take a Cadillac body, cut it in two, and add a middle segment to stretch the limousine. The result are limos of various lengths, limited only by variety. The inside is then further customized with added touches of luxury and comfort—from built-in bars and color TVs to Jacuzzis. So in demand were these stretch limos, usually costing $50,000 and up, that according to *Limousine & Chauffeur* magazine, between 1981 and 1987 production almost tripled.

By 1990, the story had changed. With the Greed Decade over and the economy souring, demand dropped off to such a degree that production of stretch limos had skidded more than 37 percent and scores of coach builders had closed their doors. The demand was again for smaller limos.

In addition to the fact that Cadillac never did make stretch limos, two other facts are not generally known about this status symbol. First, most are rented by individuals or corporations for periodic or special use rather than bought. And second, the source for many such rentals are funeral homes, which lease them out for private use during off hours.

The Status Symbol Among Savers:

The Swiss Bank Account

One of the status symbols—if not necessities—of being rich is having a Swiss bank account. In an age of easily accessed computers stuffed with personal financial information, as well as a time of an increasing number of bank failures, more and more of the moneyed are turning to the privacy and security of either a regular Swiss account or the ultrasecret numbered Swiss account, known only to a few officials of the bank. (Of course, a side benefit of a Swiss bank account is the one-upmanship of letting friends and associates know one has one's funds in "my bank in Zurich.")

Actually, banking privacy can be found in three other places—the Cayman Islands, Panama, and Hong Kong, each of which has similar laws to the Swiss restricting disclosure of information by their banks. But only the Swiss offer the security of one of the most solid banking systems in the world.

What makes the Swiss banking system so attractive to those who want secrecy are the Swiss rules in its penal code against disclosure of banking information. A large fine of 20,000 francs (or about $14,000), or a prison sentence of six months or both can be imposed on a bank employee who reveals information about a customer.

However, that does not mean a person can just walk into a Swiss bank, open a numbered account with large amounts of cash, and expect everything to be hush-hush. A relatively recent agreement among Swiss banks requires them before opening a numbered account to "interview" the depositor to see if there are "legitimate" reasons for the person wanting the high-level privacy. The agreement, however, is loosely interpreted and enforced.

Also, American depositors are now being made to agree in writing that if their deposits are being used to trade in the stock market, their records can be available to investigators. Furthermore, Swiss banking secrecy can be overturned if it can be shown that funds on deposit were stolen or gained from "crimes committed under Swiss criminal codes." But since United States income tax laws are not binding under the Swiss code, the Internal Revenue Service can get access to a Swiss account only by showing tax fraud, a much more difficult case.

All in all, if someone wants the strictest banking privacy available—

in a country known for its stability—that person wants his funds in a Swiss bank account.

How, you ask, does one go about opening such an account?

You can either appear in person at a branch of a Swiss bank in the United States (the largest all have branch offices in New York City) or, if you want to do it in style, you can stop off in Switzerland and just walk into the home office of a Swiss bank. (Note, however, that if the account is opened in the United States and you die, the United States government and your debtors get their share of your funds first, but if you open the account in Switzerland, you can appoint someone else with the power of attorney over your estate.)

More and more Swiss banks are requiring large minimum deposits, although at times and for the right reason some Swiss banking officials will lower the initial deposit requirement. Here, too, opening the account in Switzerland can be advantageous. The Swiss Bank Corporation, which requires a minimum $100,000 deposit in the United States, will accept $25,000 at home in Switzerland. The rich don't have to worry about the mechanics. The Swiss will generously allow a customer to wire his deposit from his present bank with just a phone call.

The application one must fill out is, surprisingly, often less involved than the application for a United States banking account. The Swiss banker will ask you for name, address, date of birth, and occupation. For proof of identification, a driver's license or passport will do. After that, all that needs to be supplied is that little matter of the initial deposit and then you, too, can have your very own Swiss bank account.

Although interest on a Swiss bank account is usually less than a United States bank offers, you can do anything through a Swiss bank you can do at an American brokerage house—including investing in Euro-dollars, international stocks and bonds, and certificates of deposit in any of the major world currencies.

But to help maintain your privacy and for added security, you will be required to make your withdrawals in writing.

For more information about opening your own Swiss bank account, call or write one of the following, each of which has a New York office: Crédit Suisse, Swiss Bank Corporation, or Union Bank of Switzerland.

Remember—once you open your Swiss bank account, you will have your money in as secure a place as possible. You will also have a lot of company. Swiss banks now have one trillion dollars on deposit from foreigners alone. Just don't look for the Swiss to set up an automated teller machine at your local supermarket.

•

Party! Party! Party!

The greedy do not seem to be private people. After all, why are there Rolls-Royces and Cadillacs if not so their owners and occupants can be more readily seen in public? Isn't the point of flashy diamonds and fashionable minks to make their wearers stand out in the crowd?

Which explains the rationale behind the most public, conspicuous display of the fruits of greed—the lavish party. History is replete with parties featuring copious amounts of fancy food and frivolous decor, the more expensive, overdone, and unnecessary the better. The party atmosphere is, after all, the one situation that enables the greedy not only to show off, but to involve others in the display, thereby gaining, if just subliminally, fellow cohorts in excess.

Here are a few significant milestones in the annals of partying over the past hundred years.

The Birth of the Four Hundred

On February 1, 1892, *The New York Times* published the names of the Four Hundred, a supposedly exclusive list of the cream of New York society. The list had been compiled by a man named Ward McAllister, a snobbish social climber. In 1872, he had met Mrs. William Backhouse Astor, Jr., the wife of the grandson of John Jacob Astor and the reputed queen of New York society. Together they developed the concept of the Four Hundred based upon a curious physical fact. This was the number of people who could fit into Mrs. Astor's ballroom for a party.

McAllister had first announced the Four Hundred idea in 1888 when he observed that since only that number could fit into Mrs. Astor's ballroom, then only that figure constituted society because, he noted, "if you go outside that number you strike people who are either not at ease in a ballroom or else make other people not at ease." Interestingly, when McAllister finally released his list of the Four Hundred, it had almost a hundred names less than ballroom capacity.

Eventually, Make-a-Lister, as he was derisively called by the non-Four Hundred, was shut off from high society when his views and actions were increasingly ridiculed by others. Among his choicest beliefs, which he openly expressed, was that "hospitality which includes the whole human race is not desirable" and that the most distasteful thing about America was the practice of shaking hands.*

The Vulgar Dress Ball

What has been termed one of the supreme examples of vulgar spending took place on February 6, 1897. On that date, Mr. and Mrs. Bradley-Martin, newly moved to Manhattan and eager to secure their place in New York society, threw an enormous fancy dress ball at the Waldorf-Astoria Hotel. They converted the hotel into a replica of Versailles Palace, complete with rare tapestries, and asked several hundred guests to come dressed as court figures from England and France.

Bradley-Martin himself dressed as Louis XV, with a brocade suit to complete his kingly attire. August Belmont came dressed in a suit of gold inlaid armor said to cost $10,000. The ladies came drenched in jewelry, the value of which one chronicler of the time wrote "simply baffles description."

All in all, the expenditure on the party and on the clothes was said to have been more than $300,000—at a time when the country was in a severe economic downturn and a living weekly wage was in the tens of dollars. With the Hearst and Pulitzer newspapers reporting all the vivid tales, there was a storm of public reaction to what the Bradley-Martins had done. They eventually left New York for England—and never returned.

The "Poverty Social"

The conspicuous displays of wealth lavished on balls and parties during the Gilded Age had its guilt-ridden conclusion when, in response to rising criticism about such wasteful spending on frivolity, some members of the social set hosted what came to be called the "Poverty Social." Here funds were raised for charity in what was felt to be more appropriate settings. At one such "poverty-stricken" affair, hosted by a Western mil-

*When Malcolm Forbes, as head of *Forbes* magazine, was looking for a way to top rival *Fortune* magazine's famed Fortune 500 listing of America's leading companies, he started an annual listing of the Forbes 400—the four hundred richest Americans. The 400 figure echoed McAllister's famed list.

lionaire, guests were instructed to come in tattered clothing. Upon arrival, they found seating accommodations to be battered boxes and buckets. Presented with old newspapers, dusting cloths, and worn skirts as napkins, the guests dined on scraps of food served on wooden plates and drank beer poured from a rusty tin can. The cost of the party was still considerable—it was said to be $14,000, a considerable sum for the time.

The 2,500-Year-Old $100 Million Party

Time magazine called it "one of the biggest bashes in all history." But that was no surprise to its host, who had history very much in mind when he conceived the festivities.

In October 1971, the shah of Iran, wanting to show the world that Iran "is again a nation equal to all the others—and much finer than many," mounted a celebration marking the 2,500th anniversary of the founding of the Persian empire by Cyrus the Great. Representatives from sixty-nine nations responded to the shah's invitation. Among those attending were an emperor, nine kings, five queens, thirteen princes, eight princesses, sixteen presidents (including the President of the Soviet Union), four vice presidents (including the Vice President of the United States, Spiro Agnew), three premiers, two foreign ministers, nine sheiks, and two sultans.

One head of government who did not attend was France's president Georges Pompidou. He seemed to capture the spirit of the event, which had a decided French flavor to it, by noting that if he went "they would probably make me the headwaiter."

Maxim's of Paris was the caterer serving up a lavish menu that included quail eggs stuffed with caviar, roast peacocks stuffed with foie gras, stuffed rack of roast lamb, and champagne sherbet. More than 165 chefs, wine stewards, and waiters were brought in from France, along with 25,000 bottles of wine. Decorations, by Jansen of Paris, featured Baccarat crystal, Ceralene Limoges china, and Porthault linens. As part of the festivities, guests were treated to a recreation of Alexander the Great's sacking of Persepolis, the capital of Persia more than 2,000 years ago.

All in all, it took the shah sixty-two air-conditioned tents spread over a 160-acre oasis and an estimated $100 million to put on such a pageant.

In response to those who wondered why he had spent so lavishly, the shah had the perfect answer: In hosting so many heads of state he had to treat them royally, didn't he? "We can hardly offer them bread and radishes, can we?" he asked.

Greed and ostentation have their own punishment, which helps to explain why the shah—long vilified by his subjects for his high living—was eventually forced to flee Iran by January 1979. Thus, just a little over seven years after he had thrown one of the biggest bashes in history, he himself had become, as they say, history.*

THE PARTY HOSTESS CHAMPION

Grace Vanderbilt, the wife of Cornelius Vanderbilt III, is said to have calculated she spent $300,000 a year for fifty years entertaining guests—a figure that totaled $15 million, an extravagant sum for any day.

The Case of "Diamond Jim" Brady
(His Fortune Went to His Stomach)

Talk about overdoing it. Few can match the case of "Diamond Jim" Brady, a wealthy businessman living at the turn of the century who devoted his fortune to feeding . . . and feeding . . . his face.

When Brady died in 1917, it was found that his stomach was six times the size of a normal man's stomach. And little wonder. The following was an average day's fare for Diamond Jim.

His typical breakfast: heaping portions of hominy, eggs, corn bread, muffins, flapjacks, chops, fried potatoes, and beefsteak—plus a gallon of orange juice.

At 11:30 A.M., he had a mid-morning snack—two or three dozen clams or oysters.

For lunch he then had more shellfish, deviled crabs, boiled lobsters,

*When the shah fled his country, I remember thinking at the time that there was a perfect title for his autobiography if he ever decided to write one: *I Ran Iran Until I Ran.*

a joint of beef, a huge salad, and several pieces of pie—plus more orange juice.

In the late afternoon he had tea—plus another platter of seafood and two or three bottles of lemon soda.

Then came dinner. Now he really got serious. He had two or three dozen oysters, six crabs, two bowls of green turtle soup, six or seven lobsters, two canvasback ducks, a double portion of terrapin, sirloin steak, vegetables, and for dessert a plate of French pastries—plus two pounds of chocolate.

After Brady's death at fifty-four, Charles Rector, owner of Brady's favorite New York restaurant, commented, "Diamond Jim was the best twenty-five customers we had."

◆◆

THE DECENT THING TO DO

"When you have told anyone you have left him a legacy, the only decent thing to do is die at once."

—SAMUEL BUTLER
(1835–1902), English author

◆◆

The Whims of the Wealthy Department—

Exhibit A: $300 Cola

Christina Onassis, the daughter of shipping magnate Aristotle Onassis, was considered one of the richest women in the world after her father died. She could, therefore, have probably had any drink she wished, no matter what the cost. But what she chose was the commonest of all drinks—and she literally drank it no matter what the cost.

Her favorite was first Coca-Cola and then, as she gained weight, diet Coke. She consumed it morning to night, up to thirty bottles a day. And she would make sure she had a ready supply wherever she was.

As, for instance, when she was in France, where diet Coke was not available. No problem. Each week she would send her ten-seater jet to New York to fly back to her with exactly one hundred bottles. Why only a hundred bottles? "Because," an aide told someone who once inquired, "Madame doesn't want *old* diet Coke."

At the time, the cost to transport the hundred bottles worked out to $300 a bottle—making Coke surely one of the most expensive drinks in the world.*

World's Most Expensive Hotel

At one time, the world's most expensive lodging was a Parisian hotel whose rooms ranged in price up to $7,000 a night (and that did not even include breakfast).

This was the Nova Park Élysée. Opening in 1981 and located near the Champs-Élysées, it had just seventy-three rooms, but each was luxuriously appointed. Upon arrival, each guest was greeted with a bottle of champagne and flowers. The hotel featured a gym, bars, disco, and such services for business executives as secretaries, telex machines, and worldwide access to financial information. The Royal Suite ($4,500 per night) offered five bedrooms, a reception area, seven bathrooms, a meeting room, and an office.

The $7,000-per-night accommodations were available in a three-floor layout called the Thousand and One Nights Suite. This featured not only rooms spread over three floors, but a garden and swimming pool, plus a Rolls-Royce with chauffeur provided gratis for the night.

Alas, in January 1986 the hotel folded. One of the things that seemed to do it in was its restaurant, which oddly enough had low prices and was open to the public. The crowds attracted to the restaurant turned off the hotel's upper-crust clientele, who began staying away. The lesson for other hoteliers: For $7,000 a night (which works out to almost $300 an hour), a guest wants something a little exclusive.

Trump's $25 Million Yacht

One of the playthings of the rich and greedy is the yacht—not only a high-ticket luxury item to buy, but to maintain. However, for the ac-

---

*Christina became such a consumer of Coca-Cola that it was reputed she could drink a glass of it and tell from what bottling plant it had come—especially those in Europe, where the taste and sweetness varies from one country to another.

quisitive and the avaricious, a yacht is definitely the thing to have.

One of the highest visibility yachts was purchased by Donald Trump for $25 million from Adnan Khashoggi, a Saudi Arabian businessman and arms dealer reputed to be one of the richest men in the world. Trump bought the 282-foot vessel as a forty-second birthday gift to himself. When the yacht sailed into Absecon Inlet to be delivered to him, eleven film crews were there to record the event and President Ronald Reagan sent a congratulatory telegram.

The yacht—Donald named it *Trump Princess*—has eleven opulent suites, thick superwhite carpets, 3,500 yards of chamois leather, and bathtubs carved out of white onyx. It is powered by two 3,000-horsepower 16-cylinder turbocharged diesel engines.

The yacht was assigned to Trump Castle, one of his Atlantic City Casinos, for business purposes, but this meant that Absecon Inlet, where the marina was located, had to be dredged to accommodate the vessel. The cost: more than $1 million. Various operating expenses totaled $400,000 a month. This meant that in 1989 the casino, then losing money, was paying out $5.7 million to house the yacht.

But for all this expenditure, Trump himself rarely used the *Trump Princess*. He was so terrified of being on board when it was sailing that he only went on when it was docked at the marina so he could either watch a boat race or occasionally entertain an important client or business associate. Except for the Trump-owned vessel's maiden voyage from the Azores to New York Harbor, during the first two years he owned it, Trump never sailed or slept on his $25 million toy.

◆◆

"Piggy, piggy, piggy."

—former New York City mayor, ED KOCH, referring to Donald Trump

◆◆

What's in a Name? For Trump, It's $500,000 a Letter

Donald Trump is noted for putting his name on everything he can get his checkbook around. But his preoccupation with naming things for himself one time led to an expenditure of more than a million dollars because of an apostrophe and a single letter in the alphabet.

In 1988 Trump decided that one of his Atlantic City casinos, Trump's Castle, needed major reworking because it was now losing money—its $41 million in interest payments meant the property was posting a $3 million net loss, the first in the casino's history.

So what did Trump do?

Instead of following the recommendations of the new chief executive officer of his casinos that he institute cost-cutting measures, Trump actually ordered two costly renovations. One, at an expense of $2 million, involved ripping up the relatively new carpeting in the casino and replacing it. Why? Because it did not match the carpeting in the new show-room then under construction as part of the Castle Tower project at the casino.

The second decision he made was to change the name of the property. Donald decided he wanted to change the name of Trump's Castle to . . . Trump Castle. So he ordered that the apostrophe and the letter *s* be immediately dropped. But this necessitated major changes throughout—both on the outside and inside signage and in the operation of the facility.

"Every sign, logo, decal and fixture, plus the huge letters on the outside at the top of the hotel tower, had to be replaced at a cost of more than $1 million," writes one of Trump's former casino presidents, Jack O'Donnel, in *Trumped!* (New York: Simon and Schuster, 1991).

The casino staff tried to save money by at least using for the outside sign some sign letters found in the Castle's warehouse. Costing $50,000, these letters would at least be cheaper to install than ordering new ones. So the staff took them out of the warehouse, lifted them up to the top of the casino, took down the old letters saying "Trump's," and mounted the new ones in place next to "Castle."

"But when Donald saw the new sign," writes O'Donnel, "he flew into a rage: the letters that spelled 'Trump' were slightly smaller than those that spelled 'Castle.' He immediately had the entire sign dismantled."

It was one time when Donald Trump paid dearly to put his name up in lights.

All the Greed That's Fit to Print:
"The Robb Report" Reports It All

The unabashed pursuit of materialism even has its own publication. It's a slick, glossy, four-color monthly magazine called *The Robb Report*.

With issues running well over two hundred pages, the magazine is crammed with articles and ads about luxury autos, yachts, dream vacations, art, antiques, aircraft, premium properties, food, wine, and collectibles. Subtitled "For the Affluent Lifestyle," *The Robb Report* is touted in subscription ads in the publication as "The Magazine for People with Million-Dollar Taste."

First started in 1976 as a newsletter for Rolls-Royce devotees, *The Robb Report* published out of Acton, Massachusetts, was expanded into a magazine in 1984. More than 85,000 copies are now distributed nationally and internationally each month. Largely available through the mail by subscription (the regular one-year subscription in the U.S. is $65 for twelve issues, $100 a year for foreign countries), issues are also sold or distributed through high-class hotels, specialty shops, and similarly exclusive outlets (the single-copy price is $6).

Who subscribes to and reads "The Magazine for Connoisseurs," as the publication also calls itself? In a profile sent out to ad agencies and other prospective advertisers, the average subscriber was shown by an independent market research company to be a male (91 percent of readers), forty-one years of age, with an average annual income of $422,000 and an average net worth of $2.6 million. Forty-four percent own more than four cars, 25 percent own three or more homes, 42 percent own a boat.

What do these people do for a living? Seventy-four percent are either a corporate president, CEO, or business owner, and 25 percent are either a doctor, lawyer, professional, or technical person. But these people are not all work and conspicuous consumption. While 58 percent belong to a country or tennis club, 89 percent report visiting museums, art galleries, and antique shops and 58 percent attend concerts or musical events (32 percent attend the opera or ballet).

What are the contents of the magazine that attracts them as readers? Here are some of the major articles in various issues over a six-month period: a profile of the superexpensive Bugatti 110 Supercar, playing golf in Palm Springs, all about luxury yacht charters, sport boats under $100,000, building your dream boat, ideas for fantasy vacations, a comparison of ten luxury coupes, and an annual assessment of "the world's best hotels, cars, boats and more!"

In its annual Ultimate Gifts Guide (published in December, just in time for holiday gift-giving), the magazine one year touted the latest Bentley model—the Continental R, a turbocharged sporting supercar selling for $261,000 . . . the newest Harley-Davidson motorcycle, the Dyna Daytona, selling for $12,120 . . . a rosewood cane with a twenty-six-inch Wilkinson sword hidden inside ($10,000) . . . the Golden Dream golf clubs—a set of nine irons and a matching putter made out of a Japanese-developed alloy containing almost 10 percent gold plus nickel and bronze (price: $100,000) . . . a seven-day, six-night vacation at Jamaica's newest and most luxurious resort, with special gifts daily and twenty-four-hour service throughout ($50,000) . . . even what is termed possibly the most expensive home in the world—the eight-story hundred-year-old Casa Batillo in the heart of Barcelona, Spain, that has undergone extensive restoration; once termed by a famed Spanish architect as a "vision of paradise," the residence that was built to look like an undersea palace is valued at $110 million.

But it is in the area of luxury cars that *The Robb Report* is filled with out-of-sight high-priced items. Readers and car dealers fill the pages with new and restored autos, from $93,000 Porsches to a 1958 Impala Sport Coupe once customized for Sylvester Stallone (asking price: $45,000) to a wide variety of Rolls-Royces and Bentleys (how would you like a forty-year-old Bentley convertible with 83,361 miles for $140,000?).

Plus there are of course the ads for lush, plus estate (like the $7.2 million Brach Candy Mansion in St. Petersburg, Florida, with its three sets of security gates, his and her studies, seven bedrooms, eight baths, four garages, four fireplaces, cabana, pool, spa, deepwater dock, guest house and more). And then there are the ads for watches costing thousands of dollars, for airplanes, yachts, horses, art, rare coins, wines, rare breeds of dogs, zoo animals ("the Zoo Store can provide any animal allowed by law"), custom-made pens for $12,000, even original restored Coca-Cola soft drink coolers for $1,895 (the headline reads, "You Just THINK You Have Everything!").

Why, it's enough to make you feel that Robin Leach, host of TV's "Lifestyles of the Rich and Famous," should somehow be part of this. And there he is! In the December, 1991, issue, Leach is the interviewee in The Robb Profile, a column concluding the issue. Asked why he reads *The Robb Report*, the chronicler of the moneyed set intoned, "It is the world's greatest department store of toys. It is for those whose hands can immediately reach for the wallet, checkbook or credit card. It addresses, on a monthly basis, things that even I, in the world of the rich and famous, don't know about."

Well, now we all know where to find that special little something for a gift.

But even *The Robb Report* realizes that money can't buy everything. As the editors state in an introduction to one of their Ultimate Gifts

Guides, "(W)e believe, as always, that in the final measure it's the thought that counts. . . . (K)eep in mind that the ultimate gift is often the one given with the most heartfelt intentions."

For the Magazine of "Money, Power and Greed,"

IT WAS A SIGN OF THE TIMES (THAT IT'S OVER)

Begun in 1980 in Washington, D.C., this slick, glossy magazine covered the business, political, and social worlds swirling around the nation's capital. Its name was *Regardie's*, with the subtitle "The Business of Washington." As a result of its provocative, controversial, yet stylish approach, the magazine grew and prospered, propelled in part by numerous reports on financial scandals that usually ran along with an oft-repeated label the magazine put on such doings: "Money, Power and Greed."

Among the stories it covered with hard-hitting articles were savings-and-loan scandals in the Maryland area, the failure of the National Bank of Washington, the United Way financial scandal, and the connections between First American Bank and the Bank of Credit and Commerce International. An upscale audience and advertisers wanting to reach that audience responded. Especially fueling the magazine's growth was the real estate boom in and around the nation's capital as high-rise office buildings and luxury homes for executives were built—and advertised. The average issue went to 350 pages and revenues mushroomed to as high as $8.5 million in 1988.

But then the bottom started falling out of the Washington commercial and residential real estate market, which had been the major source of advertising for the publication. In a city that was supposed to be recessionproof because of all the federal government offices and workers located there, as well as the presence of so many lawyers and associations and lobbyists that fed off the federal government, Washington at the end of the 1980s became as mired in recession as the rest of the country at that time. With the recession of the 1990s hitting with perceptible impact, Washington suddenly found itself with a stalled, then moribund real estate market. Sales started to plummet at *Regardie's*, so much so that by 1991 the monthly magazine switched to every other month and laid off almost all its employees. By 1992, sales had sunk to $1.3 million. The publisher, William A. Regardie, had tried some novel approaches to save the magazine—at one point, during the height of the recession, he even tried as a publicity stunt to hawk subscriptions to the magazine on the sidewalks of Washington, D.C., like someone selling apples during the Depression—but nothing stemmed the tide of red ink.

Facing continued losses after not seeing a profit since 1988 and having invested more than $2 million of his own, Regardie, in December 1992, announced he was ceasing publication. The magazine of "Money, Power and Greed," the magazine that had been the first to chronicle some of the major business scandals of the 1980s, fell silent.*

◆◆◆

PRESCRIPTION FOR HAPPINESS

"Annual income twenty pounds, annual expenditure nineteen nineteen six, result happiness. Annual income twenty pounds, annual expenditure twenty pounds ought and six, result misery."

—CHARLES DICKENS

◆◆◆

*On its cover for July 1989, *Regardie's* magazine showed a bloated, cigar-smoking figure sitting atop a mound of money as an illustration for its cover story: "The Greed Decade: Is It Over? What's Next?" Inside, editor Brian Kelly wrote that with that issue the publication hoped to be coining the phrase "the Greed Decade" for the 1980s. He noted that although somebody had said it before (he had "conveniently forgotten who"), no other magazine had splashed across its cover this term for what he called "the greatest chowdown that this country has ever seen."

••

IMELDA MARCOS'S SHOES AND MARY TODD LINCOLN'S GLOVES:

OUTLANDISH SPENDERS AND THEIR SPREES

Anyone who says

money doesn't

buy happiness

doesn't know

where to shop.

—ANONYMOUS, quoted in
Forbes (March 4, 1991)

Everyone knows about Imelda Marcos. The one-time wife of the President of the Philippines lived high and well and shopped often during his corrupt presidency, when the Marcoses allegedly stole and hid millions, if not billions, from the Philippine treasury. As one indication of her extravagance, it is reputed that she bought more than 1,000 pairs of shoes (some even say it was 3,000 pairs). Not as well known is the fact that she also purchased more than 300 bras—all the same style and the same color (black).

And all this was going on at a time when Imelda's countrymen and -women were existing on meager wages and living in modest means. In fact, her spending over the two decades of her husband's virtual dictatorship is said to have plunged her poor country into serious debt. Although a federal court jury in New York later found her not guilty of fraud and racketeering in what was said to be her attempt to steal $222 million from her country

134

while its First Lady, Imelda Marcos was found guilty of corruption in 1993 by a Philippine court and is now appealing a sentence of eighteen to twenty-four years.

Today, Imelda remains as the supreme example of greed through shopping. As one magazine noted in a profile of her in 1991, five years after she and her husband had fled the Philippines in panic to avoid angry rebellious mobs, "They were a brilliant couple: as Ferdinand practiced the politics of intrigue and patronage, Imelda shopped, and shopped, and shopped, and shopped."*

Here are some examples from former and present times when unbridled greed led many notable men and women to "shop until they dropped."

Mary Todd Lincoln's Urge to Splurge

Abraham Lincoln, born to poor parents, was careful with his money throughout his life. Mary Todd, his wife, was born to a banker and raised in a wealthy home, but she spent money so freely that she plunged herself deeply into debt throughout much of her life.

The penny pincher and the spendthrift. If opposites attract, the story of the Lincoln marriage is the story of two vastly different sides of the coin of greed.

There was evidence of Mary's buying sprees before she became First Lady, but once in the White House she went on what one of her biographers has called "wild shopping expeditions." Her purchases were especially surprising since they came at a time of war and deprivation for the public and the military. With soldiers "in want of blankets," for instance, Mrs. Lincoln paid $2,000 for just one gown and $1,000 for a cashmere shawl, as well as purchasing a white point lace shawl later valued at $2,000.† She even bought eighty-four pairs of gloves in one month.

Along with some women friends, Mrs. Lincoln would make regular shopping excursions to New York City, Philadelphia, and Boston. She

---

*An indication that the shopping habit dies hard can be seen in a news report in August 1992 that Imelda, while in Hong Kong to search for family assets six years after her exile, went shoe shopping and bought six pairs of crocodile shoes said to cost $5,806—or almost $1,000 a pair. The news reports also said that to protest her presence, 30 Filipino students demonstrated in front of her hotel by building what they called a "monument of shame." The "monument" consisted of piles of shoes and shoeboxes.

†These sums are especially enormous considering her husband's annual salary as president was $25,000.

While Abe Lincoln was born poor and stayed frugal (is that why he's the one on the penny?), his wife, Mary Todd, was a shopaholic, once buying eighty-four pairs of gloves in one month.

bought herself an array of bonnets, gowns, slippers, shawls, diamond ear knobs, little gilt clocks, and sets of china, silver, and crystal. Some of these items she used only once or twice—or not at all.

Her letters to others are full of her thoughts and concerns about clothing, jewelry, and items for the White House. Although as First Lady she had a budget of $20,000 for redoing the White House, she overspent this budget, too. She purchased a dinner service with the seal of the United States that so impressed her she bought a second set with her own initials in place of the U.S. seal—at a cost of $1,100. She bought bell pulls, brocades, books, draperies, ornate furniture, custom-made carpets, and wallpaper. She expended sums for cleaning, repairing, painting, and papering the mansion. She modernized the White House with furnaces and gaslights in place of fires and candles. Although the modernization may have been needed, she soon discovered to her horror that she had soared past her $20,000 limit by $6,700, most of which was owed to a wallpaper firm located in Philadelphia.

Realizing what she had done, she tried to get the commissioner of public buildings, Major Benjamin Brown French, to get her husband to understand "it is common to overrun appropriations. . . . Tell him how much it costs to refurnish," since, she hoped, "he does not know much about it." She also feared that Abe would offer to pay for the cost overrun himself, which she confided to the commissioner "he cannot afford." Finally, she implored: "You must get me out of this difficulty."

When he found out, Abe Lincoln exploded. According to Commissioner Brown in a letter he later wrote, Abe responded that he would never countenance additional appropriations to pay for the overexpenditures.

"It can never have my approval—I'll pay it out of my pocket first— it would stink in the nostrils of the American people to have it said that the President of the United States had approved a bill overrunning an appropriation of $20,000 for *flub dubs*, for this damned old house, when the soldiers cannot have blankets."

Abe, echoing many other husbands, then wondered what his wife's costly activity was all about. "The house was furnished well enough, better than any one we ever lived in. . . . "

There were other bills she ran up, and she found herself turning to wealthy men to pay for her extravagant purchases so that her husband, the president, would not know. By 1864, on the eve of Lincoln's reelection campaign, Mary had run up debts of $27,000, primarily to one New York store. She became that much more anxious about her husband winning another term, something that Abe noticed but that he ascribed to her concern for him. But she had another reason as well. "If he is re-elected," she told her dressmaker, "I can keep him in ignorance of my affairs; but if he is defeated, then the bills will be sent in, and he will know all."

Her rationale for all this spending was tortured and complex. At times she voiced the belief that she felt an obligation as First Lady to dress well for all occasions. She also felt that her purchases of imported materials actually helped the treasury and were a patriotic act. Furthermore, she believed that if anything happened to the family's financial fortunes, she could sell these purchases for much of what she paid for them.

But what also propelled her buying sprees was a growing neuroticism that may have been developing from an early age. Her mother died when she was seven and she was raised by a stepmother she detested (there were also the births of nine siblings she then had to contend with from her father's new marriage). Early in her marriage to Abe, while living in Springfield, she lost a child to diphtheria, and then in the second year in the White House, her eleven-year-old son Willie died, plunging her into prolonged grief. She also had a temper and a cool manner that alienated others and the press, who focused on her negative qualities, often over-looking her good efforts as First Lady, such as her trips to army hospitals. The resulting coldness and indifference of others drove her even further into the warming embrace of accumulating possessions.

Abe Lincoln's assassination—he was shot as he leaned over to talk to Mary and she experienced the full horror of her husband being mur-dered beside her—drove her further into what soon became a descent into insanity. Her emphasis on elegant clothing continued—her mourn-ing veils needed, she said, to be "the very finest, and blackest and light-est"—but now she implored Congress and others to pay for her upkeep because she believed she was sliding into poverty. She even advertised in the New York *World* for help and tried to sell her clothes and other personal effects at auction. This shocked and angered the public.

Finally, a New York businessman, Joseph Seligman, came to her as-sistance. For several years, Seligman and his brothers sent her money, and Joseph pushed Congress to pass a pension bill to care for the widows of presidents. The bill finally passed in 1870. Later, the benefits were upped by $2,000 a year and a one-time bonus of $15,000 paid.

Even with this pension and bonus and even with the sixty-four trunks and crates of possessions she kept stored in a room in her sister's house, Mary Todd Lincoln died believing she was poor. But after she passed away

July 15, 1882, at the age of sixty-four, it was found that at the time of her death she was worth $90,000.

Her estate was more than her husband's when he had died. Frugal Abe Lincoln left an estate valued at $80,000.

◆◆◆

"It is a great thing to make a fortune. There is only one thing greater, and that is to keep it when made."
—BENJAMIN DISRAELI (1804–1881),
Prime Minister of England

(Disraeli was so deeply in debt by the time he was twenty-one it took him thirty years to get out of it. In fact, his political career was propelled by his debt problems since he was able to avoid debtor's prison by being elected to the House of Commons.)

◆◆◆

Jacqueline Kennedy Onassis:
First in the Hearts and Shops of America

One of the most glaring examples of shopping-spree mania can be found in the case of Jacqueline Kennedy Onassis, who exhibited the trait before, during, and after she served as First Lady. Based upon eyewitness testimony over the years—plus the exhaustive research by author C. David Heymann reported in *A Woman Named Jackie* (New York: Lyle Stuart, 1989)—Jackie appears to have gone through millions of dollars in purchases of clothing and furnishings alone.

In the early days of her marriage to John F. Kennedy, even while he was a young senator from Massachusetts, she would spend inordinately for expensive clothes and furnishings for their home. It led an exasperated John F. Kennedy to exclaim: "She's breaking my ass."

George Smathers, a family friend who observed Jackie's actions and John's reactions, told Heymann how the two haggled over bills. "In that sense, they had an entirely average marriage—she spent and he seethed."

When JFK reached the White House, his wife seemed to reach even higher spending heights. During the spring of Jack's first year as president, Jackie spent more than $35,000 just on clothes. And this figure did not include her White House clothes allowance, which JFK's father, Joseph, was funding.

Among Jackie's practices as First Lady was to wear clothes once and then return them—or even sell them. But such actions did not compensate for the accumulation of bills (one time, an item appeared on Jackie's clothing account marked, "Department stores . . . $40,000," but neither Jackie nor anyone else could explain it). As a result, JFK at one point retained an accounting expert and friend to review spending records and put some controls on Jackie's account. The expert JFK turned to was no slouch: He had worked on various Senate subcommittees to decipher the financial records of the Mafia.*

But still the spending went on. By the end of 1961 and her first year in the White House, Jackie had personal expenditures of $105,000. The next year she even topped that—$121,000. At one point, a frustrated President Kennedy queried a friend, "Isn't there a Shoppers Anonymous?"

Later, as JFK's widow, Jackie found a new source of funds for her spending—one of the richest men in the world, the Greek shipping magnate Aristotle Onassis. Her marriage to the short, inelegant Onassis stunned much of the world. One explanation for her actions—a common sentiment voiced in France at the time—was that "this woman has a bank vault for a heart."

At first, Onassis gave her huge gifts—for her fortieth birthday he gave her a 40.42-carat diamond ring valued at $1 million—and provided her with a $30,000 monthly tax-free allowance. But when she soon overspent even this sum, Onassis cut it down to $20,000 monthly and closely monitored it.

But Jackie was not to be denied. She soon developed into a speed shopper, plunging into a store, buying things, and leaving—all in ten minutes.

"She didn't bother with prices, just pointed," Heymann quotes a source. "She bought anything and everything: music boxes, antique clocks, fur coats, furniture, shoes." She particularly liked to visit the international fashion shows and buy up the entire collection.

The bills that came into Onassis's office shocked his financial overseer: $5,000 for slacks, $6,000 for the care and feeding of pets, $7,000 for

---

*Robert Kennedy had somewhat the same spending problems with his wife, Ethel, and he too used the accounting expert to try to control her. But Ethel was no match for Jackie, and, in fact, at one point Ethel complained to her sister-in-law that she was damaging the Kennedy family name "with all that reckless spending."

items from a local pharmacy. Once she purchased two hundred pairs of shoes for $60,000. Onassis complained: "She orders handbags, dresses, gowns and coats by the dozen—enough to stock a Fifth Avenue specialty shop."

After buying all these clothes, Jackie would often revert to a practice from her White House days—she would sell the clothes to such second-hand stores as Encore in New York. According to columnist Jack Anderson, who once looked into the spending—and selling—habits, Jackie would then "stash the cash."

She also tried to get department stores to give her a reduction on her clothing purchases because, she told them, it would be good for their business for people to see her wearing their merchandise. Or she would return items soon after buying them on impulse. One Bergdorf Goodman salesman recalled her buying three dozen pairs of shoes one day, then returning them the following day.

Another herculean spending effort by Jackie occurred over a nine-day stay in Teheran with an entourage consisting of her husband and several friends and business associates. She ran up huge purchases of Persian rugs, clothing, jewelry, and art objects, topped off by a large quantity of golden caviar as a souvenir of the trip. The total bill for the nine days: $650,000. Although Jackie promised to leave a $700 check for tips to the hotel staff who had provided round-the-clock room service, she departed without doing so.

When Ari Onassis died in 1975, leaving an estate valued at between $400 million and $1 billion, he was contemplating divorce, but advisers to Onassis's daughter, Christina, worked out an agreement with Jackie's lawyer. She received $26 million, with $20 million going directly to her and the rest going to cover estate taxes. This was twice what she would have gotten under the will and seven times what she would have gotten had Onassis lived to complete divorce proceedings, but far less than what she could have received. The sum, however, was in addition to the $200,000 a year of lifetime income he had bequeathed to her in his will. It is estimated that during the six years of her marriage to Onassis, Jackie grossed $42 million.

The settlement made Jackie a millionairess in her own right—a far cry from the near penniless state in which she married John Kennedy (although seemingly from monied background, her parents had divorced when she was eleven, and whatever monies her father had were dissipated over the years). It also came nearly twenty years after an interview printed in the December 1957 issue of *Ladies' Home Journal*. Jackie, posing with her sister, Lee, for a fashion layout, had told the magazine: "I don't like to buy a lot of clothes and have my closets full. A suit, a good little black dress with sleeves, and a short evening dress—that's all you need for travel."

When a First Lady Became "Second Hand Rose" to Boost Her Popularity

Nancy Reagan was another First Lady widely accused of overspending, especially in her early days in the White House. Her wardrobe for the inauguration was reputed to have cost $25,000 (it consisted of a red dress by Adolfo, a Bill Blass black dress, a James Galanos gown, and a full-length Maximillian mink coat).

She added to her spendthrift image by prodding major Republican contributors to put up $800,000 to add special touches to the White House mansion and used a similar approach to buy a 220-piece set of gilded china for more than $200,000.

As a result, her image plummeted. A *Good Housekeeping* poll in 1981 failed to show Nancy Reagan among the top ten most admired women in America.

Nancy, however, took an unusual approach to deflate her critics. She decided to poke fun at herself by performing a surprise skit about her spending habits at the March 27, 1982, annual dinner of the Gridiron Club, an event that brings together the nation's most powerful press and political figures for an evening of spoofing the high and mighty.

Arranged secretly in advance with those who organized the evening's performances (even President Reagan did not know), Nancy performed a parody of "Second Hand Rose" entitled "Second Hand Clothes."

The skit began when Nancy, dressed in a green skirt with red and yellow flowers held together by safety pins, a large hat of feathers, and a boa, sprang into view through a rack of clothes. The former movie actress then sang the following song:

> Second hand clothes,
> I'm wearing second hand clothes.
> They're all the thing in spring fashion shows.
> Even my new trench coat with fur collar,
> Ronnie bought for ten cents on the dollar.

> The china is the only thing that's new.
> Even though they tell me that I'm no longer queen,
> Did Ronnie have to buy me that new sewing machine?
> Second hand clothes, second hand clothes.
> I sure hope Ed Meese sews.

Her performance—and her self-deprecation—were an instant hit and, according to Hedrick Smith in *The Power Game*, a major factor in resurrecting her image among, first, the press and later, the public. By January 1985, especially after she lowered her clothes profile and raised her antidrug efforts, one major poll found her approval rating was actually higher than her husband's—71 percent to 62 percent.

If everyone loves a winner, Nancy Reagan had shown that when it comes to criticism, no one loves a whiner.

◆◆◆

"I am living so far beyond my income that we may almost be said to be living apart."

—SAKI (1870–1916),
British author

◆◆◆

THE QUEEN OF MEAN WAS ALSO A CRIMINAL CONSUMER

"The basic elements—greed, avarice and sheer nastiness—are just too wonderful, aren't they?"

The remark was made by a British reporter covering the highly publicized 1989 tax fraud trial of Leona Helmsley and her husband, Harry. The Helmsleys owned a vast real estate and hotel empire, and Leona had made a name for herself posing in ads as "the Queen" of the luxurious Helmsley Palace Hotel in mid-Manhattan. But during the trial she had also come to be seen as a tightfisted employer who terrorized her workers, exploited suppliers, and engaged in lavish spending on herself.

After a long trial (in which her lawyer even tried what was called "the bitch defense"—that Leona's former employees testified against her because Leona *was* a bitch to work for), "the Queen" was convicted of thirty-three felonies, including conspiracy to defraud the IRS, evading $1.2 million in federal taxes, filing false tax returns, and mail fraud. At the time, she and her husband were reputed to be worth over $1 billion.

And yet personal items large and small had been illegally charged to their businesses, including $2,000 for a pink satin dress (said to have been "uniforms"), $1 million spent on construction of a swimming pool enclosure at their mansion home, a $45,000 birthday present from Leona to her husband, and a $12.99 girdle from Bloomingdale's.

Her problem may have been found in the remark she made to a former head housekeeper of her mansion, a remark that made headlines when it surfaced during testimony at the trial: "We don't pay taxes. Only the little people pay taxes."

Her problem may also have been part of a shopping compulsion. As the reporter who covered her trial and later wrote a book about her noted, "The Queen was an obsessive consumer."*

One of her maids said that if Mrs. Helmsley liked a sweater she would buy as many as twenty-four of the same kind in various colors. She did the same with dresses, pants, blouses, and skirts. The clothes had to be kept clean and ready for wearing, although few were worn: Just having the right color available at a moment's notice seemed enough for "the Queen."

The same was true of stockings—hundreds of them were kept clean and ready for wearing. Another former employee reported that Leona would purchase ten gross of stockings—1,440 pairs—in one color at a time. One day, a truckload of stockings was delivered to the mansion. Leona, laughing, said she had made a mistake and had ordered twelve gross of three or four colors. The amazed employee stated that it was not twelve gross all together but twelve gross of each color, which meant a total shipment of at least 5,000 pairs of stockings.

Another outlandish purchase was lipstick—a very red lipstick. This same employee once counted twelve cases of the same red lipstick—over 2,000 tubes.[†]

As her former employee remarked, "There was this insatiable quality about Mrs. Helmsley. There was always a hunger for *more*—there was never enough of anything."

In her case, it also got her something else—a criminal record.

The Queen of Mean: The Unauthorized Biography of Leona Helmsley by Ransdell Pierson (New York: Bantam, 1989).
[†]The astonishing aspect of this statistic is that even if Leona used up a tube a week, she could not have gone through her stash of lipstick in less than 38 years.

How the World's Biggest Spender Spends $120 Million a Year

How does one of the richest men in the world spend his money?

Adnan Khashoggi, the Saudi Arabian wheeler-dealer and arms merchant, is reputed to have made more money more quickly than anyone else in history—and to spend it more rapidly than anyone else. Born July 25, 1935, as the son of a prosperous doctor who was the personal physician to Abdul Aziz, founder of modern Saudi Arabia, Khashoggi had the connections to the Saudi royal family, as well as the business acumen, to serve, beginning in the 1960s, as middleman on Saudi defense contracts and the purchase of arms and airplanes from Western manufacturers, pocketing huge multimillion-dollar commissions in the process.

In on the ground floor of Saudi development in the 1960s and 1970s, he owned the Saudi agencies for Rolls-Royce airplane engines, Marconi, Fiat, and Chrysler. He represented such American companies as Lockheed Corp. (by the mid-1970s his commission from Lockheed totaled more than $100 million) and Lockheed's rival, the Northrop Corp. (which brought him $54 million). On the Saudi army's purchase of $600 million worth of armed cars from France, he made $45 million. He was also the first Arab to develop land in the United States (he organized and invested in a $450 million industrial park and foreign trade zone in Salt Lake City). He assembled nearly fifty companies into a worldwide conglomerate, with investments in banking in California and South Korea, cattle ranching in Arizona, a giant meat-packing plant in Brazil, a chain of hotels in the Pacific, a shipping company in Indonesia, a furniture manufacturer in Liberia, and a ready-to-wear clothing manufacturer in France. He is said to be the model for the high-flying Arab tycoon in Harold Robbins's best-selling novel *The Pirate*.

Khashoggi's personal wealth has been estimated at times as high as $4 billion. Such a prodigious fortune has enabled him to spend at a prodigious pace.

As one chronicler of the Arab world has noted, his less-than-discreet spending may have come from a long-remembered statement his father once made to him: "Throw coins on the carpet. You hear nothing. Throw them on a stone floor. They make a noise. My son, always put your money where it can be heard." He appears to have taken this advice to heart—and magnified it.

A biography by an award-winning investigative journalist and *Washington Post* reporter—*The Richest Man in the World* by Ronald Kessler (New York: Warner books, 1986)—spells out how he would spend an estimated $300,000 a day, every day of the year. His American Express bill alone would often top $1 million in a month.

One area he splurged on was his residence. At one time, he had twelve luxurious homes around the world—in the Canary Islands, Monte Carlo, Rome, Cannes, Jeddah, and Riyadh. Each was fully staffed at all times. The most sumptuous was his villa in Spain, which was set on 5,000 acres overlooking the Rock of Gibraltar. It not only had its own helipad, rifle range, disco, and ten marble bathrooms, but also a reserve for 20 Arabian stallions, 200 African animals, and 70,000 pheasants for hunting. It was here that he hosted lavish parties that attracted celebrities like Frank Sinatra and Brooke Shields and heads of state like King Juan Carlos of Spain.

He also had his own game ranch in Kenya (with a pool for his pet crocodiles), a duplex in Paris housing much of his $30 million art collection, and a two-floor Manhattan residence valued at $25 million (it was so big it had its own swimming pool and was so lavishly appointed that *House & Garden* magazine gave it an eighteen-page color spread in a 1984 issue).

Another of his possessions was one of the biggest and most lavish yachts afloat. A 282-foot gleaming vessel that required a crew of forty and was built at a reputed cost of $70 million, it was used in the James Bond movie *Never Say Never Again*. He eventually sold it for $25 million to Donald Trump so he could replace it with a $100 million yacht.

He had also had his own helicopter and three commercial-size jet airliners, including a Boeing 727 and a $31 million DC-8 that, originally equipped to carry 259 passengers, was converted by Khashoggi at a cost of $11 million into a custom flying machine capable of flying fifteen hours nonstop, complete with forty-foot, carpet-walled sitting room, double beds, video machines, and triangular chinaware costing $600,000. His annual jet fuel bill alone was said to be more than $1 million.

But in addition to spending on clothing—he has been known to buy a half dozen suede and leather jackets lined with fur and cashmere for $2,000 each and to spend $60,000 in a one-hour shopping spree in Cannes—Khashoggi has spent lavishly on one other indulgence: pretty girls. Not just one at a time, but as many as eight or ten at a time.

"They came in from California or Texas, or from France on the Concorde," writes Kessler. "As if handing out Tootsie Rolls, Khashoggi always gave them gold bracelets."

A witness is reported to have seen him go from one bedroom to another, visiting each of the girls in turn or two or three of them at a time. Although married, he found his thirst for beautiful women growing as his wealth grew, and he easily arranged to purchase nights with the most beautiful call girls around. He eventually arranged through a madam with connections to meet various *Playboy* or *Penthouse* playmates that he had seen in the magazines (many of those who responded did not always measure up in person to their retouched magazine photos and had to be specially prepared by the madam).

Khashoggi would pay up to $1,000 for a night and $2,000 to $3,000 for a weekend, plus give presents that might include jewels, furs, or more cash. Centerfold girls cost more—as much as $15,000 plus their travel costs. It was estimated that with one of the madams who arranged these liaisons he spent more than $500,000 in ten months.

But Khashoggi did not always purchase the services of these girls for himself. He often provided them to his friends, business associates, or, writes Kessler, members of the Saudi royal family.

Indeed, Khashoggi tired of the parade of female flesh. "Over time, he became corrupted by his own wealth. The more girls he bought, the less they satisfied him. He always wanted fresh new faces and women who would outdo the previous ones," says Kessler.

Today, with the drop in oil prices and with the Saudis dealing more and more directly with arms merchants, Khashoggi's wealth no longer places him among the world's richest. However, at the height of his earnings, Khashoggi's annual personal expenses, as listed by AK Holdings Ltd. for items ranging from telephone bills (as high as $300,000 a year) to parties, butlers, limousine expenses, and gambling (he has been known to gamble $250,000 on the roll of a dice), were $120 million, which, writes Kessler, "clearly dwarfs any other known level of spending."

Khashoggi's days as the world's biggest spender may be over. When last seen, his personal fortunes as well as his monetary fortune had seriously slipped. He had been indicted on racketeering and fraud charges, then arrested and imprisoned in Switzerland (where, it is said, he was made to clean the prison toilets). He eventually had to sell his yacht, saw his jet impounded by creditors, and was forced to spend money on lawyers to fight the charges against him. In March 1992, *Parade Magazine* reported that Khashoggi was living in Spain, still waging legal battles, and was "down to his last $54 million."

●●

"Unless you can communicate with other human beings, I don't care how much money you have, you have nothing for the other person."

—ADNAN KHASHOGGI,
quoted in *The Richest Man in the World*

●●

These, of course, are stories about the buying habits of famous or wealthy people. How does the average person compare when it comes to shopping? Not much better. Let's look at the situation in our shopping malls and in our use of credit cards.

Who Told You You Can't Have It All?:
The Story of America's Biggest Mall

When it opened on August 11, 1992, in Bloomington, Minnesota, a suburb of Minneapolis, nearly 150,000 people came to see and shop at the largest mall ever to open in America, and by the end of the first week more than a million people had come to this retail mecca. The Mall of America, as it is called, quickly became known as the Mega-mall, and for good reason. Built at a cost of $650 million on 78 acres and containing 4.2 million square feet, with 400 specialty stores and huge versions of a number of national department store chains, the Mall of America offers shopping over what is said to be the equivalent of 41 football fields.

In addition, in an effort to be a tourist attraction and a destination for the entire family, the Mall houses Camp Snoopy, the world's largest indoor amusement park, with seven acres of rides (including a roller coaster), trees (400), plants (30,000), a mountain, and a waterfall (four stories high). Plus there are more than a score of restaurants (fast food and expensive), a movie house (14 screens), nightclubs, and parking for 13,000 cars.

The Mall of America would have been the largest in the world, but the developers, the Ghermezian brothers, had to scale back their initial plans because of changes in their financing and local skepticism that retailing on such a grand scheme would work. But the builders had no qualms. In fact, the major partners in the project are the same ones who built the $1.1 billion West Edmonton Mall in Alberta, which still ranks as the world's largest. Their plans for America's largest mall call for it to draw more people eventually than Walt Disney World or the Grand Canyon.

The concept behind such a gargantuan monument to marketing is the hope that the shopper is endlessly ready to be lured by the fantasy of merchandising hoopla. As the theme song for the Mall of America expresses it, "You've got to see it to believe it. Who told you you can't have it all?"

The first cathedral built for shopping—the first fully enclosed shopping mall, that is—was constructed in another suburb of Minneapolis. In 1956, a covered shopping center called Southdale was opened in Edina, Minnesota. It is still standing, but the size and nature of malls have expanded considerably since then.

But the shopping habits of Americans may now be shifting away from giant malls. It appears that the peak year for sales per square foot of retail space in the nation's enclosed malls occurred in 1978. According to studies by Management Horizons of Chicago, sales averaged $197 a square foot back then. By 1992, that figure had fallen to $163 per square foot, a drop of 17 percent. What's more, surveys have shown that although shoppers spent an average of twelve hours a month in malls in 1980, a decade later, in 1990, the shopping time in malls had lessened to four hours— just a third of what it had been.

These figures show that Americans may no longer be seeing shopping at a mall as a leisure-time activity. But they have not cut back on their shopping, as can be seen from the credit card statistics.

THEY DROPPED A LOT SO YOU COULD SHOP TILL YOU DROP

Why is the world's largest shopping mall located in Alberta, Canada, where it can get to 40 degrees below zero?

Because that's where four Iranian-born brothers—the same people behind the largest mall to be erected in the United States—

decided in the Canadian oil boom days of the 1970s to spend $650 million to build a 110-acre mall with more than 800 shops.

Named the West Edmonton Mall, it was eventually opened in 1981 at a cost of $1.1 billion. The Ghermezian brothers, not known for being reticent, later boasted that this was "the Eighth Wonder of the World." Their idea was to create not just a destination for shoppers but for tourists as well. In addition to the hundreds of stores were a 360-room hotel, amusement park with more than 20 rides, a 10-acre area for swimming, a miniature golf course, 34 movie theaters, nearly 25 restaurants, and a 400-foot lake with submarines and real sharks, monkeys, and tigers.

The tourist attractions are vital to the success of the world's largest mall because it is estimated that less than one fifth of the population needed to support such an enterprise lives in the shopping area being served.

The West Edmonton Mall was built on some of the 15,000 acres of land they bought originally for $200 an acre after coming to the United States from Iran in the 1950s. By the 1980s, the land was worth $40,000 an acre. The Ghermezians obviously know how to shop.

The Big Fear:
A Nation of "Credit Card Junkies"

In one of the most famous motion pictures of the 1960s, *The Graduate*, the hero, played by Dustin Hoffman, is advised upon graduation to "go into plastics." That 1960s advice could now be supplanted, after the widespread use of credit cards in the 1980s and beyond, by another piece of advice: "Avoid plastic as much as possible."

Indeed, American society's shopping spree in the last decades of the twentieth century has been fueled by an overreliance on credit, especially the easy but high-interest credit provided by the flip of a plastic credit card. However, many people have come to realize that they have not handled their credit cards well—and that the schools should teach teenagers how to avoid becoming "credit card junkies."

This was the finding of a survey of credit card users conducted in March 1992 by two consumer groups and AT&T Universal Card Serv-

150

ices. At that time, 40 percent of cardholders said they were "very concerned" about meeting their current monthly credit card bills and another 14 percent were "somewhat concerned." That means that more than half of credit card users worry about being able to pay for their purchases made with credit cards, a situation that indicates the extent to which card owners do not know how to handle the purchasing power—or, more precisely, the debting power—of these cards.

This widespread lack of ability to handle credit was underscored by another finding—92 percent of those polled said that high school students should be *required* to take instruction in the management of money and credit.

Indeed, learning about managing money may be as important as managing credit. The head of Bankcard Holders of America, one of the consumer groups involved in the survey, said that many consumers use their credit cards just to maintain their standard of living during difficult economic times. "They know it's not a great way to go . . . but for many there's no other option," said Elgie Holstein, president of the organization.

◆◆◆

"Always live within your income, even if you have to borrow money to do so."

—JOSH BILLINGS (1818–1885),
American humorist

◆◆◆

Shopping and Buying:
By the Numbers

Here are some statistics on the nature and scope of the shopping and buying going on in America.

THE BIGGEST SPENDERS

Where are the nation's biggest spenders? According to the "Statistical Abstract of the United States" published by the United States Government Printing Office in 1992, the city with the most retail sales per house-

151

hold was St. Cloud, Minnesota, which in 1990 saw each family spend an average of $36,640. Second place went to Portland, Maine, with $32,650 a household. Honolulu, Hawaii, was third at $31,340.

WHAT THE AVERAGE HOUSEHOLD SPENDS

Nationwide, the average household in the United States in 1990 generated $19,488 in retail sales.

THE MOST POPULAR CREDIT CARD

The most popular credit card in America is the Visa card, with the MasterCard a distant second. Visa was launched in the 1960s by Bank of America in San Francisco as BankAmericard. Bank of America then signed up other banks across the country to issue the card on a franchise basis, with each financial institution free to charge its own rates and establish its own terms. By 1977, BankAmericard became Visa International, a totally separate company. Now nearly 150 million Visa cards are in use, issued by 6,000 banks. By 1991, just thirty years after being first issued, these cards were used by consumers to charge $171 billion in purchases. Using MasterCard, consumers charged another $99 billion. Thus, with just these two cards alone, Americans spent as much in one year as the United States government had run up in the national deficit in that same year.

THE GROWING CREDIT CARD DEBT

The use of credit cards is mushrooming. Total credit card debt outstanding went from $4.1 billion in 1970 to $194.1 billion in 1991. Interest payments made on credit cards in 1991 totaled $33 billion—a sum that for the first time in history exceeded interest payments made on all automobile and other consumer installment loans (according to a study by the Boston Company Economic Advisors). From all this charging, the credit card industry made an after-tax profit in 1991 of $2.4 billion.

THE INCREASE IN PERSONAL BANKRUPTCIES

With all this spending going on, it has led inexorably to more of another thing—personal bankruptcies. While the average car loan in the 1920s was one year and in the 1950s three years, by the beginning of the 1990s it had become five years. The number of bankruptcies has grown with all this borrowing. In the mid-1940s, personal bankruptcies totaled nine thousand in the nation. By 1987, this figure had grown to nine thousand a week. During 1992, more than nine hundred thousand Americans filed for bankruptcy.*

The Ten Signals of Credit Card Danger

The size of credit card debt has gotten so high in the United States that financial counseling services are seeing an increasing number of people—including executives, doctors, lawyers, and other well-educated professionals—who have accumulated huge balances on a score or more of credit cards. Total outstanding balances, which used to be considered high when they reached $30,000 or $40,000, are now reaching $60,000 or more, even $100,000 for some people on as many as thirty credit cards. While job layoffs, salary freezes, and high mortgage payments sap a family's funds, experts in the credit card field say that "financial literacy is very low" and that many individuals lack the know-how for handling credit and get overextended. It is not how much money a person has that ensures a sound financial situation, but how a person manages available money.

Here are ten signs that you are headed for charge card danger:

1. You pay only the minimum balance on your credit card each month.
2. You pay one charge card with a cash advance from another.

---

*The state with the most bankruptcies on a per capita basis is Nevada. Rounding out the top five are Tennessee, Georgia, California, and Indiana.

The state with the least bankruptcies per person is Vermont. The next four with the fewest bankruptcies are Massachusetts, Connecticut, New York, and Pennsylvania—all in the Northeast.

3. You pay other bills with cash from your card.

4. You go shopping when you're bored or depressed and then put the purchase on your card.

5. You seek higher lines of credit.

6. You need to take out a debt consolidation loan.

7. You constantly dip into a home equity credit line.

8. You never seem to have any money left at the end of the month after paying your monthly bills.

9. You buy even your groceries on a credit card.

10. You are getting dunning letters for late or nonpayment of bills (and even worse, you don't open the letters).

To help you get out of debt and put your spending on a proper basis, you should talk to a financial counselor, a nonprofit credit counseling service, or a group like Debtors Anonymous. One thing you should *not* do, according to many experts, is respond to a company touting itself as a credit repair service that charges a high fee. That's just another expenditure you don't have to make.

The Compulsive Spender:

Just Trying to Buy Love?

Studies of compulsive shoppers have found that psychologically such people are not buying things, but buying love and self-worth. Their trips to the store are really escapes from loneliness, despair, and anxiety.

The compulsive shopper in this scenario is defined as someone who purchases things he or she later regrets or simply ignores—often doesn't even use. These people cannot control the urge to buy even though they might be suffering from huge debt. While the general population spends an average of 22 percent of household income aside from mortgage or rent to pay for past purchases, the compulsive spenders lay out an average of 40 percent.

And the compulsive shopper can be found in all income levels, representing an estimated 6 percent of the population. The problem, however, seems to be more prevalent among women than men, as reflected in attendance at self-help groups formed in recent years to help people deal with shopping compulsions—although this may be because women are more willing to go to self-help groups. In such meetings, women represent three-quarters of participants, but estimates are that in the general population women represent at least 60 percent of compulsive shoppers.

Research has found that compulsive spending may well be driven by the same impulses that drive other addictions. One key motivator is low self-worth, with shopping used to bolster self-confidence. Indeed, interaction with sales clerks is found to be very important for such people, for the clerk gives the shopper a feeling of importance. Some compulsive shoppers will list sales people as among their best friends, with one woman shopper telling researchers that her most important possession was a thank-you note from a sales clerk at a store she frequented.

It has also been found that compulsive shoppers often have a strong tendency to fantasize. They either ignore the consequences of their spending or delude themselves that they will be able to cover the purchase with extra money that will come in.

In all this spending, the process of buying matters more than the items being bought. Characteristically, items are either ignored, put away, or hidden and forgotten after being bought. When asked what purchase has been especially meaningful, compulsive shoppers usually cannot think of one, even though thousands of dollars might have been spent.

But don't let this picture of the compulsive shopper delude you into thinking only a few people exhibit these traits. According to one researcher, Dr. Alain d'Astous, a business professor at the University of Sherbrooke in Quebec, "Almost all of us are compulsive buyers to some extent, some more than others."*

Curing "the Gimmes"

Good shoppers are made early, according to an article in the October 1990 issue of *Parents* magazine. Author Lynn Schnurnberger, who interviewed a number of child psychologists, gives advice on how parents can help their children "curb their covetous impulses . . . although there's no vaccine against greed."

---

*Much of the research cited here comes from a 1989 study by Dr. Thomas O'Guinn, an associate professor in the College of Communications at the University of Illinois, and Dr. Ronald Faber, a researcher in the School of Mass Communications at the University of Minnesota, as reported by Daniel Goleman (New York Times News Service, July 17, 1991).

She begins by stating that "child-development experts agree that the gimmes are a perfectly natural, if exasperating, part of growing up." It's also natural for acquisitive traits to emerge as early as the age of two. Since children that young tend to feel more secure with more possessions, and since they have no concept of cost and value and no sense of moderation, they expect to be given what they want. "In a sense, you might say kids are born to shop, accrue, and want more," writes Schnurnberger.

AN EXPENSIVE LESSON—TEXAS STYLE

"It's not a sin to be rich anymore, it's a miracle."
—Message embroidered on a pillow put in his bedroom by the late John Connally, former three-time governor of Texas and President Nixon's Secretary of the Treasury, after he went bankrupt in 1987 owing $93 million (against assets of $13 million, mostly in real estate). Said Connally at the time: "One lesson I learned out of this bankruptcy is that not only is fame fleeting but so are possessions."

She quotes psychologists who give such advice as teaching the child to delay gratification and cope with frustration so that he or she will learn early that one cannot have everything one wants. Even trinkets and other inexpensive items should not be given to a child whenever demanded because this only reinforces the child's acquisitive behavior. "A child who is used to getting what he [or she] wants is going to strongly resist any attempts the parent makes to be less compliant. The time to buy your child a treat is when you decide you would like, not when he [or she] insists that you do so. Otherwise, if you do relent, you will only reinforce a child's out-of-control behavior," says one child development expert.

To avoid problems, it is suggested that you not take children into stores where the merchandise may be too tempting for them or, if they must be taken along, to explain before-hand what specifically will be bought—and only that. If the child still winds up throwing a tantrum because he or she has seen something he or she wants, the best strategy is not to yell at or argue with the child, but calmly take him or her out of the store and, after the child has quieted down, acknowledge his or her feelings of frustration but stick to the original shopping plan. Writes Schnurnberger, "It's how the parent acts in these situations that communicates to a child the futility of tantrums."

It's also all right, according to psychologists, to explain to children when something is too expensive or out of the financial reach of a family. Such an explanation is actually better understood and accepted by the child than an outright, abrupt "No!"

One strategy to make better consumers of children is letting them draft realistic wish lists and then having them earn some money toward purchases by doing odd jobs for which they are paid or save up allowance money. It is also a good idea to make family members aware of the wishes so they can use the list to get ideas for gifts at birthday time. The requests, of course, have to be realistic, but when a child contributes his or her own money toward a purchase, it has that much more meaning. This method is also effective in teaching children how to manage their money as well as how to become better shoppers. Certainly, it's a good way to curb a child's endless moans of "Gimme, gimme."

◆◆

SHOPPING FOR SOMEONE REALLY SPECIAL

Gloria Rubio, the wife of financier Loel Guinness who inherited approximately $200 million in 1947, was herself born in poverty in Mexico. Yet she set herself on a schedule of spending for clothes that has been called one of "extraordinary vigor," as if to make up for lost time and opportunity in her upbringing. Asked by a reporter if she had a hobby, she responded: "Yes, one. Myself."

◆◆

●●●

HE, SHE, AND IT:

A LOOK AT MONEY AND THE SEXES

All heiresses are

beautiful.

—JOHN DRYDEN
(1631–1700), English
dramatist (from
King Arthur)

"**M**en and women deal with money differently. They perceive it, use it, speak about it, and live with it in surprisingly diverse ways," says Dr. Victoria Felton-Collins, a psychologist and certified financial planner, in her book *Couples & Money: A Financial Guide for Surviving & Thriving in the '90s* (New York: Bantam, 1990).

One reason men and women differ in how they handle money is because they earn or possess different amounts. In 1987 *Money* magazine surveyed 2,250 households and discovered that men had on the average $54,700 in financial assets, while women had $26,000 in assets.

Because men have more earning power, they can invest, lose, and recoup faster than can women, who on the average earn less. So women are basically more cautious in their investment decisions than men.

Dr. Ruth Berry of the University of Manitoba, in studying how the sexes view the quality of their lives, found that women place their relationship with their mate first, while men view their financial status as contributing most to the quality of their lives.

With this different perspective and background when it comes to money, is it any wonder, then, that the sexes often battle over money-related matters? And the battle is only increasing in our times. Dr. Felton-Collins writes, "Everything I read in the press and heard from my colleagues confirms what I am seeing in my own office. Couples are fighting more about money than ever before. And those fights are raging among the rich as well as the poor."

Indeed, in a survey of 86,000 married people reported by *Reader's Digest* in 1990, 37 percent cited money as the number one cause of problems in their marriage, and another study of married couples found that not sex but money caused the most fights. (Other studies have found as much as 78 percent of couples argue about money as contrasted with 24 percent arguing about sex.)

What follows are some insights about how the sexes deal with money and money-related matters.

●●●

SOME THINGS NEVER CHANGE

When the Bible listed the price to be placed upon a human being's work, a man's worth was listed at fifty shekels and a woman's at thirty shekels. In 1987, *Money* magazine reported that for every dollar earned by a man, a woman earned approximately 64 cents—a ratio of virtually the same 3 to 5 experienced by women 3,000 years ago.

●●●

●●●

"Some couples go over their budgets very carefully every month. Others just go over them."

—SALLY POPLIN

●●●

Finding True Love Is Hard When Digging for Gold

Greediness may find its fullest bloom in the gold digger—the female or male bent on marrying a wealthy person out of love . . . for the other person's money. One who was particularly exposed to and abused by this practice was heiress Barbara Hutton. She went to the altar six times without finding true love, only true deceit and heartbreak (except possibly for one husband, actor Cary Grant, but when the two married they were often referred to by Hollywood wags as "Cash and Cary"). After her fourth marriage, Hutton told a reporter, "You can't believe the depths to which some people will stoop for money."

The desire to marry for money appears so widespread that seminars have even been offered on how women and men can find that very special someone with a fortune. In its September 8, 1991, issue on the then current listing of the world's billionaires, *Fortune* magazine ran a side article reporting on how a former E. F. Hutton stockbroker from Dallas, Texas, was offering sessions on "How to Marry the Rich." For a price of $25 for a three-hour course taught nationwide or $125 an hour for a minimum of two hours for a private consultation, Ginie Polo Sayles, a "self-admitted shameless gold digger," according to *Fortune*, teaches women (her usual students) the not-so-fine art of finding and marrying money. But she also instructs men ("she has reeled in a lot of Material Men, particularly accountants," as students. "Those CPAs are *fascinated* with money," she notes).

In that *Fortune* sidebar, entitled "How to Marry a Billionette," Sayles offers advice to the male gold digger on how to pan for a wealthy wife. Among her ideas, as recounted by writer Patricia Sellers,

- *Know the field.* Divorcées frequent bars and clubs, widows like opera and ballet, so these are the places to go. Many executive businesswomen look for househusbands. "The key is to appreciate what these women like and to let them show you off." Just make sure, says Sayles, that any divorced rich women you encounter are living off assets and not alimony.
- *Dress well.* Among her suggestions: Buy a good watch with a leather strap, avoid wearing diamonds, and keep up with the fashions in magazines like *Esquire* and GQ.

- *Live where the rich live.* Do it even if all you can afford is a rented attic, she says. And if you are uncomfortable with your name because it "doesn't mean success to you," change it.

- *Hang out where the rich hang out.* This is an obvious suggestion, but it needs to be said. Sayles adds a special insight: "Sign on for a class with a prominent artist. It will be filled with rich widows."

- *Accept gifts graciously.* According to Sayles, there's a special way to handle the offer of an expensive gift from a wealthy woman. "Pause, fold your arms, frown, look at her, smile, take her in your arms, and say, 'You're wonderful.'"

- *Dare to defy her.* The advice here is Machiavellian. Sayles says you should never try to please a rich person because this is what everybody else always tries to do. Instead you should give *her* orders (okay, "small orders") or just balk when she tries to tell you what to do (but balk "with humor"). As for any thoughts of going along to get along, Sayles advises: "Start a fight every eight weeks or so just for stimulation."

- *Remember, you are the asset.* An example cited is the case of Larry Fortensky, the blue-collar husband of Elizabeth Taylor. She once said of her beau: "No boy is poor if he's rich at heart."

I guess the moral of this seminar is that with this information and these insights, a man can go out in the world and truly make his fortune.

One who seems to have put the gold digger in his or her place was John D. MacArthur, the multimillionaire. Once asked what he thought of the phenomenon of wealthy older men marrying young women from a far lower social stratum, the octogenarian replied: "I think it's ridiculous when a loaded old man takes up with a young working woman. You and I both know that the only thing she could possibly be after is what's in his pockets, not what's in his pants!"

◆◆◆

"There is only one thing for a man to do who is married to a woman who enjoys spending money, and that is to enjoy earning it."

—ED HOWE

◆◆◆

Folklore Advice on How to Marry a Rich Man

The Old Farmer's Almanac offered a sampling of folklore from many regions of the country on a number of topics. One such topic was entitled, "How to Marry Money." Among some of the words of wisdom were these pieces of advice and prophecy to hopeful brides-to-be:

- Dreaming of a future husband bringing the dreamer a gold or silver cup filled with water would mean that the dreamer would marry a rich man.
- Snap an apple with the fingers while eating the fruit and then name the apple for the loved one, after which count the seeds in the apple. "If there are fourteen, you will become rich."
- Shoes worn out on the sides mean the wearer will marry a rich man.
- Spotting a goldfinch on a holiday means an eventual marriage to a millionaire.
- Hairy arms and legs on a girl foretell that she will marry a rich man.

And then there is advice on what to do on the wedding day to ensure wealth:

- "Marry in September's shrine, all your days are rich and fine."
- During the wedding ceremony, a bride should have an old coin in her shoe, preferably one handed down from mother to daughter. To do so will ensure prosperity.

The Pursuit of an Heiress

In her day, Barbara Hutton was one of America's richest women. She was heir to a fortune estimated to be $50 million. Her life was marked not only by a parade of husbands (six), but by a line of gigolos and fortune hunters of the most outrageous nature. Wracked with the effects of tranquilizers, smoking, and drinking, she aged conspicuously in later life, but

162

this did not stop men from congregating in the Wilshire Hotel bar to greet her on her daily trips there. According to one biographer, "they would line the bar two and three deep and wait for Barbara to make her entrance." Once she was found the next morning bound and gagged in a vacant hotel room. A playboy had stolen her clothes, her purse, and her jewelry.

Hutton also received entreaties through the mail. It is reported that she had a continuous stream of letters from throughout the world. Enclosed with such letters were photographs of the senders—both with and without clothing. The men also described themselves, often in an erotic way. Barbara Hutton would read the letters and look at the photos with what was said to be great merriment.

All this male attention did not stop the wasting away of Barbara Hutton, who spent lavishly on her husbands, her divorces, her boyfriends, and herself. At the end, on her deathbed, she asked, "Is it all gone yet?"

Out of her $50 million fortune, she died with less than $3,500.

THE WORLD'S HARDEST WORKER

"Nobody works as hard for his money as the man who marries it."
—KEN HUBBARD

The Wrong Side of Paradise

Greed may have both made and broken not only a marriage, but a great literary career.

F. Scott Fitzgerald was a struggling young writer when he met the love of his life, Zelda Sayre. But she refused to marry him because she did not think he had enough money. Crestfallen, the young Fitzgerald abandoned his job as a copywriter in a New York advertising agency and went back to his home in St. Paul to write a novel in hopes of earning enough money to get Zelda to say yes. The result was *This Side of Paradise*, one of Fitzgerald's greatest works. The result was also a $5,000 advance, enough to convince Zelda that F. Scott might be the wage earner of her dreams after all.

But the experience greatly affected Fitzgerald. As he confided in his diary, the fact that the girl he loved turned him down initially over the matter of money made him distrust the wealthy. It also caused him to resent Zelda over the course of their marriage and he blamed his failures and his bad luck on her. Those failures and bad luck eventually led to an early death.

However, his experience with Zelda also led him to write another novel, possibly his greatest—*The Great Gatsby*—which explores an individual's self-destructive pursuit of money and status.

What Couple Doesn't Fight About Money?

When two people live together, they tend to disagree at times. And there is no more potent an issue to fight over—except maybe sex—than money.

But there is one type of couple—and only one—for whom money is not usually an issue at all, and that is the lesbian couple.

For *American Couples: Money, Work, Sex* (New York: Morrow, 1983), Philip Blumstein and Pepper Schwartz studied the attitude of couples toward various matters. When it came to money, the amount earned by a person established his or her power in the relationship. Except for one notable situation.

Blumstein and Schwartz found that lesbians strive not to have money affect their relationship. One reason may be that women do not usually judge themselves by how much they earn. In a lesbian relationship, then, the tendency is for one partner to treat the other in the same nonjudgmental way.

HOW TO DRESS FOR SUCCESS . . . IN MARRIAGE

DEAR ABBY: Do you think married women dress to please their husbands?
—*Mazook in San Francisco*
DEAR MAZOOK: If they do, they are wearing last year's clothes.
—DEAR ABBY COLUMN,
July 28, 1993

Some Inside Tips About Tipping

What better place to discover truths about how the sexes handle money than at Donald Trump's Plaza Hotel in New York City. Ranked among the top luxury hotels in the world, the Plaza is surely the place where the habits of moneyed men and women can best be studied. Consider, for instance, tipping.

In *The Hotel: A Week in the Life of the Plaza Hotel* (New York: Simon and Schuster, 1989) by *New York Times* reporter Sonny Kleinfield, interviews with bellmen and doormen revealed the following:

- Men tip better than women.
- Women traveling alone tip better than women traveling in pairs.
- A man with his mistress or girlfriend tips better than a man with his wife (surprise).

No matter what the sex:

- Show business stars skimp on their tips.
- The best tippers are Americans—except for doctors and lawyers, who are, according to a veteran bellman, "cheap, cheap, cheap."
- Clergymen are generous tippers. And within this group, "Catholic priests head the list, rabbis come next, and Protestant ministers are last."

Bellmen have learned some techniques for extracting bigger tips. Two such techniques:

- They carry change for at least $100 so a guest cannot avoid tipping by saying he or she has a large bill and nothing smaller but "will get back to the bellman later."
- When being tipped by a man traveling with his wife, bellmen try to block the wife's view since wives generally think their husbands tip too much.

●●

CONFUCIUS SAYS:

"A gentleman has three things to guard against. In the days of thy youth, ere thy strength is steady, beware of lust. When manhood is reached, in the fullness of strength, beware of strife. In old age, when thy strength is broken, beware of greed."

●●

Conspicuous Consumption in a Bottle

Gold, pearls, caviar, and cashmere are expensive items, offering a certain luxury aspect just at the mere mention of their names. Marketers of high fashion know this and try to associate their products with these elements, but various cosmetic companies have tried to capitalize on this conspicuous consumption in ways that border on the ludicrous.

For instance, Guerlain came out with a "beauty enhancer" called Divinaura that was touted to be flecked with bits of real gold—actually, 6 milligrams of 24-karat gold in each bottle. But the cost of Divinaura was $56 for one ounce at a time when gold was trading for $363 a troy ounce (or 31 grams), which means that 6 milligrams of gold was worth 7 cents.

Christian Dior sold a mascara containing real cashmere at $13.50, which seemed a real steal since cashmere can cost $275 or more in a sweater or jacket. But while cashmere gives warmth in a coat or garment (after all, it comes from the coats of goats bred in Kashmir), it is hard to see what cashmere is doing on eyelashes.

●●

WHY DIAMONDS ARE FOREVER FOR ZSA ZSA

"I never hated a man enough to give him back his diamonds."
—ZSA ZSA GABOR

●●

While these two products at least had some of the substance of the status symbols in their bottles, two other similar products did not. La Prairie Skin Caviar cost $90 for just two ounces, but the caviar reference came from the fact that it had salmon-roe-sized beads of allantoin providing the moisturizing elements. In comparision, real Beluga caviar at the time was going for $69.50 for one sixteenth of an ounce.

And Yves Saint Laurent offered Hydra Perles Hydro-Protective Day Cream looking very much like real pearls, but the beads were really only "perfluorine," "silicone," and "aqueous" pearls. Yves was charging $40 for one ounce of his product, actually more per ounce than a 30-inch strand of cultured pearls, which at the time was priced at $1,500.

Are the prices of these products reminders that, as the adage goes, beauty is painful?*

A Cologne for the Times?

In 1991, when the business climate was getting rocky, a new men's cologne was introduced. It had an unusual name and an even more unusual—albeit appropriate for the times—slogan and packaging statement.

The fragrance was called Recession, and it was touted as being for "the man who used to have everything." In fact, at $22.50 per two-ounce bottle, it was billed as the first "Owe de Cologne."

The package carried an even more profound message: "The economy stinks. You shouldn't have to."

Parade magazine, in its "Best & Worst" issue of 1991, hailed it as the year's best new product.

◆◆◆

"Kissing Doesn't Kill, Greed and Indifference Do."
—Ad on buses in New York, San Francisco, and Chicago showing two lesbians, two homosexual men, and an interracial couple kissing (ad paid for in part with $10,000 in funds from the National Endowment for the Arts)

◆◆◆

*These products are discussed in "Expensive Habits," *New York Times Magazine*, June 6, 1991, in the Beauty column by Penelope Green.

Till Divorce Settlements Do Us Part

The sexes often find their biggest battles over money come not during marriage but after it—during divorce proceedings. All a divorce settlement often seems to settle is how much money one spouse can extract from the other.

According to *The Guinness Book of World Records* (New York: Bantam, 1992), the largest divorce settlement on record occurred when the wife of Adnan Khashoggi was awarded $950 million plus property in 1982. But don't weep for Adnan. Although Khashoggi, an arms dealer and go-between for Arab oil sheiks, has since fallen on less lucrative times, in those days, as shown in a previous chapter, he was spending over $100 million a year and had a personal worth of several billion dollars.

The largest claim for alimony was made by the twenty-three-year-old Belgian wife of a Saudi Arabian sheik, Mohammed al-Fassi, twenty-eight. Filed in California, where the couple had lived for awhile, the suit asked for $3 billion. It was noted that the sheik could well afford it since among his many possessions were fourteen homes in Florida. In June 1983, the court awarded her $81 million.

The record for largest-divorce-settlement-rejected-because-it-wasn't-enough may belong to the former wife of Texas billionaire Sid Bass. Anne Bass was reputedly offered and turned down a settlement worth $535 million. She was said to have sniffed at the offer because it would not enable her to live in the manner to which she had become accustomed. Although the final divorce settlement in October 1988 was sealed, it is estimated that after all the in-fighting Mrs. Bass was awarded $200 million in cash and another $75 million worth of automobiles, jewelry, art, and real estate.

These are record-setting situations. For the average American couple splitting up, it is estimated that only 25 percent of spouses are awarded alimony. And don't forget that in these days of working women, some of those who ask for and get alimony are the husbands. When it comes to divorce, few are those who can divorce themselves from thinking about money.

••

"Love lasteth as long as the money endureth."

—WILLIAM CAXTON,
The Game and Playe of the Chesse

••

A Summing Up

Perhaps the pithiest comment on the link between money and the sexes comes from Satchel Paige, the great black baseball pitcher and common-sense philosopher, who once said about man's dual drives for wealth and sex: "Money and women. They're two of the strongest things in the world. The things you do for a woman you wouldn't do for anything else. Same with money."

••

HAS MONEY REPLACED SEX?

"It used to be that sex was fun. It isn't any longer. What's happened is sex has become dangerous and money has become fun."

—JERRY STERNER, author of the play
Other People's Money: The Ultimate Seduction (1989)

••

••

"GREED IS GOOD!":

WALL STREET BULLS, BEARS, AND PIGS

There are two occasions when a man should not speculate. When he can afford it and when he can't.

—MARK TWAIN

Wall Street has long been viewed in two ways—as either a place where prudent investors can purchase a part of American business and realize a more-than-fair return on their investment over the years or as an arena where sharp and shrewd trading can realize a fast buck. On one side is the picture of a little old lady or man who follows sound, sober investment advice and patiently invests and clips coupons or dividends; on the other side is the hotshot in-and-out trader who tries to make a financial killing with rapid buy and sell orders based on insights or gut feelings.

In the millions of trades and the exchange of millions of shares that take place each day on Wall Street, both types of scenarios occur. But it is an axiom of Wall Street that money can be made with various approaches except one. Bulls—those who feel the market or an individual stock will go up—and bears—those who believe the market or a stock will go down—can make money. But pigs—the

170

greedy in pursuit of too much profit—will never prosper.

It is more than coincidental that the most compelling statement in recent years on behalf of greed—that "greed is good"—came from a character in the movie *Wall Street*, who in turn seemed to echo a denizen of Wall Street, Ivan Boesky, the trader who was found guilty of using insider information to build his vast fortune. With huge sums to be made on Wall Street, the lure of an extra edge in trading, even if it comes from illegal means, is often too much for the "pigs."

What follows is a look at some of the sound and unsound practices that have been followed on Wall Street as both the prudent and the imprudent have tried to make money make more money. Nowhere else can it be better seen what greed can do to affect human behavior. After all, Wall Street, as do other streets, comes with a gutter.

Great Investment Advice from a Man Who Lost $800,000 in the Market

Bernard Baruch (1870–1965) was known as one of America's greatest financiers. A Wall Street partner at twenty-five and a millionaire before he was thirty-five, Baruch was also a statesman who served as unpaid adviser to every president from Wilson to Eisenhower. Yet even he was not immune to experiencing major losses in the stock market.

In his autobiography, *Baruch: My Own Story* (New York: Holt, 1957), he tells of losing $800,000 when he invested heavily in coffee. He had learned that restrictions in 1902 on planting for five years and poor weather prospects in Brazil made coffee a good buy on margin in 1905. But the weather proved better than expected and the 1906 crop was exceeding expectations. Although the Brazilian government bought up millions of bags to keep them off the market and prop up the price, the market price soon began slipping. By selling out then, Baruch would have minimized his losses. Instead, he began selling more profitable stock to raise more margin money for coffee in hopes the trend would reverse. Only later, when his losses reached $800,000, did he get out.

"One of the worst mistakes anyone can make is to hold on blindly and refuse to admit that his judgment has been wrong," he wrote. "This I knew, but instead of acting sensibly, I did as good a job of taking leave of my reasoning powers as any amateur in a market squeeze."

He pointed out that many a novice, eager to make a big profit, will sell one stock in which he has a profit to protect a stock in which he has a loss. With a bad stock, since its loss is likely to be severe, the tendency most people have is to stay with it in hopes it will rise and wipe out the loss.

"Actually, the procedure one should follow is to sell the bad stock and keep the good stock. With rare exceptions, stocks are high because they are good, and stocks are low because they are of doubtful value," Baruch noted.

His experience with the coffee purchase retaught him that lesson, as well as taught him another one—that greed distorts intelligence.

"[O]ften we become so carried away so much by the desirability of an end that we overlook the impracticability of its accomplishments. In such cases the more one knows about a subject—the more inside information one has—the more likely one is to believe that he or she can outwit the workings of supply and demand." In that case, he wrote: "Experts will step in where even fools fear to tread."

But Baruch is one "expert" who succeeded much more than he failed on Wall Street. In fact, he is one of the few who got out of the stock market largely unscathed before the Crash of 1929 (one reason: An old beggar outside Baruch's Wall Street office, to whom he would give gratuities, one day during the pre-1929 Crash period told him: "I have a good tip for you." Baruch notes that when beggars and shoeshine boys can "tell you how to get rich it is time to remind yourself that there is no more dangerous illusion than the belief that one can get something for nothing.")*

In his autobiography, Baruch offers his own ten-point investment advice based on his own errors and hard-earned lessons in the market. Distilled from his ten points are the following "rules" of his investment philosophy:

1. Speculating in the market is a full-time job. Don't do it unless you can devote yourself fully to it.
2. Beware of "inside" tips.
3. Find out all you can about a company before buying its stock.

---

*About tips on the stock market, Baruch points out that they become more frequent during a booming market, which just builds to the eventual bust, since "in a rising market, for a time at least, anyone's tip will seem good. This only draws people deeper and deeper into the market."

4. "Don't try to buy at the bottom and sell at the top. This can't be done—except by liars."

5. Don't think you can always be right, and if you make a mistake, take your loss quickly.

6. Buy a few investments rather than many so they can be watched closely.

7. Periodically review all investments for changes in developments that might affect prospects.

8. Keep in mind your tax situation to know when is the best time to sell.

9. Never put all your funds into an investment, but always keep a cash reserve.

10. Invest in the field you know best.

Baruch expands on these pointers:

- Get the facts of a situation before acting; "getting these facts is a continuous job which requires eternal vigilance."

- "In no field is the maxim more valid—that a little knowledge is a dangerous thing—than in investing."

- No speculator can be right all the time; in fact, being right "three or four times out of ten should yield a person a fortune if he has the sense to cut his losses quickly on the ventures where he has been wrong."

- "I have found it wise to periodically turn into cash most of my holdings and virtually retire from the market. No general keeps his troops fighting all the time; nor does he go into battle without some part of his forces held back in reserve." A cash reserve can help pay for any error in judgment, as well as provide the opportunity to take advantage of new possibilities.

- A common illusion is that people think they can engage in a number of activities—such as playing the stock market, buying real estate, conducting a business—simultaneously. "My own experience is that few men can do more than one thing at a time—and do it well."

- "Success in speculation requires as much specialized knowledge as success in law or medicine or any other profession." No one, he points out, would open a store in competition with a major department store or build cars in competition with General Motors without preparation. "Yet the same man will cheerfully toss his savings into a market dominated by men who are as expert in their line as Macy's and the automakers are in theirs."

- Almost all amateurs make two mistakes in the market—not having ample knowledge of the company in which securities are being purchased and trading beyond one's finances "to try to run up a fortune on a shoestring."

- In speculating in stocks, the emotions often set traps for reasoning powers. This is why "it is far more difficult to know when to sell a stock than when to buy" and why most people "find it equally hard to take either a profit or a loss." The reason is that if a stock goes up the individual wants to wait for even a further rise and if it goes down the individual wants to wait for the stock to rebound. "The sensible course is to sell while the stock is still rising, or if you have made a mistake, to admit it immediately and take your loss."

What, then, can the individual investor with modest savings do who is looking for a fair return but cannot give full time to a study of the market?

Baruch's advice is to seek out an unbiased, trusted investment counselor, which during his time was an emerging profession, "one of the more constructive and healthy developments of the last half century."

It's not an exciting approach for the person who wants to make a killing in stocks, but then the investor won't get murdered in the market either.

For Baruch, who passed away at ninety-five after a long and glorious career on Wall Street, this advice comes at the cost of an $800,000 cup of coffee.

The Biggest Loser in the Crash of '29

What individual suffered the largest loss in the stock market crash of 1929?

The answer: Clarence H. Mackay, chairman of the board of International Telephone and Telegraph.

Mackay, who had inherited wealth (his father was John Mackay, one of the richest men in America), sold his controlling interest in the Postal Telegraph to Sosthenes Behn, president of ITT—a move his lawyer advised against. When the two companies merged on March 29, 1928, in a $300 million deal, Mackay took his multimillion-dollar share totally in stock. He was, of course, trying to capitalize on what seemed an ever-rising market, but the decision, essentially based on a greedy attitude for more, left Mackay vulnerable to a collapsing market.

A year and a half later, on Black Thursday, Mackay encountered a market that collapsed with sickening fury. In only a half hour, he lost $36 million. But that was just the beginning. Mackay eventually lost several times that amount of money in the Crash.

As a result of his losses, Mackay had to close his 100-acre Long Island estate, Harbor Hills, and shutter his fifty-room, $6 million mansion, with its thoroughbred horses and stables, tennis courts, and servants. After selling his horses and letting his 134-member staff go, the formerly powerful member of the business establishment wound up moving into Harbor Hill's gatekeeper's cottage.

Mackay has one other distinction. At the height of his wealth before the Crash, he became the father-in-law of famed American songwriter Irving Berlin. It was a marriage he strongly opposed because Berlin was Jewish. But after the wedding, when Mackay's daughter was asked by reporters about how she felt marrying someone not from her social circle, she responded: "I feel good. I married above myself."*

•••

THE BRIGHTEST AND FUNNIEST WERE MARKET LOSERS

The 1929 stock market fever was so widespread and catching that it pulled in some unlikely victims.

Among those who lost large sums of money in the Crash of 1929 was Winston Churchill, who had put his recent earnings from his writings into the market in hopes of financial security (he invested "every shilling he could spare"). As a consequence of his losses in

*Berlin did not do too well in the stock market crash of 1929, either. He lost $5 million worth of stock bought with his songwriting income.

175

the Crash, Churchill had to plunge into an extensive writing effort during the 1930s.

Other big losers were the Marx Brothers, especially Groucho, who saw $250,000 vanish. Ironically, of all the brothers, Groucho had been the most concerned about not squandering the considerable money they were making in show business. He waited until he could buy his house in cash and made few purchases of luxury items. Yet he freely followed hot stock market tips and wound up putting all of his excess cash at the time into buying stock, only to see it all disappear in the wave of selling.

Groucho, along with his brother Harpo, once passed a hot stock market tip to playwright George S. Kaufman, with whom they were working on a script. Kaufman followed their advice, invested $10,000 and soon came to lose the whole amount. He later remarked that "anyone who buys a stock because the Marx Brothers recommend it *deserves* to lose $10,000."

Another comedian who had unhappy experiences in the Crash was Eddie Cantor. He wound up with just $60 in his pocket—and a debt of $285,000 on margin calls. At one point, as the market started to slide, he quipped before an audience, "If the stock market goes any lower, I know thousands of married men who are going to leave their sweethearts and go back to their wives." And then, with his own stock losses already at several hundred thousand dollars, he added: "As for myself, I am not worried. My broker is going to carry me; he and three other pall bearers."

One of the few who got out in time was Will Rogers, the cowboy humorist. On the advice of Bernard Baruch, the financier, Rogers had reduced his stock market holdings to a small amount when the Crash hit. Thereafter, he always spoke appreciatively of Baruch. Rogers, who presented himself to audiences as an untutored person, proved to be one of the most astute stock market players in the country. He certainly was the smartest of the comedians.

The Biggest Loser in the Crash of 1987

The biggest loser in the stock market in the Crash of 1987—a heart-stopping event when in one day the Dow Jones industrial average plummeted a record 500+ points—is said to have been a man reputed to be one of history's smartest and most successful investors. His name: George Soros. His loss: $800 million during the course of the day of the crash and in the ensuing two weeks as he tried to get out of his stock index futures contracts.

Soros was later able to show an overall profit for the year, which proves either that you can't keep a good man down or that even the best and brightest can lose a whopping amount in wild and woolly Wall Street trading.

••

"A broker is a man who runs your fortune into a shoestring."
—ALEXANDER WOOLLCOTT (1887–1943)

••

••

HE LOST A BILLION

One of the biggest losers in stock market history is H. Ross Perot, the Texas businessman who gained his greatest notoriety as a candidate for president of the United States during the 1992 elections. During just one day—April 22, 1970—the value of his stock as founder and chairman of Electronic Data Systems plunged $450 million. All in all, during a three-month period from March through May of 1970, Perot lost $1.2 billion.

What led to this loss was a scenario in which Perot, in taking his company public in 1968, saw the value of his stock soar to as high as $162 a share by March 1970, making him then the wealthiest individual in America. But then the stock price fell to $85 in April and plunged as low as $29 by May.

Eventually Perot bounded back, selling 46 percent of his shares in EDS to General Motors in 1984 for $1 billion and getting 11.3 million shares of class E GM stock, which he then sold back to GM in 1986. With the formation in 1988 of his own company again (in competition with EDS), Perot saw his worth climb back eventually to over $2 billion. As for the $1 billion loss in the value of his stock in the 1970s, he later airily termed the tumble as being "Mickey Mouse."

How to Invest Like "the Investor's Investor"

Warren Buffett is the only member of the Forbes 400 to have made his fortune the new-fashioned way—through investing.

Called the investor with "the Midas Touch" (*The New York Times*) and "the investor's investor" (*Financial World*), Buffett, after years of service as head of the Berkshire Hathaway investment group, was said by Forbes in 1993 to be worth more than $4 billion—making him the richest person in the United States that year. When Salomon Brothers needed help restoring its image in the wake of a Wall Street scandal, Buffett is the one who was called in. Indeed, so successful has Buffett been that a person putting $10,000 into Buffett's original investing partnership at its inception in 1956 would have had thirty years later, in 1986, a fortune worth more than $5 million.*

Buffett, who has been described as pleasant and genial, grew up in Omaha and did much of his investing from his base in Nebraska, 1,000 miles west of Wall Street. A follower of Benjamin Graham, a noted financial writer and thinker who headed a successful investment company, and an adherent of his value approach toward stocks, Buffett formed his own investing partnership in 1956 at the age of twenty-five. His results over the years have been astonishing—and very lucrative for those who placed their money in his hands or followed his advice (Omaha itself has fifty-two "Buffett millionaires").

What, according to Buffett, does it take to be a good investor? And how can one avoid being a bad investor? Here is how Train encapsulates

---

*Buffett is modest about his accomplishments and riches. In a paraphrase of Buffett's philosophy, John Train points out in *The Midas Touch: The Strategies That Have Made Warren Buffett America's Pre-eminent Investor* (New York: Harper & Row, 1987), a book about Buffett's investment approach, that the financial genuis does not act rich. "Of course, as Buffett well knows, being immensely rich (as distinct from just being rich) objectively does you more harm than good. It isn't logical, any more than endless body building or an oversized chair. From the conspicuously rich everybody wants something. . . . If you get hugely rich, most or even all of the people around you are, beneath their flattery, envious and resentful."

Buffett's philosophies based upon his writings and statements in interviews with journalists.

"Investing calls for much the same qualities as those required to become a first-class ballet dancer or concert pianist," writes Train, who enumerates Buffett strategies that advocate prudence and planning rather than speculation and the gamble for the quick and big market payoff. The great investor has a "ruling passion" to excel, just as a great artist does, and, like an artist or master chess player, will work diligently to overcome difficulties and frustrations in order to triumph.

There is one attribute, though, of the great investor that ties directly to the pursuit of money. According to Buffett, such a person's ruling passion "is usually greed—typically deriving from a less-than-prosperous childhood." But such greed is tempered by the real pursuit, which is that of mastering the very craft of investing, "sometimes without caring whether he only gets rich or immensely rich." The distinction is important. "It has been rightly said that the reward of the general is not a bigger tent but command," writes Train in a paraphrase of Buffett. "It is, in other words, succeeding in the process itself that fascinates the greatest investors."

Another attribute is that of originality, since the largest sums are earned in the market by doing the opposite of most everyone else at propitious key times or by being the only major buyer of stock while building a position: "Committee investing is almost always mediocre investing."

One should also be sure about the stock one is investing in. Only with such confidence will an investor be able to withstand the actions of the crowd at critical times. In the same regard, one should buy a stock in the same careful way as one buys a house. Buffett would many times list the reasons why he found a stock interesting, study the list for a while, and only then make up his mind to buy or pass.

Buffett also looks for an investor who has the energy and determination to be "a fanatic" about dedicating himself to the job of investing. Notes Train, great investors like Buffett are always fanatical about their work.

And finally, one should heed Buffett's main message to "be thorough, cautious, and risk-averse." Such a cautionary approach is summed up in Buffett's "two key rules for successful investing":

Rule Number 1   Never lose money.
Rule Number 2   Never forget Rule Number 1.

179

Buffett's views of what makes for a bad investor (which usually means a "poor" investor, in more ways than one) is often the person who exhibits just the opposite characteristics:

- He does not do his homework with a stock, but rather switches from one stock to another based on a story or the whims of the investing crowd.
- He buys a stock on a hot idea when the stock is already high and near its top and sells in despair when the stock reaches its lows.
- He does not know how to value a company and therefore does not know how to gauge an appropriate price.
- He has a high turnover rate in his stock selections.
- He is more gambler than investor, acting as though a stock is "a thing to bet on like a racehorse, rather than what it is—a share of a business, whose fortunes derive from the success of that business."

Indeed, Buffett is not a betting man in his private or public life. His value-oriented approach to the market, in which he follows two principles (favorable odds and many bets), makes him more like the casino than the gambler. In this way, Warren Buffett has reduced his risk—and made his $4 billion fortune.

Never on Mondays:
Some Market Insights by Today's Most Famous Stock Picker

Another very successful stock market figure shares the same investment approach as Bernard Baruch and Warren Buffett.

Peter Lynch, the portfolio manager of the highly successful Fidelity Magellan Fund for thirteen years, was considered the most famous stock picker in America during the 1980s. From 1977, when he was named to his position, until his retirement in June 1990 at the age of only forty-six, the mutual fund he managed recorded an amazing return of more than 2,500 percent (the Standard & Poor's 500, the benchmark against which funds and money managers are measured, during this time posted a return of just over 500 percent).

To what did Lynch ascribe his success?

He pointed out that he did not try to predict the future but studied hard and did not let emotion rule his decisions. "When your gut says it's now time to get in the market, you're probably wrong. You've got to get your gut out of it," Lynch told *The Best of Business Quarterly* in an interview published in the magazine's Spring 1991 issue. He then offered a revealing insight that showed how emotion rather than learning a company and following the fundamentals of its stock's value can lead to losses in the market.

A study of the stock market from 1955 to 1985, Lynch said, showed that during that thirty-year period the market—which gained 900 points during that time—was actually down 1,500 points on Mondays, but up 2,400 points the rest of the week.

Lynch called this "a staggering statistic on the psychology of [a person's] brain."

To what did he attribute the Monday phenomenon?

Lynch saw it as part of the human swing from pessimism to optimism, from fear to hope about the future.

"The reason for the Monday decline is that on the weekend everybody becomes an economist," he said. "They read the Sunday papers, they think, and they basically get depressed. Then they get to work, and they sell on Monday." He pointed out that it was not just a coincidence that the biggest one-day drop in stock market history, the 500 plus plunge in October 1987, happened on a Monday.

But Lynch had built his success on not trying to forecast the economy, not looking at and worrying about overall trends and becoming a so-called weekend economist. Instead he followed the facts about a company—was its business good?—and facts about the economy—were car loadings down, were help-wanted ads up?—rather than whether a recession is coming or the threat of global changes.

His rational, unemotional, nonspeculative approach to the market obviously paid off for Peter Lynch. And yet, at the age of forty-six, he was able to free himself from the daily pressures of managing his multi-billion-dollar fund (with holdings of $13 billion, it had grown to be the largest mutual fund in America by the time Lynch resigned). Although staying active in the business, he retired from fund management because, he said, he had not lived a normal life since 1982. Until then he had never worked weekends or nights and could watch one of his daughters grow up. But from 1982 on, he found himself traveling two weeks each month, working every Saturday, and getting to the office at 7:00 A.M.

"These things start to get to you. There are lots of other things I'm interested in," he said. The "other things" did not involve making more money.

Said Lynch: "When you start out in this business, you hope to achieve a net worth of X. I reached several times X, and I didn't want to make 110X or 400X. I never understand these people who make incredible amounts of money yet want to make eight times more. What good is it?"

••

GREED FACTOR QUIZ: THE STOCK MARKET

Question: In what year was the record set for trading volume on the New York Stock Exchange, and how many shares changed hands in that record year?

The answer: The annual trading volume record was set in 1987, when nearly 48 billion shares were traded (the actual figure was 47,801,308,660). After this high was reached at the height of the Greed Decade of the 1980s, by 1990 the trading volume slipped by 8.2 billion shares to 39,664,516,030 shares.

Question: In what year and for how much was the record set for the purchase of a seat on the New York Stock Exchange?

Answer: Again it was in 1987. The high was reached for a NYSE seat on September 21, when one was sold for $1,150,000—a record in the long history of the stock market. However, by 1990, the price of a seat had dropped significantly. On November 27, one went for $250,000—nearly a million dollars less in just three years.

The Greed Decade of the 1980s is defined by these record-setting statistics about the stock market. The dramatic drop-off in volume and in the value of a stock exchange seat occurred as the decade ended and the 1990s began.

••

Boesky and Milken:
Star Players of the '80s

The midpoint—and perhaps low point—of the Decade of Greed came on September 12, 1985, when Ivan Boesky, the Wall Street financier and arbitrageur who eventually went to jail for his illegal use of inside information, spoke on the Berkeley college campus and told his youthful audience: "Greed is all right" and that "everybody should be a little bit greedy. . . . You shouldn't feel guilty."

The crowd cheered.

Boesky was invited back to give the commencement address at Berkeley's business school graduation ceremonies, and on May 18, 1986, he elaborated on his theme, declaring, "I urge you as part of your mission—to seek wealth. It's all right. Does anyone disagree with that? No!" But he went on to caution his audience in a way that has often been overlooked: "But do it in a virtuous and honest way. . . . Having wealth, if you aim high, can allow you to be what you want to be in this great land. You could be more of a person who could make a difference. As you accumulate wealth and power, you must remain God-fearing and responsible to the system that has given you this opportunity."

Six months later, November 14, 1986, the Securities and Exchange Commission announced that Boesky had agreed to a plea bargain and was cooperating with authorities on investigations into widespread abuses of insider stock-trading activities. He was eventually convicted and punished with a three-year jail term and a fine that was until then the largest in history—$100 million. It was a fine that Boesky was able to pay in cash.

What did Boesky do that was illegal? How had he made such huge sums that he could be fined—and pay—$100 million?

Boesky was not alone in illegally manipulating and making hundreds of millions of dollars during the Decade of Greed. He was joined by such others as Michael Milken and Dennis Levine of the Wall Street firm Drexel Burnham Lambert. Together they had developed a new way of issuing junk bonds—bonds at higher-than-average rates of return because they were securities of less-secure companies—as a way of financing businesses, then buying up such bonds before trading them later to hostile takeover dealers at huge profits. The key was their inside knowledge of company prospects and their willingness to trade on that knowledge, a criminal activity according to SEC regulations. What it meant was that companies were now left with massive debt, while Wall Streeters like Boesky and Milken and others cashed in.

Boesky profited, but no one profited like Milken, who had been the one in the late 1970s to seize on the concept of junk bonds as a way for small and midsize companies to get financing. In 1987, for instance, Milken was paid $550 million by Drexel Burnham. This figure, according to calculations by *The Wall Street Journal,* was the most ever paid an American in the history of the nation. In fact, it far surpassed John D. Rockefeller's earnings in his peak years of 1910 to 1913, when he annually earned $400 million in comparable dollars to Milken's. And Milken's compensation from Drexel Burnham does not include money he made from his own trading account and from returns from other investments and partnerships he had. This figure has been estimated as equaling another $500 million, which means that Milken, who had become a billionaire before he was forty, earned more than a billion dollars in 1987.*

WHAT HAPPENED TO BOESKY'S $100 MILLION FINE?

Ivan Boesky's $100 million fine, the largest such fine in history until Milken later paid $1 billion in fines, took a dual route. Half of the money went into a fund to compensate his victims. The other $50 million went to the United States Treasury.

In addition to the fine, Boesky paid in other ways for his greediness. He served twenty-two months in federal prison, and upon his release he was sued for divorce by his wife of thirty years. He later returned the favor, suing his spouse, the daughter of a successful real estate developer, for $1 million a year in alimony. And not only was he barred forever by the Securities and Exchange Commission from ever making a living in the securities industry, he also was said to be without funds. "I'm virtually wiped out," he said in connection with his need for alimony.

The New York Times calculated that Drexel Burnham paid Milken at the rate of $1,046 a minute in 1987. If we figure in his other earnings, then Milken was making $120,000 an hour that year.

THE "GREED IS GOOD!" SPEECH

The statement "Greed is good!" is obviously an echo of Ivan Boesky's "Greed is all right" declaration in 1985. It comes at the beginning of a speech by the main character, a business tycoon, in the 1987 motion picture *Wall Street*. That speech is usually remembered in the way in which the latest edition of *Bartlett's* presents it (which can be found at the beginning of this book). But that is just an excerpt; the full speech uses the word *greed* as indicative of the drive for other things than just wealth. Here are the actual remarks delivered by actor Michael Douglas as the tycoon Gordon Gekko in a scene at a stockholders meeting of Teldar Paper:

"The point is, ladies and gentlemen, that *greed*, for lack of a better word, is good!

"Greed is right!

"Greed works!

"Greed clarifies, cuts through, and captures the essence of the evolutionary spirit.

"Greed in all its forms—greed for life, for money, for love, knowledge—has marked the upward surge of mankind, and greed—you mark my words—will not only save Teldar Paper but that other malfunctioning corporation called the U.S.A.!

"Thank you very much."

In the movie, the speech is greeted with applause by the gathering of stockholders. The movie itself went on to be well received. Michael Douglas won an Oscar for best actor for his role as Gordon Gekko. Oliver Stone, who co-wrote the screenplay with Stanley Weiser and directed, went on to direct such other popular films as *JFK* and *Heaven and Earth*. But *Wall Street*, coming as it did at the height of the Greed Decade, reverberated throughout the public with its dramatic portrayal of the aggressive pursuit of money on the stock exchanges that led to insider trading and other criminal activity. As Oliver Stone no doubt intended, the movie served to criticize the increasingly acquisitive atmosphere that had pervaded America in the 1980s.

The $64 Million Question:

Was It Greed?

In all the discussions about the stock market highfliers of the 1980s who were brought low—about why Boesky, Milken, Levine, and others did what they illegally did—a question often raised is, Why did they keep going after more and more money when they had so much already? Was greed motivating them to manipulate the market or to trade on unlawfully gained insider information—or was it something else?

One of the culprits asks himself this very question in his autobiography of his fall from Wall Street grace. In *Inside Out: An Insider's Account of Wall Street* (New York: Putnam, 1991), Dennis B. Levine, a managing director of Drexel Burnham who was convicted of trading on insider information and who was imprisoned and fined for his indiscretions, tells that he was earning more than $2 million a year at the time he went astray and had $10.6 million in his bank account. He concludes therefore that "there was more at work here than simple greed."

But his extended answer shows that while the desire to use more money to purchase more things may not have been his driving purpose, money was the means by which the score was kept—and therefore greed and avarice *were* part of the mix.

"Something deep inside forced me to try to catch up to the pack of wheeler-dealers who always raced in front of me," he notes. The drive forced him to work sixty to a hundred hours a week, with little time for reflection, creating a "narcotic effect" within him.

When he would learn that he had just made several hundreds of thousands of dollars on an insider trade, the result for him was "a rush of euphoria that had to be akin to a drug high." But then the high would wear off because he would soon remember "that there were so many ahead of me on the scoreboard."

In looking back at his career, Levine writes he now realizes that at every level of his career he kept pushing his goals higher. Being an associate led him to wanting to be a vice president, but becoming a vice president soon made him want to be a senior vice president. And so on up the ladder—senior vice president, partner, managing director.

And as he earned more, he thought of earning still more. At $20,000 a year he envisioned making $100,000. At $100,000 he thought he could make $200,000. When he earned $1 million he dreamed of making $3 million. And yet he never seemed satisfied. "There was always somebody one rung higher on the ladder, and I could never stop wondering: Is he really twice as good as I am?"

He discovered his ambition clouding his judgment and his sense of fulfillment unable to be assuaged by realistic limits. "One frenetic meeting followed another. One deal was piled atop the next. The hours grew longer, the numbers grew bigger, the stakes grew more critical, the fire grew ever hotter."

He even wondered if Ronald Perelman, a man with whom he had major dealings and who was ranked number three on *Forbes* magazine's list of four hundred wealthiest Americans, was content or "was he obsessed with catching the two individuals above him?"

And yet Levine could see that such obsessions had to stop, that by the time he had become a managing director of Drexel he was out of control and so were such people as Boesky and Milken.

So although they were intoxicated by the deal and moved more by ambition and competitive spirit than by money, still, as Levine writes: "To those of us who raced along the Wall Street treadmill of the 80s, money assumed a mystical aura." That aura was manifold, for as Levine also writes: "Once you achieved a modest level of success . . . money simply became the way you gauged your level of success, compared to those about you."

Human beings will always search for ways to make names for themselves, to determine who is more successful. In the world of Wall Street, money becomes a measuring rod of success. Because money can symbolize success so readily in its numbers—as it did to Levine and company—the lust for those numbers is as avaricious a pursuit as the drive for the raciest of sports cars, the gaudiest of clothes, or the grandest of homes.

Oh, the Wages of Wall Street

Laura Pedersen, barely out of high school and not yet twenty, made a million dollars on Wall Street during the 1980s as an options trader—which means that while she was trading options for her firm she was not old enough legally to directly buy, sell, or own for herself a single share of stock (the Securities and Exchange Commission requires that a person be at least twenty-one to do so).

From 1984 through 1989, Pedersen was responsible for trading many millions of dollars' worth of stock index options, and at the age of twenty she became the youngest person in the history of Wall Street to get, courtesy of her employer, her own seat on the American Stock Exchange.

Her career, however, was marked by the wild up-and-down swings of Wall Street. On the day of the October 1987 crash, she actually made $100,000 for her firm, then lost $1.3 million on the following Monday, then lost another $350,000 the day after. She was also fully exposed to the screaming, arm-waving, cussing, spitting, stomping, and phone-throwing that marks the life of options traders in the pit on the floor of the American Stock Exchange.

"I did everything my parents told me never to do," she writes in *Play Money* (New York: Crown, 1991), her account of what she subtitles *My Brief but Brilliant Career on Wall Street*. "Bad enough that I would antagonize, curse, spit, slug, kick, and terrorize, and fight with my colleagues— many of them older and probably wiser than I—but that I would do these things gladly and for a price struck me as ironic, given my abhorrence of confrontation of any kind."

The options traders work in what is called the pit, an area set aside from the rest of the trading floor that is only sixty-five square feet in space but must accommodate upwards of three hundred people. And these people, from 9:30 A.M. to 4:15 P.M., must make rapid buying and selling decisions involving thousands, if not millions, of dollars, all the while calling out their orders and trying to be ahead of other traders. The result is invariably an atmosphere of bedlam leading to physical abuse of many kinds.

Pedersen talks about how some days, within a first mad hour of trading, her "sweat-stained" blouse would be "torn to ribbons." She would often have to discard her working outfits after only one wearing. Other hazards of the pit were being poked by ballpoint pens and pencils, drenched by spilled coffee or cans of cola, lacerated by staples and subjected to paper cuts, sometimes requiring a trip to a nearby hospital for stitches.

But the physical problems that loomed the largest came from the internal damage done by the stress and working conditions. One warning signal cited by Pedersen: When she and fourteen other traders went to the hospital to donate blood for a fellow trader who had undergone heart surgery, all fifteen were rejected as blood donors because of colds or liver or cholesterol problems. And two of them were told they needed to be admitted for further testing.

A major threat to the health of the traders is what the constant shouting does to their voices. Many of them resort to over-the-counter throat sprays. Pedersen herself became a "throat spray junkie" to ease the pain and rawness stemming from yelling out her buy and sell orders. A throat specialist finally told her that her recurring polyps, strep throat, and swollen glands could be cured but he predicted she could develop throat cancer in several years. Her dentist discovered a strange decay pattern in her mouth, explainable finally by the six Lifesavers she would wedge between her teeth and the inside of her mouth each night to ease her burning throat.

And then there was her hearing. A special auditory examiner at Manhattan Eye, Ear & Throat informed her that she had lost three frequencies in her hearing, representing 10 to 20 percent of her hearing capability. "Some of the other traders wore the kind of earplugs doctors recommended to Con Edison tunnel drillers or shipyard sandblasters, but I hadn't done this, as I worried about missing a critical trade," she writes. And then she ruefully notes that unlike throat problems, ear problems don't clear up so readily. "Once it goes, hearing doesn't come back."

Her eyes also were affected. Watching eight computer screens at a time while also keeping tabs on two electronic tapes had caused her eye muscles to contract and not relax. She noticed that after a day of trading, people seemed to be "jumping up and down" before her, and other times she was bothered by a glare that distorted objects. One ophthalmologist, observing her condition, asked if she refereed tennis matches. When she told him what she did do and then described her day, of how her "eyes would dart from trader to trader, up to the broad tape, the ticker, down and to the side monitors, the market minders, then back to the traders— all within seconds," the doctor warned her: "You're abusing yourself."

And finally her podiatrist, ordering her to wear special shoe inserts he fabricated for her, told her she was "the most anxiety-ridden patient" he had ever treated.

Throat. Hearing. Eyes. After just four years, her body was trying to tell her something about her career path. And she was not alone in this physical reaction to the stresses of her Wall Street job. A friend functioning as a clerk nearly caused a major debacle when she inexplicably signaled to a trader to buy six thousand options—a huge number—when in fact she meant six hundred (although she caught her mental error in time, the friend resigned a week later). A young trader, the week after the stock market crash of 1987, experienced the shock of having his hair turn prematurely gray. Many of the traders worried about dying of a coronary during trading (one trader with a strange sense of humor walked around with a tape measure offering to fit anyone for a body bag, which could then be kept ready in the coat room).

What also changed her attitude about working on Wall Street was a combination of the market's second major crash in two years—this one the 190.58 drop on October 13, 1989—and a growing sense that the stock market needed closer regulation to stop the excesses she had witnessed in the decade of the 1980s.

Starting in 1984 as a $120 a week clerk on the main trading floor of the American Stock Exchange, Pedersen left in 1989 as a highly successful options trader making six figures annually. She told her supervisor that she was leaving because "it was either my money or my life, and I valued my life more."

When Pedersen quit her job for a career away from Wall Street, she had just turned twenty-four.

The Other Side of the Street

When people think of Wall Street, they don't usually think of religious institutions. But the editors of the magazine "Institutional Investor" did when compiling a book about finance. In *The Way It Was: An Oral History of Finance 1967–1987* (New York: Morrow, 1988), the editors interviewed the spiritual leaders of three religious sanctuaries in the Wall Street area. One is Trinity Church, an Episcopal church that has hovered over the Wall Street area for nearly three hundred years. Another is Our Lady of Victory, the parish church for the New York Stock Exchange. The third is known as the Wall Street Synagogue.

The three spiritual leaders interviewed each had witnessed the effects of a Wall Street environment increasingly ruled by greed as the decade of the 1980s entered its last years. But they had also seen signs of increased religious practices as well.

Vicar Richard May of Trinity had observed a great change between what he termed the "old-style money managers" and the new. The old-style types were very conservative because they were dealing with either their own money or family or trust funds and saw themselves as having a fiduciary responsibility. Even at the trading level their attitudes were more mechanical and more directly involved in helping others to invest. "Nowadays there are more strivers—out to make money for themselves or to make a reputation," he noted.

He saw the competition in the schools, the desire to get ahead, the striving for supremacy among their peers, the rampant materialism as causes of the insider-trading scandals and the lust for money. "With some insider traders, I think the desire to succeed becomes a compulsion, even if they don't need the money," he said. "Their goals get set early, and they don't really question them until they get to the top . . . [and then] they find out that all these things really don't bring happiness.

"Achieving can become greed when you do it for its own sake and not for any useful purpose," he concluded.

The result of the Wall Street pressures can be seen in two ministries offered by Trinity Church. One is an Alcoholics Anonymous program and another is a methadone clinic. Providing these services in a church building enables Wall Streeters to come to such a clinic in their suits "and not stand out."

But Wall Streeters were also showing more religiosity during the closing years of the 1980s. Monsignor Edward Mitty of Our Lady of Victory reported that his church was conducting eight masses a day for some 2,000 attendees, not to mention additional numbers during the Lent season. And Rabbi Meyer Hager said he saw a decided increase in practicing Jews on Wall Street. Noting the overt discrimination Jews faced in banking and insurance when the Wall Street Synagogue was formed in 1929, he stated he had not seen similar prejudice since he had come to the synagogue in 1965.

"In fact, I have noticed that the number of Jews who are working here has increased greatly, especially among those who are Orthodox," he said. "When I came, it was practically unknown to see men walking around with yarmulkes and working in banks or financial houses."

Monsignor Mitty felt that the insider-trading scandals then erupting represented "a very, very small fraction" of those who worked on Wall Street. Rabbi Hager declared, "There is no subsitute for plain integrity" and that "in Judaism our prophets denounced greed throughout ancient history."

••

THE GREATER FOOL THEORY

One of the theories guiding wily Wall Street stock market traders is termed "the Greater Fool Theory." This concept was probably best summed up by Donald J. Stockings, a member of the Securities and Exchange Commission, in 1925. Said Stockings: "You don't buy a stock because it has real value. You buy it because you feel there is always a greater fool down the street who will pay more than you paid."

CRIMES OF PASSION (FOR MONEY):

SCHEMES TO GET RICH EVEN QUICKER

Whenever I am

asked what kind

of writing is the

most lucrative, I

have to say,

ransom notes.

—H. N. SWANSON,
Hollywood literary
agent, in *Sprinkled with
Ruby Dust*

One thing about the greedy—they always seem in a hurry to get more and more. Greediness appears to be associated with impatience. Maybe that's why the phrase "get rich" is almost naked without adding "quick."

And quite often schemes to get rich quick involve dubious if not outright fraudulent practices. Whether it's in the stock market or the marketplace, whether it's with a gun or a pen, the criminal is after as much return for as little investment of time and effort as possible. And his prey, who shares a common interest, often makes it even easier for him.

While this aspect of human nature has not changed, the type of criminal actions in the pursuit of money and possessions have changed over time. Today we have a host of sophisticated electronic-based crime, including fraudulent use of computers, telephones, and credit cards. We also have the S&L scams, phony billings, government rip-offs, and insurance fraud. Here are a few notable examples.

◆◆

THE THREE WAYS TO WEALTH: TWO BY HOOK, ONE BY CROOK

"There are only three ways by which any individual can get wealth—by work, by gift or by theft. And clearly the reason why the workers get so little is that the beggars and thieves get so much."

—HENRY GEORGE,
Social Problems

◆◆

The Ponzi Scheme:

Robbing Peter to Pay Greedy Paul

He was a thirty-year-old immigrant, with just $200 to his name in 1919, and yet within six months he had $15 million in the bank, a chauffeur-driven limousine, crowds of supporters, and the police and postal inspectors up in arms.

His name was Charles Ponzi and the get-rich scheme he concocted would enter his name into the annals of confidence games that prey on greed. For the "Ponzi scheme" is based on using the money of later investors to pay high rates of return to a few earlier ones, thereby creating the illusion of a very successful enterprise—when the truth is that a classic pyramid scheme is under way in which Peter, the later investor, is robbed to pay Paul, the early investor. The problem with such a scheme is mathematical: eventually the scheme runs out of Peters to rob, and Paul soon finds out that his original investment, while paying a high rate of return initially, is virtually nonexistent. The money that has disappeared from Paul, not to mention Peter, has been pocketed—in this case, by Ponzi.

Ponzi based his scheme on the International Postal Reply Coupon then in existence, an instrument whereby a person sending a letter to another country could purchase a coupon good for redemption in stamps in the other country that could be sent along to be used to send a return message. This was especially helpful earlier this century, when there was much immigration splitting apart families, who kept in touch by mail.

194

Ponzi realized that because of the difference in value of the currencies among countries, the coupons, while good for stamps, could also be exchanged for a slight profit for cash in a country with a higher exchange rate.

To capitalize on this, Ponzi set up a company he called The Securities Exchange Company that would purchase the coupons and redeem them in other countries at a profit. He began selling shares in his company, saying he could return investors as much as 50 percent profit in forty-five days—guaranteed. As the money began trickling in from ads he placed in newspapers, Ponzi made good on his boast of large and quick profits to his earliest investors, and soon, as he expected, word spread of this great investment. People eventually began clamoring to be allowed to invest— it reached 20,000 investors within six months—and a grinning Ponzi collected millions of dollars, all the while claiming that the investment was sound. Ponzi quickly became a national hero.

But by 1920 the postal authorities noticed something was amiss. The traffic in coupons had not increased noticeably. Where, then, was Ponzi's company putting all this investment money? When word spread that the government was investigating Ponzi, the whole enterprise began unraveling. It was soon discovered that he was pocketing investors' money. Ponzi was eventually convicted and sent to jail for larceny and mail fraud. He was later deported for engaging in land fraud in Florida and eventually wound up in Brazil. Most of the investment money was never returned to investors.

As one business magazine has noted, the Ponzi scheme now "lives on in spirit in such well-established schemes as pyramid games, chain letters, and the Social Security system."

The $100 Million Swindle of the Rich and Famous:
The Ponzi Scheme in Action

Ponzi schemes—in which money is returned to initial investors at a high rate of return in order to sucker these and other investors into putting in larger sums that are then diverted to other uses and never returned—did not stop with the downfall of Charles Ponzi. If anything, they have been cropping up in recent decades in various forms, such as in chain letters, pyramid sales schemes, offshore mutual funds, private hedge funds, real estate partnerships, and the sales of commodity contracts and gold coins.

One of the most spectacular uses of the Ponzi scheme—spectacular because of the amount of money lost by duped investors and because of the number and prominence of the duped—was the Home-Stake Production Company swindle that began in the mid-1950s and lasted for eighteen years. Home-Stake was an oil-drilling company based in Tulsa, Oklahoma. An Oklahoma lawyer, Robert S. Trippet, was the mastermind behind the swindle, which involved offering wealthy individuals an always enticing incentive—a legal tax dodge. Rich investors were sold tax shelter partnerships in Home-Stake that Trippet said could generate through its oil-recovery operations a return of as much as 300 percent or more, as well as realize a considerable tax savings on the company's deductible oil-drilling leases.

An elaborate artifice was created around the company. Trippet carefully cultivated his image as a conservative, well-to-do businessman/lawyer. He hosted prospects at swank places like New York's "21" Club. By offering consulting fees, finders fees, and loans, he enlisted accountants, lawyers, and business advisers to help him sell investments in Home-Stake. And he utilized a number of ploys to hoodwink others. One example: To promote the oil-drilling operations in his company, he inflated oil production figures to potential investors and even had the irrigation pipes on a California farm where only minimal drilling was being done painted a bright pink to make it look like the aboveground part of an active underground oil pipeline. Another device (and the one that made it a Ponzi Scheme): he used money from later investors to boost the return paid to early investors, thereby building word of mouth about the great investment in Home-Stake. But only a small part of the payment was coming from oil revenues.

As a result of these and other devices, combined with the lure of high profits and lowered taxes, from 1955 until 1973, when the company collapsed in bankruptcy amid charges of fraud by the Securities and Exchange Commission and the Internal Revenue Service, hundreds of some of the leading figures in show business, commerce, banking, and law wound up investing and losing more than $100 million in Home-Stake.

Here are just a few of the prominent people who were influenced to invest in Home-Stake:

In the entertainment field—Alan Alda, Jack Benny, Candice Bergen, Jacqueline Bisset, Oleg Cassini, Tony Curtis, Sandy Dennis, Phyllis Diller, Faye Dunaway, Bob Dylan, Mia Farrow, Buddy Hackett, Shirley Jones, Walter Matthau, Liza Minnelli, Ozzie Nelson, Mike Nichols, Barbra Streisand, Barbara Walters, Andy Williams, Jonathan Winters, and

CRIMES OF PASSION (FOR MONEY)

a number of other performers, producers, writers, and agents.

In the business world—such top executives as the chairman of Pepsico; the chairman of Norton Simon; the president of Bethlehem Steel; the chairman and president of Western Union; the chairman, the president, and the former chairman and president of Citicorp and Citibank; the president of Time; the chairman and former chairman of General Electric, as well as more than thirty other officers and managers at GE (one of the GE executives put in $640,000).

In politics—two U.S. Senators (Javits of New York and Hollings of South Carolina) and a former governor (Kirk of Florida).

In law—at least thirty-seven attorneys, many of whom were partners in New York or Beverly Hills law firms (including the brother of the former mayor of New York City, John V. Lindsay; William Shea, for whom Shea Stadium is named; a former Attorney General of New York; the judge on the U.S. Court of Appeals who wrote the decision in the Pentagon Papers case; and Thomas E. Dewey, former Governor of New York and Republican candidate for President of the United States in 1948).*

In the aftermath of the Home-Stake swindle, the Federal government began looking into abuses involving tax shelters and Congress started a process of severely tightening up the use of shelters to limit or defer taxes.

But Home-Stake also showed how vulnerable even the wealthy and the financially and commercially successful are to being defrauded of their money. Many of the Hollywood figures, upon learning they had been duped, said they left the management of their money largely to others and often went along because of what a friend was doing with his or her money. Said comedienne Phyllis Diller, "I had it checked out by my Harvard-educated New York lawyer, the fastest brain in the East, and I knew that anything Andy Williams was into had to be pure gold." Buddy Hackett, the comic, said he didn't have "the vaguest idea" why he invested, that his lawyers and accountants usually looked into such things "and explain them to me in baby talk. If it sounds okay we go ahead."

Another investor moaned about how he would now shy away from any tax shelter proposal. "You know what is the best tax shelter?" he asked. "Don't make any money."

As for Trippet, in his 1977 criminal case he pleaded "no contest" and

---

*A comprehensive list of the prominent investors in the Home-Stake Production Company can be found in *Stealing from the Rich: The Home-Stake Oil Swindle* by David McClintick (New York: Evans, 1977).

was convicted of conspiracy (one count) and mail fraud (nine counts). He was fined $19,000 and assessed $100,000 toward a fund for the civil claimaints. But the jail sentence he received drew considerable scorn. The judge, noting the government's poorly presented case, the fact that the wealthy who should have known better lost little because they were seeking to shelter income from taxes anyway, and Trippet's ill health, sentenced him to one day in jail and three years of supervised probation. The day after the sentencing, *The Tulsa Tribune* published a scathing editorial criticizing the judge for the "one night in jail" sentence as "topping himself in the matter of trivial sentences." The paper noted that "for most Home-Stake investors there were real obvious losses" and that a big loser in Home-Stake was the U.S. Treasury since "any write-offs for bad Home-Stake investments reduced income taxes." Andrew Tobias, the financial writer, commented, "The judge should be shot."

Alan Alda, who said he went into the investment not to speculate but because he was told it was very safe, summed up the pain and suffering caused by such a colossal swindle. "I'm really sore. It's going to take me a lot of time to salvage what I've lost. I'll have to work harder now. I'm told this was a classical swindle. That doesn't make it any easier. I'm not used to being conned—except by people I vote for."*

The Infallible Forecaster:

Half Wrong, Always Right

It is estimated that Americans lose $10 billion a year to investment fraud. According to the National Futures Association, the two most prevalent methods used by the unscrupulous to separate investors from their money are the Ponzi scheme and the "infallible forecaster" ploy. We've seen how the Ponzi scheme separates people from their money by the use of lies and deception. The infallible forecaster ploy is a scam based upon an artful understanding of human psychology.

The perpetrator selects two groups of people and, usually by phone, introduces himself as an investment adviser. He then offers free advice about a commodity or stock, but to one group the adviser predicts that the item will go up in price and to the other group that it will drop in price.

*Stealing from the Rich: The Home-Stake Oil Swindle, p. 251.

When the price changes sufficiently in one direction or another, the scam artist calls back the people in the group to whom he gave the correct prediction and makes a further prediction about this or another item, telling half of this group that the price will rise and the other half that the price will drop.

After the price has changed again, the con man contacts the people in the group who have now received two "correct" forecasts in a row and makes the case that based upon his successes in picking winners, he should be retained as an investment adviser and entrusted with the now duly impressed investor's funds.

Once those funds are turned over to the "adviser," they will slowly be stolen through poor if not fraudulent advice about other investments.

••

"Behind every great fortune is a crime."
—HONORÉ DE BALZAC
(1799–1850), French novelist

••

Crimes of Greed:
The Statistics and the Scope

Question: What costs stores more—shoplifting or employee theft?
Answer: Employee theft.

Studies have found that 30 percent of inventory losses at retail stores are due to shoplifters, but 43 percent of stolen inventory is due to employees. (The value in lost merchandise is said to be $27 billion annually.)

This is just one of the surprising statistics about crimes of greed. Here are some other numbers that show the enormous scope of these types of criminal activities:

- Organized crime rakes in $50 billion a year, according to the President's Commission on Organized Crime.
- White-collar crime is not far behind organized crime. Here the estimates are that it represents at a minimum $40 billion a year in activity and may go as high as $100 billion.

199

- The illegal drug industry worldwide takes in $300 billion a year, generating $240 billion in profits, according to estimates by the U.S. State Department. And the drug trade may be growing by $10 billion a year.
- The underground economy—the amount of untaxed and unlawful income—is estimated to be $550 billion, a figure that is about as large as 10 percent of the nation's Gross National Product.

Thus, between white-collar, organized, underground, drug, and retailer-ripoff crimes, the greedy criminal economy represents $1 trillion of activity.

And we have not even figured in the amount of cheating on taxes, which during the 1980s found 25 percent of the population admitting to fudging on their tax returns to save money. The estimate is that this represents $100 billion in tax fraud annually in the United States.

Another drain on the economy is fraudulent workers' compensation claims. Fraud and exaggerated claims are driving up the cost of workers' compensation insurance by billions of dollars a year and are now a significant part of continuously increasing health-care costs. It is now estimated that cheating is involved in 20 percent or more of worker claims. Presently, $60 billion is paid out annually by employers to public and private insurers for workers' compensation. In the decade of the 1980s alone, claims doubled, the cost of claims went up by 154 percent, and the cost of insurance programs to cover workers injured on the job increased more than 150 percent—which was 50 percent faster than health-care costs overall.

Then, too, there are securities fraud and insider-trading illegalities, which represent another $10 billion in criminal activity in this country; credit card fraud, which has been mushrooming and is now costing banks and cardholders more than $700 million annually; and banking fraud, especially the savings-and-loan debacle, which it is said will take at least $325 billion to rectify, with outright fraud costing taxpayers from $5 billion to $20 billion.

Violent crime may grab the headlines, but crimes of greed rob the lifeblood of individuals, businesses, institutions, and governments. And businesses themselves rob others. Corporate crime is seemingly so widespread that in the ten years between 1975 and 1985 two-thirds of the companies listed as Fortune 500 companies were found guilty of serious criminal acts. Such crimes can include price fixing, which means higher costs in the billions of dollars for consumers, and bribing officials with kickbacks. Acts of bribery and offers of kickbacks have been estimated by the American Management Association to range up to $10 billion annually with at one time five hundred American firms said to offer $1 billion in bribes to foreign officials.

What all this means is that because of increased costs in the marketplace for higher insurance rates, beefed-up security, uncollected taxes, stolen goods, and fraudulent claims, crimes of greed may or may not pay, but they all cost everyone.

The Savings & Loan Scandal of the 80's Cost the Nation Billions of Dollars

The Greed Decade of the 80's was particularly besmirched by the savings and loan scandal that has cost depositors, investors, and taxpayers billions of dollars through fraud and manipulation of a largely unregulated industry.

Consider what happened in my home state of Maryland. The president of one of the highest flying savings and loans in the nation—Old Court Savings & Loan, which at its height was attracting a huge inflow of funds by setting its interest rates at the top (I remember nearly 16 percent at one point) and then advertising these rates in national publications—was known for his lavish lifestyle. He even had his own golf cart built with a mock Rolls-Royce grill. Local gossip had it that he and his wife, both grossly overweight, once dined out in a fancy Baltimore restaurant where they consumed six desserts at one meal. In 1985, his S&L finally collapsed amid rumors of serious mismanagement problems. He was eventually indicted in 1986 and pled guilty to swindling $14.6 million. As a result, he was sentenced to thirty years in prison. After he began serving his term, his wife, ashamed and humiliated, moved to Florida, where in her forties she soon died of a heart attack.

The scandal that erupted over the Old Court S&L spread to other S&Ls in Maryland, eventually causing the shutdown of many of the state's S&L's and a restructuring of its financial institutions. But Old Court and Maryland were not alone. Because of lax regulations, lapses in federal and state governmental oversight, poor management, and a powerful S&L lobby, a feeding frenzy developed among unscrupulous S&L executives who, through poor investments, shady deals, and outright theft, drained many S&Ls throughout the country of billions of dollars—and cost taxpayers additional billions needed to bail out the industry to prevent a collapse of the nation's financial system.

A leading figure in the country's savings and loan debacle was Charles H. Keating, Jr., a Phoenix, Arizona, millionaire who in 1984 bought Lincoln Savings & Loan in Phoenix for $51 million and then within several years defrauded Lincoln and its parent company, the American Continental Corporation, on such a massive scale that it resulted in the nation's biggest S&L failure. Twenty thousand investors claimed losses after the collapse of American Continental. The cost to the federal government to bail out Lincoln was $2.5 billion, the most expensive bailout in history.

On the federal level, Keating, who was later found to have enlisted the questionable support of five United States Senators with large contributions (they came to be known as the Keating Five), was eventually convicted of 73 counts of fraud, racketeering and conspiracy. On July 8, 1993, he was sentenced to twelve years in federal prison and fined $250,000. At the time, he was already serving ten years in a California prison on state charges of defrauding American Continental Corporation.

Who was at fault for allowing this mess to happen, and how much would it cost taxpayers to clean up?

In 1990, Congress created a commission to investigate the causes of the S&L collapse and suggest reforms. When issued in July 1993, the commission's 117-page report blamed Congress, the presidency, regulators, lobbyists, the thrift industry, and even the news media (for being "largely silent . . . when most of the damage was being done"). At a news conference after the report was issued, a member of the commission, Elliot Lentas, a former five-term Democratic member of Congress, known for his hard-nosed anticorruption attitude, stated that he believed the true cost of the debacle would eventually reach a half-trillion dollars—with another collapse possible unless more stringent reforms were made.

❖❖

BANK ROBBERY — THE QUICKEST GET-RICH-QUICK SCHEME — IS BACK WITH A RECORD YEAR

Willie Sutton, a bank robber of the 1940s and '50s, is famous for having supposedly said he robbed banks because "that's where the money is." After a drop-off in bank heists, this crime is coming back. More than 9,000 were reported in 1991—an increase of 10 percent over 1990 and a record year for bank robberies in American history. The leading city: Los Angeles, with more than 2,000 bank holdups in 1991 (one fifth of the national total) and as many as 67 in one week. The average amount taken was $3,244.

But banks are fighting back with cameras, exploding bundles of cash, and a plastic transmitter that tellers can put in a stack of money to track thieves. As a result, most robbers are quickly caught (85 percent in Los Angeles).

Now, however, robbers are turning to the 77,000 automatic teller machines, breaking into them or waylaying bank customers after they make a withdrawal or, in some cases, stealing the entire ATM by using a forklift and truck. As *Newsweek* noted in a story about the bank robbery boom, "The S & L thieves didn't get all the money. Now stick-up men want the rest."

◆◆

In Our High-Tech Age, Watch Out for Postcard Fraud

Although much of modern get-rich frauds are based on high-tech approaches, one of the most widespread techniques today involves the use of postcards. This simple, seemingly innocent device is actually the culprit in a flood of phony approaches by fraudulent marketers. They use the lowly postcard to sell often shoddy merchandise by means of such come-ons as contrived sweepstakes and supposedly free prizes involving cash, trips, cars, jewelry, vacations, and real estate.

According to a Harris poll in July 1992, the phony postcard ploy has reached such a tidal wave of usage that nine out of every ten consumers in America has received such offers. What is even more surprising—and indicative of the ease with which people's desire for something for nothing can be tapped—it was found that 33 percent of the public (almost 54,000,000) have responded to the offers.

According to postal inspectors and Federal Trade Commission officials, the schemes have one or more of the following characteristics:

- The recipient is told he has qualified for a prize, but to claim his winnings he has to put up money for a "processing" or "registration" fee, which has been known to be as much as $1,000, or else the recipient is required to buy an item, which turns out to be vastly overpriced.

- The prize is awarded only after the recipient comes to the sales office and hears the pitch, but the prize is far different than originally touted on the postcard—or sometimes no prize is given at all.

The top five postcard scams, according to a coalition of ninety government, consumer, and corporate representatives known as the Alliance Against Fraud in Telemarketing, are said to be:

The Sweepstakes/Free Prize   A recipient is informed he has won a Cadillac or cash, but to qualify for his free prize he has to buy what turns out to be a $600 camera. The eventual prize is neither a Cadillac nor cash, but cheap jewelry.

Travel and Vacations   The recipient is told he has been chosen for a free vacation, but to claim the prize of free airplane tickets the person finds he has to pay for costly hotel accommodations (in one case the FTC fined the company behind the promotion $12,000 because they did not disclose that the two free airline seats came with a requirement to pay for two weeks of hotel rooms).

Prize Recovery   Those who enter sweepstakes often find themselves later informed that "unclaimed funds" are waiting for them. Such recipients constitute what are called "sucker lists."

Credit Cards and Credit Repair Offers   These are usually targeted to the poor and financially strapped, holding out the hope for a credit card or help with fixing bad credit reports. The cards, however, turn out to have a cost of $35 to $50 and are usable only at one store, while the credit repair involves a charge for printed materials that credit counseling services offer free.

Government Money   The recipient is notified a refund is available from the Internal Revenue Service, but the notification and further specific information is accompanied by a $10 charge.The IRS, however, makes refund claims available at no charge.

The victims of these postcard promises that turn into costly shams are usually the elderly and the poor. But also being victimized are the gullible greedy, who are often blinded by the con artist's waving of his new calling card—the postcard. As the head of the National Consumers League, a consumer advocacy group, said in issuing warnings about promotions by strangers through the mail, "The only time a consumer should take a postcard sweepstakes offer seriously is when Ed McMahon shows up in person at the door."*

Affinity Fraud:
The Major Investment Problem for the Future

The Wall Street Journal reported it is a confidence scheme that is "spreading like a virus across the U.S." Securities officials, it was noted, "think this type of investment fraud will be their major problem" in coming years.

The scam they were talking about is termed "affinity fraud."[†] It is one in which con artists sell phony investments to the members of a particular group that is based on common ethnic, political, religious, or professional interests, with a specially targeted message and approach for that group. The idea behind the fraud is that people tend to drop their defenses when approached by someone seemingly from within their own kind or by others within their group who have been duped into being early endorsers.

The type of group does not matter, so long as its members share the same beliefs or characteristics. And both inexperienced and experienced investors are proving to be easy prey to this approach. Among those who have been defrauded are shrewd business executives, doctors, nurses, professors, other professionals, and affluent immigrants. The types of fraud have ranged widely, from investing in real estate to buying silver and gold to speculating in futures contracts and foreign currencies. And the vehicles to sell these schemes have included professional and foreign language publications and periodicals, cable TV, and other media that can be targeted to a select group.

The horror stories abound. One retired businessman with conservative political leanings found himself losing more than six figures in a fraudulent silver investment after he was led to believe in the investment by attendance at a three-day seminar run by what he took to be fellow Republican conservatives. It later turned out that the company running the seminars never delivered the silver, but diverted the money to other uses, including buying a conservative magazine to lure more prey from the conservative affinity group. A federal grand jury wound up indicting

---

*" 'Guaranteed Winner!' postcards promise trips, cars, cash to millions of sure losers," *The Sun*, Baltimore, Md., November 18, 1992, p. 1A.
†" 'Affinity' Groups Are Targeted by Con Artists," by Earl C. Gottschalk, Jr., *The Wall Street Journal*, December 11, 1992, p. C1.

the company for racketeering, mail and wire fraud, and, since some of the money from new investors was used to pay off early investors to build a facade of success, operating a Ponzi scheme. All in all, hundreds of people were said to have been defrauded of close to $37 million.

Thousands of doctors, nurses, and medical technicians in Utah, Nevada, and California were found to have been duped into investing $50 million of pension money in a real estate investment firm that subsequently went bankrupt, after which its president was found guilty of eighteen counts of securities fraud and was sentenced to nine years in prison. These professionals invested their money because they said they had heard about the investment from other doctors and thought therefore that "the investment was sound." So far, few have gotten any of their money returned. One seventy-year-old physician is still awaiting word as to whether he will get back any of his $200,000 from the bankruptcy payout, saying he has been told he might get back only two cents on the dollar. He had, he told the *Journal,* been expecting to retire on that $200,000 but now had to continue working. "It's one thing to be old and sick. But it's another thing to be old, sick and broke," he said.

One affinity group especially vulnerable seems to be successful immigrants, and it does not appear to matter from where they originate. In an investment scheme that used free seminars on setting up Indian restaurants, immigrants from Pakistan and India were found to have been swindled out of $3.7 million—and the swindler turned out to be a broker who himself had immigrated from India (he was sentenced to three years in prison). Chinese and Vietnamese immigrants, as well as Chinese-Americans, are also being targeted, especially in California, where numerous companies selling highly risky commodity investments have been found to be operating. The San Francisco District Attorney's office alone looked into 30 such firms over a two year period, finding that most of them had folded. But professors, college students and shop owners had invested—and lost—$12 million in supposed investment clubs that had been set up to speculate in futures contracts, foreign currencies and gold. The president of the commodity trading firm that catered to Chinese-Americans has since vanished.

How can one guard against such schemes and their schemers? Regulators offered four pointers:

1. Be wary of testimonials of success from others in your group. The citing of high rates of return on an investment in the initial stages may be the sign of a Ponzi scheme at work.

2. Get as much information as possible, including a prospectus, so that you are fully aware of the risks and of how you can get to your money.

3. Get an outside expert—not someone in your group—to determine the advisability of the investment.

4. Check out the seller of the investment. You can do this through the security regulator's office in your state government or by contacting the National Fraud Information Center (1-800-876-7060).

Finally, remember that invariably the higher the rate of return the higher the risk of any investment, especially an honest one. Only the dishonest promise high, fast and sure returns. It's called a get-rich-quick scheme. The problem is that the one who is going to get rich quickly is probably not you.

♦♦

GREEDY ROBBERS

"It's almost an axiom in police work. What gets somebody in trouble is their greed. Rather than being a conservative thief, most thieves get caught because they don't know when to stop."

—CONNIE FLETCHER,

What Cops Know: Cops Talk About What They Do, How They Do It, and What It Does to Them

♦♦

GAMBLING:

THE ODD WHO BATTLE THE ODDS

Love is the most

important thing

in the world.

Fortunately, I

love money.

—TV STAND-UP COMEDIAN

The gambler seems to possess an overabundance of the get-rich-quick attitude. Gambling presents the opportunity to acquire large sums of money with little hard work or persistent labor. There is much evidence that for many of those addicted to gambling it is the excitement of betting rather than the money itself that makes them gamble. Still, it is money—with its promise of a free-and-easy lifestyle filled with possessions—that attracts the casual as well as the compulsive gambler, over and over, to continue to wager.

What is intriguing, however, is that since the odds are always against those who gamble, the end result of continuous gambling must be a loss. Some gamblers do win some of the time, but all gamblers must eventually lose if they gamble long enough. Rare is the gambler who, having wagered and won, is willing to call it a day at the races or at the casino. Instead the gambler often overstays at the track or the table, betting again and again in hopes of win-

With the legalization of gambling by so many states, more and more people are being attracted to wagering. The odds, though, are stacked against players, with the worst odds at a casino being at the slot machines.

ning more and more. And what so often happens is that, either that day or over time, less and less is kept, first of winnings and then of the sum originally slated for wagering.

Why is the gambler so blind to this eventuality? Why do so many buy lotto tickets when, as we will see, the chance of winning a big payoff is literally less than that of being hit by lightning?

Because the key ingredient in gambling is greed, along with the eternal hope for a lot of something for little or nothing.

The Portrait of the Compulsive Gambler:
It's Not a Pretty Picture

When Dr. Valerie Lorenz testified in 1984 before a United States Senate subcommittee studying state lotteries and gambling, she had already had fourteen years' experience researching and working in the field of compulsive gambling. She reported that national trends emerging in gambling were "cause for alarm" and that the number of compulsive gamblers in the United States was "rapidly increasing"—rising from an estimated 1.1 million in 1975 to as much as 6 to 10 million by the time of her testimony.

Dr. Lorenz listed a number of reasons for the escalation:

- **The growing availability of legalized gambling**—Legal gambling, previously confined to horse or harness racing in most states, dog races and jai alai in a few states, some state lotteries, and casino gambling in Nevada, had now become readily accessible and financially possible for almost everyone and was no longer confined to just the people with the time and money to travel to Nevada or go to a racetrack.

- **Video and gaming machines tied into payoffs**—Video machines on which can be played poker, blackjack, or other games of chance billed as "for amusement only" are often tied illegally into payoffs by the establishment in which the machines are located. The machines can now be found in heavily trafficked areas, such as arcades, restaurants, and bowling alleys, as well as more private places, such as bars, clubs, and pool halls.

- **State lotteries**—New Hampshire offered a state-sanctioned lottery to raise money for education in 1963 and thereby started a trend eventually followed by many other states. The result is that the airwaves and newspapers and magazines are filled with advertising promoting not only lotteries but the excitement and thrill of gambling.

- **The women's liberation movement**—The change in the status of women and their emancipation has led to a growth in the numbers of women gambling. Their increased earning power means easier access to cash for gambling, and they move more freely now into casinos and bars without a male escort. The same is true also of minorities and low-income groups, for whom many social barriers have been lifted.

- **Social acceptance of gambling**—The previous concept of gambling as illegal and sinful has largely eroded as legalized gambling became more widespread. Bingo, for instance, has spread beyond just the churches and fire halls. It can now even be found in schools and shopping malls.

As a result of these factors, the profile of the typical compulsive gambler has shifted from that of the middle-aged, middle-class white male betting on horses, sports, cards, or casino games. As seen at Gamblers Anonymous meetings, it now includes females, blacks, and lower-income people.

Gambling addictions also now involve lottery and poker machines. "Poker machine addicts now include teenagers, retired people, men and women, usually lower-educated people, and individuals from all levels of vocations, from unskilled laborers to clerks, bartenders, salespersons, and professionals," Dr. Lorenz testified.

The disquieting statistic involving lottery and poker machine addicts is the much shorter time period in which the addiction sets in as contrasted to the more traditional compulsive gambler. Instead of a pattern of typically ten to fifteen years from the onset of gambling to compulsive gambling involving "hitting bottom," the time span with lottery and poker machine addicts is dramatically reduced—to as little as a few months.

Dr. Lorenz's conclusion: With more and more states looking to lotteries for revenue, with the widespread push for legalized gambling, the nation faces "the urgent need" for prevention programs, community education, training of mental health professionals schooled to treat gambling addiction, and treatment for the compulsive gambler and his or her family. Dr. Lorenz pointed out that at the time of her testimony less than a dozen professional inpatient treatment programs existed in the United States for the millions of compulsive gamblers—with a bed capacity of approximately a hundred. And the number of professionally trained mental health therapists with experience or training in the field of compulsive gambling numbered less than a hundred.

And yet, she noted, "compulsive gambling behavior results in broken homes, serious medical problems, suicide attempts, domestic violence, and child abuse. Financial problems result in loss of home, bankruptcies, increased welfare costs, and a variety of crimes, both violent and nonviolent."

What is needed is for the nation "to seriously consider the impact of legalized gambling on the community, on the family, and on the individual." She called for a national policy on compulsive gambling.

A decade later, little has been done except that state governments have made legalized gambling even more widespread in our society.*

Lady Luck Has No Place at a Gaming Table

The greedy impulse is so strong in gambling that everything is marshalled in pursuit of the payoff—even, or especially, luck. If the gambler is on a hot streak, he tends to go with his "luck" and continues doing the same thing and taking the same action as before. (Who has not heard of the gambler who finds he or she has a lucky piece of clothing and keeps wearing it during a winning streak?) The reverse is certainly true—a run of bad luck will drive the gambler to try anything different to make the gaming table a luckier environment. But greed is so blinding that few seem to understand the full nature of "luck" versus the laws of probability.

Consider that run of good or bad "luck." Say you have just rolled a series of dice, each totaling an odd number. You now have to bet on the next roll. Will the total be odd or even? Many people, especially those who believe in good or bad luck, will say that since their luck is hot the hoped-for result of another incredible roll of odd-numbered dice will hap-

---

*The increase in compulsive gambling can be seen in the growth of Gamblers Anonymous. First formed in Los Angeles in 1957, Gamblers Anonymous had 170 chapters by 1972, 524 in forty-two states by 1983, and 870 chapters in all fifty states by 1994—plus another 600 worldwide. Canada, England, and Germany have the most chapters outside the United States.

pen. Others will say that their luck, no matter how good or bad it is, cannot hold out for such a length of time and will bet the next roll will come out with an even number.

Tests have actually been done to determine the answer to this question. In one such experiment,* a machine was used to toss dice over two million times, during which time the results were closely surveyed. What was especially studied was what happened after an extended run of odd or even totals. Here is the breakdown:

- In the 7,461 times in which seven odd totals occurred in a row, 914 times (12.25 percent) the seven odds were followed by three more odd totals.

- Another 926 times (12.41 percent) seven odds were followed by three even totals.

- A total of 5,621 times (75.33 percent) the seven odds were followed by a mixture of odds and evens in the next three rolls.

- On 11,158 occasions (49.85 percent) an odd total followed seven odds in a row, while an even total followed seven odds in a row 11,225 times (50.15 percent).

In other words, there was virtually no difference in the occurrence of odd or even totals after a string of seven odd totals. And the reason is obvious: Since the dice do not have any emotions or feelings, they are not affected by what they just did or what they did over any length of time. Each roll of the dice is therefore independent of the other, and the chances of an even or an odd total emerging on any throw of the dice are always the same—fifty-fifty—no matter what has happened in the near or distant past.

No one, when it comes to the laws of probability, has any more or any less luck than any other human being. What separates us is our intelligence and our abilities. Greed blinds the gambler to that fact, leaving him or her in blind pursuit of Lady Luck to make the all-important difference.

There is a name for this. It's called . . .

*See a discussion of the psychology of luck in *Winning Monopoly* (New York: Harper & Row, 1985) by Kaz Darzinskis, who reports on the results of this experiment.

The Monte Carlo Fallacy

The reliance on the "law of averages" to bring someone success at gambling is referred to by statisticians as the Monte Carlo Fallacy. It is the notion that somehow the past and future results of a spin of the wheel or play of dice showing even or odd numbers will eventually result in odd and even numbers turning up equally.

But the scientific truth is that on each spin or roll there is the same fifty-fifty chance that the next roll or the rolls thereafter will turn up an even or an odd number. There is no way to predict a future result based upon a past happening in a game of chance.

All You Need to Know About Gambling in Las Vegas

Mario Puzo, the author of the runaway best-seller *The Godfather*, is by his own admission a lifelong gambler—a degenerate gambler, he calls himself—who while an advocate of the pleasures of gambling acknowledges that "gambling has been terribly destructive to certain periods of my life." In fact, he says, his second novel took ten years to write partly because he spent so much time gambling.

Puzo's insights about gambling, then, are noteworthy. And they can be found in his narrative in a book with 150 photos of Las Vegas entitled *Inside Las Vegas* (New York: Grosset & Dunlap, 1977).

What are some of his findings about gambling, especially gambling in Las Vegas?

Stay away from slot machines, he says. Casinos make most of their money there. Rather, he advises blackjack for a surprising reason—it is "the only casino game in which, believe it or not, the player can work a percentage or edge against the house." In short, blackjack provides the only game of chance in a casino in which it is mathematically possible for the player to win more times than lose.

A computer has been used to prove that the player can legitimately beat the house in blackjack, according to Puzo. This happened when scientists at the Atomic Energy Laboratory in Los Alamos, New Mexico, used idle computer time to explore such a possibility. And a Maryland man at the Army's Aberdeen Proving Ground built an electronic box with a computer that told him when to "take a hit or not" while playing blackjack. Also, Puzo tells of Edward Thorpe's book on beating the dealer, which was based on computer analysis. But in all such cases, points out Puzo, "All this stuff means nothing because if anyone does figure out how to beat the dealer the rules will be changed or the cards reshuffled after each hand."

Puzo's ultimate message about Las Vegas is one of warning. "I love Las Vegas but I must tell you that you cannot wind up a winner there over any period of time. It's just that the house percentage or 'Edge' cannot be beat by an honest player," he writes.

"Sure, you may win on some trips. You may win five, six, or seven trips in a row. But eventually you will get wiped out. Remember, a losing streak is far more deadly than a winning streak is benevolent. And that's all you have to know about gambling in Vegas."

In Roulette, Does Red Have the Edge?

The gambler's straining for the edge, no matter how slight, can be vividly seen in an intriguing possibility raised by Mario Puzo in *Inside Las Vegas*.

Puzo relates that red and black paint have different chemical compositions and cause different reactions when applied to a surface. Red paint soaks into the wooden fibers of the roulette wheel, thereby causing the pockets painted red to be less resilient than otherwise. The result: The roulette ball will tend to stick in a red pocket rather than jump out. Black, on the other hand, causes the painted wood fibers of the slot to become harder, thereby making the roulette ball more likely to bounce out.

Although Puzo points out that "this is not a proven theory because the percentage is so small and tests have not been made to prove it out," his message is that playing red more than black may prove to give the player the longed-for "edge."

However, as Puzo notes later, such tactics "do not overcome the house percentage of 5 plus." For experienced gambler Puzo, the message about roulette, whether red or black, is the same: "If you are looking to cheat the house or beat it legitimately, forget about roulette. It's basically a sucker's game."

215

●●●

ANOTHER REASON WHY IT'S HARD TO WIN AT GAMBLING

" . . . the whole recorded history of gambling in every civilization shows that when you have gambling you have cheating."

—MARIO PUZO,
Inside Las Vegas

●●●

Bet-a-Million Gates May Have Been One in a Million

Over the course of a lifetime, gamblers do not usually come out ahead. One who defied these odds was a gambler known as Bet-a-Million Gates.

Gates made a fortune in the production of barbed wire that had proved useful in the open spaces of the West for keeping cattle penned in. This wealthy American, however, was also a compulsive gambler who would bet freely on horse racing and any other activity where he could place a wager.

He won his nickname when he actually won not a million dollars but six hundred thousand on a horse race—the Stewards' Cup won, appropriately enough, by Royal Flush, a horse named for another gambling activity.

One story about Gates that shows his compulsive gambling nature tells of a man approaching him as he arrived in Kansas City. Knowing of Gates's reputation, the man asked him if he would like to bet $40,000 on a coin toss. Without pausing, Gates agreed, took the coin, and tossed it into the air, calling out his choice. When the coin landed, Gates was the winner of the huge bet—all in the space of seconds.

Gates had the ultimate victory in gambling. When he died, he was worth more than $50 million. He was one gambler who at least had more winners than losers at the end—even if he couldn't take it with him.

●●●

"Nobody ever bet enough on a winning horse."

—RACETRACK ADAGE

●●●

A Greed Moment in History

The largest slot machine jackpot in Las Vegas history was a $5.1 million jackpot on March 12, 1991, at a $1 Megabucks progressive slot machine at the Mirage Hotel. A retired machinist from Kaufman, Texas, had been playing for ninety minutes when four "Lucky 7" symbols suddenly lined up.

"I was so excited I couldn't say anything," said Harold Williamson. "I realized I had won, but I think all the blood went out of my head."

The irony in this is that veteran bettors look down at slot machines, saying they offer the worst odds of all the betting possibilities at a casino.

The Pursuit of Happiness, Lottery Style

Those who play the lottery may not realize it, but the odds of hitting it big are so slim that a person is more likely to be struck by lightning in any one year than win the lottery.

If people viewed lottery wagers as a form of taxation—which it is, since without lotteries most states would have to raise taxes to supplant lottery revenues they have now come to rely on—then people would revolt. The best payoff in America is offered by Massachusetts, and they offer only 59 cents on every dollar wagered. Which means the people of Massachusetts lose on the average 41 cents every time they bet a dollar. And Massachusetts, remember, is the best-paying state of all.

At least one thing is gained by such a payout. Massachusetts also racks up the highest per capita wagering on its lottery: $235 per person is spent on their lottery. This is followed by Washington, D.C., with $197; Maryland, $185; Connecticut, $162; New Jersey, $155; Michigan, $132; Ohio, $128; Pennsylvania, $121; Illinois, $113; and, to round out the top ten, Delaware with $89.

To see how much is being spent—and lost—just multiply those numbers by the number of people in each state. The problem with the state lotteries is that they have been set up to stimulate greed, but the odds have been rigged to make certain that lightning will readily strike . . . elsewhere.

••

THE GREED DICTIONARY

"**Moneygrubber**—Anybody who grabs more money than you can grab."

—LEWIS AND FAYE COPELAND,
10,000 Jokes, Toasts & Stories

••

Are They More Than Just Spectator Sports?

The popularity of gambling can be seen in how many attend those sporting events that also have a betting component, such as horse racing, dog racing, and jai alai, as opposed to sports in which the pleasure is in the watching (or supposed to be, since betting on these games is illegal), such as baseball, football, and basketball.

America's most popular spectator sport, ranked by attendance, is horse racing, with nearly 70,000,000 annual attendance. Greyhound racing ranks number five, with 26,477,000, and jai alai number nine with 6,414,000. The annual attendance in the three highest-profile sports— major league baseball (number two with 53,800,000), professional football (number six with 17,000,000), and professional basketball (number seven at 13,700,000)—totals 84,875,000, a figure easily beaten by the nearly 103,000,000 attendance at sports events built around gambling.

The Most Popular Forms of Gambling

At the beginning of the 1990s, the following forms of gambling were ranked by *Gaming & Wagering Business* as the ten most popular (in terms of dollars wagered in 1990):

1. Casinos ($195.9 billion)
2. Illegal sports ($27.3 billion)
3. Lotteries ($19.4 billion)
4. Illegal horse books ($8.1 billion)
5. Illegal numbers ($5.5 billion)
6. Charitable games—nonbingo ($3.9 billion)
7. Cardrooms ($3.8 billion)
8. Bingo ($3.77 billion)
9. Greyhounds ($3.2 billion)
10. Legal books ($1.4 billion)

The total amount wagered in just these ten activities in 1990 was more than $270 billion—which was more than the U.S. deficit that year.

'TIS BETTER TO BE ON A RECEIVING LINE— BUT SLOWER

"When it comes to spending money, society makes life easy.

"Yet when it is our turn to be on the receiving line, things get complicated, drawn-out and delayed.

"For instance, count the number of people served per minute in crawling unemployment and welfare lines; now, see how rapidly the lines of waiting customers are served at racetracks and casinos. The profit motive is a good reason to run things with true efficiency."

—THEODORE LIPPMAN, JR., columnist,
The Baltimore Sun

Cut the Cards: Fascinating Facts About Gambling

Monte Carlo is an international gambling center that is part of the principality of Monaco. Everyone is allowed to gamble in Monte Carlo except one group of people—the citizens of Monaco themselves.

*   *   *   *

Gambling debts are not legally collectible.

*   *   *   *

In Las Vegas, casinos are set up to keep 18 to 20 percent of the money wagered.

*   *   *   *

The first known public lottery—sponsored by Augustus Caesar—was used to raise money to repair Rome. And the sailing of the *Mayflower* to colonize the New World was financed by a lottery in England.

*   *   *   *

On the average, bettors at horse racing tracks get back 83 percent of what they wager. Which means that over a period of time, for every $2 bet a horse player is given back only $1.66 by the track.

*   *   *   *

Expenditures on gambling have been found to be regressive—the lower-income groups spend a greater percentage of their income on gambling than do higher-income groups. In other words, with gambling, the poor get poorer—and the rich get slightly less rich.

*   *   *   *

Studies have found that the moral upbringing of gamblers differs from that of nongamblers. More than 50 percent of nongamblers were taught as children that gambling was sinful, whereas only 35 percent of gamblers were so taught.

*   *   *   *

The only major American religious body that teaches that gambling is inherently sinful is the Baptist church. The Methodist church strongly opposes all forms of commercial gambling, although it does not teach that gambling is a sin. Other religions, such as Judaism, teach that gambling is wrong in excess or take no position on the issue. Whatever their religious denomination, many people believe that gambling is sinful (40 percent of nongamblers gave this as a reason why they don't gamble).

*   *   *   *

A large motivating factor for many people to gamble is because it is exciting to wager money. "Excitement" or "to have a good time" are usually the most frequently given reasons in surveys of why gamblers gamble. And the most exciting form of gambling, according to survey responses, is horse racing—for bettors and nonbettors. The least exciting? Numbers playing.

*   *   *   *

Surveys have shown that when more forms of gambling are legalized in a state, an increase in gambling behavior occurs—both legally and illegally. Thus, legalizing gambling may not be an effective policy to combat illegal games and may in fact encourage such behavior. "Legalization increases public exposure to gambling and legitimizes the gambling activity; exposure to more types of gambling reduces negative attitudes toward other types of gambling. Both factors create favorable dispositions toward gambling and thereby encourage wider participation," wrote the Commission on the Review of the National Policy Toward Gambling in its final report entitled, *Gambling in America*. Corroborating this is the fact that gamblers report far more exposure to gambling as children than nongamblers and thus began life with less negative attitudes than nongamblers. The Commission reported: "For gamblers, their exposure to the activity apparently neutralized the moral teachings."

*   *   *   *

Although a significant number of Americans felt that gambling was wrong on religious or secular moral grounds, almost 80 percent of those surveyed favored legalization of some form of gambling. Thus, as the Commission discovered about this complex social phenomenon, "gambling is inevitable. No matter what is said or done by advocates or opponents of gambling in all its various forms, it is an activity that is practiced, or tacitly endorsed, by a substantial majority of Americans."

*   *   *   *

Gamblers have the highest suicide-attempt rate.

Bingo!

Of all forms of gambling, bingo has a number of intriguing facts and misconceptions about it.

Consider the following:

- Many people do not consider bingo gambling, but it is. In fact, in terms of participants, next to lotteries, bingo is the most popular form of gambling in the United States.
- In many places where bingo is openly conducted, much of the bingo operations are not sanctioned by state law and the bingo playing is actually illegal.
- Bingo's appeal cuts across sex, age, income, and education, with one governmental study showing that 19 percent of the United States population plays bingo.
- Only three forms of recreational activities are more popular than bingo playing—swimming, bicycling, and camping. In 1934, 70,000 people played in one game in New Jersey (another 10,000 were turned away).
- The stereotype of the bingo player is a middle-aged or elderly woman, but a federal study found that 16 percent of the male population plays bingo—more than bet on horses or place sports bets with bookies.

••

LAS VEGAS AS SEEN BY HENNY YOUNGMAN

- "I have property in Las Vegas. Caesars Palace has my luggage."
- "Las Vegas isn't a city—it's a garbage disposal for money."
- "Las Vegas is always crowded because no one has the fare to leave."
- "I love to go to Las Vegas—to be near my money."
- "I'm really unlucky. In Las Vegas, I even lost $10 on the stamp machine."
- "In Las Vegas the odds are you won't get even."

—HENNY YOUNGMAN,
The Encyclopedia of One Liners

••

- The same study also found that the highest proportional represen-tation of players was among those 25 years of age or younger—with players over the age of 65 having the lowest proportional representation.

- Bingo is a multibillion-dollar industry played by millions of people in all parts of the country, but it is also the most unregulated—or loosely regulated—form of gambling we have. This has led to abuses of proper policy of the games and to lost government rev-enues.

- Bingo is associated with charities because it is often sponsored by churches and service clubs, but few people seem to play the game because of its charitable aspects. The reasons most often given by bingo players for their participation is that the game gives them excitement and offers the chance to make money.

- Although seen as a form of fundraising, bingo games are many times operated by outside firms, with charities receiving only a small portion of the funds. Also, racketeers have been known to muscle into the operation of the games, with a recurring problem being the illegal skimming of funds (the practice of underreporting game income and pocketing the difference).

- Finally, bingo may seem a harmless enterprise, but scams by crooked bingo operators occur. One such scam: to avoid paying off jackpot or large money prizes, the operator arranges for a hired shill to use a card recorded earlier with the bingo parlor announcer. During the game, the announcer calls out numbers on the planted card so that the shill becomes the first to shout, "Bingo!" The prize money is then kept by the bingo operator (who probably then silently mouths "Bingo!" to himself).

Welcome to the innocent world of playing bingo.*

◆◆

SUPPORT BINGO
And Keep Your Grandmother Off the Streets
      —BUMPER STICKER SEEN BY AUTHOR ON BACK OF AUTO

◆◆

*In the aftermath of the successful bombing of Iraq during the Persian Gulf War of 1991, a joke making the rounds posed the question: What number when announced clears out an Iraqi bingo parlor? Answer: "B-52."

••

"Frankly, the idea of risking hard-earned money on the toss of the dice or the spin of a wheel seems slightly ludicrous to me personally."
—DONALD J. TRUMP,
owner of the Taj Mahal and several other casinos, in *Trump: Surviving at the Top*

••

♦♦

THE GREAT MISERS:

PEOPLE WHO WON'T DO ANYTHING TO A BUCK

A rich miser and a fat goat are of no use until they are dead.

—POLISH PROVERB

The ultimate greediness may be seen, ironically, in those who do not want to do anything with their money. They don't want to acquire possessions, live extravagantly, travel widely, or eat well. They just want money—money to have and to hold. These are the misers—defined by one dictionary as "a greedy, stingy person who hoards money for its own sake, even at the expense of his own comfort; a miserable person; wretch." In other words, these are people who literally will not do anything *to* a buck.

In our excursion through the many manifestations of greed, we have seen how avariciousness can lead to opulence, overindulgence, waste, frivolity, and, in the pursuit of excess, even crime. At the other end of the spectrum of greed are the miserly—people who so value money that they will not employ it for the good it can do for themselves or for others.

And as we will see, not even great wealth

225

protects against miserliness. From a woman reputed to be the richest nonroyal woman in the world to an oil tycoon considered when he was alive to be the richest man in the world, examples abound of misers denying themselves and others the benefit of their wealth—with sad results for those involved. For while greediness is a sorry trait to be avoided, so too is the miserliness that can result from what is essentially inordinate love of money.

As in most areas of life, when it comes to spending or not spending, the extremes are to be avoided. Moderation in matters of money is still the golden mean. After all, the miser gets his or her name from the Latin *miser*, or "miserable."

THE RESULT OF THE MISERLY APPROACH

"It is not economical to go to bed early to save the candles if the result is twins."

—CHINESE PROVERB

Getty's Miserliness Was Just a Phone Call Away

That wealth is no guarantee against miserliness—in fact, a number of cases suggest it may even cause it—can be vividly seen in the story of J. Paul Getty.

This oil tycoon generated a net worth that at his death in 1976 was placed at $6 billion, making him, when he lived, the world's richest person. Twenty years before, in October 1957, *Fortune* magazine deemed him the wealthiest American, with an estimated net worth then of $700 million to $1 billion, making him richer than Howard Hughes, Joseph Kennedy, or any of the Rockefellers, Mellons, Du Ponts, Whitneys, or Astors.

And yet, Getty engaged in the following miserly practices:

- He paid the gatekeeper to his estate $5.60 a week because, he figured, that was a proper multiple for the number of times needed to open and close the gates.

- Although he amassed a large art collection and eventually donated it to a museum that he formed (basically as a tax write-off), he rarely if ever gave personal charity ("You should use the money for your own business and not for charity," he told a journalist).

- Asked for charity, he would respond with a standard letter in which he "apologized" for not giving: "I don't have large sums of ready cash not required for my business. . . . There may be lots of people that have more money than I have and there certainly are lots of people that have more cash than I have."

- He continuously sought ways to avoid paying income taxes—so much so that in 1936, when his income was $122,000 (worth about $1 million today), he paid $258 in federal income tax. In 1961 he paid $503.69 in income taxes.

- He rarely turned on the heat at Sutton Place, his home in England, forcing guests to wear warm clothing, even overcoats, in their rooms. His explanation to visitors: the cold "was good for the art."

- When he stayed at the Ritz Hotel in London, he took the smallest and cheapest suite of rooms.

- He rarely if ever picked up the tab for dinner. Once, when Elsa Maxwell held a dinner party in Maxim's in Paris, he was handed the dinner bill. He looked at it, paid his own portion, and left. Maxwell, the gossip columnist who had invited the group of international figures, was furious.

- He hired art experts to authenticate art he had purchased largely for tax purposes but paid them at the smallest fees possible.

- Once sent a pocket watch as a gift from someone in another country, he asked that the parcel be refused, then inquired if it could be returned with someone who was traveling there so he could avoid the customs duty.

- He instructed a hotel where he had been staying to forward any mail to him in its original envelope so that he would not have to pay for stamps in a new envelope.

But Getty's most memorable act of parsimony—and the one that got the most publicity—was his installation of a pay telephone in his mansion, Sutton Place, soon after he purchased it in 1959. The phone, he said, was for use by his guests who might want to make a local or long-distance call. He even put up a sign on a wall nearby saying PUBLIC

TELEPHONE, and put locking devices on all other phones in the house. Although a call to London at the time cost only eighteen cents, Getty told inquiring reporters, "When you get some fellow talking for ten or fifteen minutes, well, it all adds up."

Getty, who allowed the press to photograph the coin-operated phone, defended his actions by saying he himself always used a nearby pay phone when staying with someone rather than use their phone. He also later told the *Saturday Evening Post,* "I had the pay phone installed in my place because I knew that guests preferred it that way. It saved them the trouble of settling with me afterward, or of attempting to pay for their phone calls."*

••

"The meek shall inherit the earth, but not the mineral rights."

—J. PAUL GETTY

••

What He Needed Was a Good Stiff Drink:

The Miser Wine Maker

Samuel Tapon was a wealthy French wine maker, with large vineyards in Cognac. In 1934 he lost $75,000 in a speculative venture.

Distraught, Tapon went to a village shop, haggled over the price of a long piece of rope, bought the rope, and then went home and hung himself.

At the time his estate was worth $2 million.

Even the Kennedys Had Their Miserly Side

It may come as a surprise, especially since they were a family of great wealth, but Joe and Rose Kennedy had their miserly moments.

In his biography of Jackie Kennedy, C. David Heymann quotes Judge

*See *The Great Getty: The Life and Loves of J. Paul Getty, Richest Man in the World* by Robert Lenzner (New York: Crown, 1985) p. 128–129. Lenzner notes that back in the late 1930s, Getty made aides working in the basement of his home in California use a pay phone for personal calls.

James Knott, former director of the Palm Beach Historical Society, as saying of the family that they were "incredibly frugal." He elaborated that he didn't mean in a strictly financial sense, as much as "they were ungiving—they never entered wholeheartedly into the social life of Palm Beach."

One case in point of frugality in a financial sense: The Kennedy home was in dire need of repairs, but Joe Kennedy would have only the front painted; since no one could see the side and back of the house, these were left as is.

Rose Kennedy was considered an even greater penny-pincher than Joe. She was notorious for not putting more than one dollar into the church collection plate, although she attended Mass every day. As for her treatment of the hired help, she would make the servants pay a dime for any bottle of Coca-Cola taken from the pantry between meals. So paltry was their pay that the servants called the Kennedy home "The House of the Minimum Wage."

History's Greatest Miser

At her death in 1916, she was considered the world's richest woman. Termed the "Witch of Wall Street," she also may have been the most eccentric.

Her name was Hetty Howland Green. Born in New Bedford, Massachusetts, in 1834 into a wealthy Quaker family, she had a strict upbringing combined with a grounding in business. She eventually inherited $5 million from her father's estate as a young woman and invested the money in railroads, real estate, and government bonds. She also added to her wealth when at thirty-two she married Edward Henry Green, a millionaire.

Eventually she accumulated a fortune worth close to $100 million. But after her husband died, her eccentricities and miserliness emerged full-blown. In fact, when her son hurt his leg, she searched so long for a free medical clinic that eventually he had to have his leg amputated.

But at least she didn't splurge on herself either. She often wore rags, lived in dilapidated boardinghouses, and regularly ate cold oatmeal because she didn't want to spend anything on heating it. She would argue with shopkeepers over small purchases and died, it is said, from apoplexy over an argument concerning the benefits of skimmed milk.

For these reasons, *The Guinness Book of World Records* gives Henrietta Howland Green the distinction of being history's greatest miser.

Your Money or Your Life:
The Big Question for Any Miser

One comedian built his comedic character around the trait of miserliness. He was Jack Benny, one of America's biggest stars in first radio, then television. In fact, so ingrained did he become in the public consciousness as the Great Miser that the following classified ad once appeared in a Sacramento newspaper:

> Two women, about Jack Benny's age, would like small unfurnished house. Would like to pay what Benny would like to pay.

Benny himself told the story that when he was a patient in Cedars of Lebanon Hospital he was given an empty bottle and asked to give a urine specimen. Having previously gone to the bathroom, he found it difficult to give more than a few drops of liquid. The nurse, upon returning and seeing such a small amount of urine, remarked, "You never give *anything* away—do you?"

The masterpiece of his "stingy jokes," as Benny referred to them, was also in his opinion the finest joke he ever did on radio. As he recounted in a manuscript he worked on but never published during his lifetime,* the joke involved his walking home one night when he is confronted by a crook. The holdup man presses a gun into his side and barks, "Your money or your life." There is then a long pause as Benny suddenly falls silent. The impatient holdup man then snarls, "Come on, hurry up."

In response, Benny blurts out, "*I'm thinking it over.*"

According to Benny, the laughter that erupted in the studio was clocked at over two minutes. "It built and built—stopped—and went on again. On a thirty-minute comedy show, this spread is as carefully budgeted as the salaries of performers."

But in his private life Benny was quite generous. And he treated

---

*See *Sunday Nights at Seven: The Jack Benny Story*, a biography of Benny by his daughter, Joan.

230

himself in unmiserly fashion to one possession of the rich: He owned a Rolls-Royce.*

Why You Can't Take It with You

Dorothy Parker, the writer with a crackling wit, once castigated a stingy producer who asked her to write a movie script but offered what she thought was too meager a payment. Snapped Parker, "You can't take it with you, and even if you did, it would probably melt."

The Fable of the Miser and His Gold

One of Aesop's fables deals with the personality of the miser, who would rather hoard wealth than use it:

Once upon a time there was a miser who used to hide his gold at the foot of a tree in his garden; but every week he used to go and dig it up and gloat over his gains. A robber, who had noticed this, went and dug up the gold and took it. When the miser next came to gloat over his treasures, he found nothing but the empty hole. He tore his hair and raised such an outcry that all the neighbors came around him, and he told them how he used to come and visit his gold.

"Did you ever take any of it out?" asked one of them.

"Nay," said he, "I only came to look at it."

"Then come again and look at the hole," said a neighbor. "It will do you just as much good."

The moral: Wealth unused might as well not exist.

*In his carefully created miserly world, Jack Benny had a valet named Rochester whom he paid little. On one show, Benny was heard musing about what to get Rochester for Christmas. Asked Benny: "What do you give a man who has nothing?"

••

OUR HERO:

THE MAN WHO CONQUERED GREED

Money is a good

servant, but a

bad master.

—FRENCH PROVERB

Money is not only dollars and cents, gold and silver. For many people it is also a symbol of self-worth, of self-esteem. In that sense, money and wealth can be easily misunderstood and misinterpreted. It has been shown that there are four primary motivators for amassing money—love, power, security, and freedom. But this can lead to the misperception that money can actually gain its possessor a full and lasting measure of love, power, security, and freedom—when in reality money itself raises doubts about love and causes its own insecurities.

"He that loveth silver shall never be satisfied with silver," said the preacher Koheleth in Ecclesiastes over 2,500 years ago. And nothing seems to have changed since then.

We say glibly that "money cannot buy happiness," but we throw ourselves headlong into the pursuit of money. And yet, we can only feel secure, loved, happy, and free when we finally have freed ourselves from greed, when we do things not out of our love for the value of money, but out of our love for life's higher values.

In this regard, let us end this survey of greed with a celebration of one who peered into the pit of avariciousness, who teetered on its precipice, and who then rescued himself from its destructive depths. A writer, he not only chronicled one of America's most flamboyant periods of greed (from 1860 to 1890), but gave it its name—the "Gilded Age." He is. . . .

Our Hero:
Mark Twain (1835–1910)

One person who lived through the ups and down that greed can cause—and yet who learned from the experience—was the great American author and humorist Mark Twain. His attempts at get-rich-quick schemes were no laughing matter. He went from being poor to being rich to being heavily in debt to being bankrupt to being financially sound—all during a lifetime marked by enormous success as a writer and dismal failure as a get-rich-quick businessman and investor. But because he came to see the error of his ways, strove successfully to pay his bills, and ended his avaricious pursuits, he truly triumphed over greed.

The first time Twain tried for great wealth was as a young man, when he went to California to seek his fortune amid the silver and gold fervor then building. He owned a trunkful of Nevada silver mining stocks that he believed eventually would be worth at least $100,000. Reaching San Francisco, he lived high, spending money freely while living at the city's best hotel. During a bull market for mining stocks, he bought on margin stock valued at $300 a share and waited for it to soar. And soar it did, going to $1,000 a share, then $2,000, then even higher and higher. But instead of selling, twenty-seven-year-old Sam Clemens held on, watching as the stock soared to $6,000 a share. And still he held on, expecting the stock to go even higher.

But it didn't. Suddenly, the stock reversed direction and started to plunge. And plunge. Twain was trapped and could not get out until the stock crashed. When the dust cleared, Twain found his stock was worthless. After he paid his hotel bill, he had only $50 to his name. He moved to a boardinghouse and, to survive, got a job as a reporter on a local newspaper.

Years later, Twain tried again. Now a world-famous author with considerable income and savings from his writings and lecturing, Twain became fascinated with the publishing business and with inventions. But the Webster Publishing Company, of which he was a director, eventually became caught in the panic of 1893–94 and went into bankruptcy on April 18, 1894, with debts of $94,000 owed to ninety-six creditors. Although Twain's wife had given over $65,000 of her personal inheritance in the last days in hopes of saving the company, and although Twain himself was not legally liable for the $94,000, he felt a personal obligation. At the age of fifty-eight, he was bankrupt. Ironically, his father had also been debt-ridden during his lifetime and to pay his debts had had to sell off, according to one biographer, all of his household goods, "down to the very spoons."

Compounding Twain's problem at the time was that he had been fascinated with an invention—a typesetter—and had sunk $190,000 of his own money over fourteen years into making the invention marketable. (At one point, Twain was putting $3,000 a month into the typesetter.) A test of the machine at a Chicago newspaper was disastrous. With 18,000 movable parts, the invention proved impractical. The machine never went into production, even though its inventor, James W. Paige, had spent twenty years building it and a total of $2 million overall was put into it by various investors. As the Twain biographer points out, "it was the costliest unworkable machine ever invented."

When Twain received the news that the machine would not prove to be his financial salvation, he wrote to a friend and financial adviser that "it shows how little we know ourselves and how easily we can deceive ourselves."

But Twain carried on, plunging himself into his writing and lecturing to pay off the $94,000 debt. He and his family also scrimped and saved to provide more money to debtors. However, Twain found this part of his situation consoling. He wrote to a friend that "there is such solid pleasure in *paying* the things that I reckon maybe it is worthwhile to get into that kind of hobby after all. Mrs. Clemens gets millions of delight out of it; and the children have never uttered one complaint about the scrimping from the beginning."

By the end of January 1898, Twain was able to pay off all the money owed by the Webster Publishing Company. In less than four years since his bankruptcy, he was free of debt. The achievement did not go unnoticed. The event generated considerable newspaper coverage, and editorials praised Twain's honorable payments.

Ironically, Twain once had a chance to invest in Alexander Graham

Mark Twain, the humorist, did not find humanity's greediness funny, since he himself went bankrupt pursuing get-rich-quick schemes. He eventually paid off his debts, however, and overcame his greedy ways.

Bell's telephone. He was offered a sum of stock at $500, but he turned it down, saying he had lost money before on newfangled dream devices.

Why do so many human beings always seem haunted by what they do not have and driven to want more?

It is one thing to have ambition to better oneself, to want fine possessions and to provide amply for one's family. It is another, as we have seen so often in these pages, to be unhappy with what by any sane measure should be measure enough.

Indeed, why have we witnessed repeatedly in history that periods of excess—on both personal and national levels—lead so often to sorrow and misery?

One intriguing insight into the avaricious personality comes from some ancient religious sages, as recorded in the Talmudic literature of close to two thousand years ago. Here in the Midrash (Koheles Rabbah 6:7) is the statement that "the soul is not satisfied" with human pleasures because it yearns for the heavenly realm. According to this view, this is why we are never truly fulfilled by wealth or riches. Mankind's urge for material possessions is, in fact, a thirst for the spiritual; the desire, for instance, to build and possess great, enduring structures—from the days of the pharaohs and their pyramids to our days of multimillionaires and their mansions—is really a reflection of the soul's eternal need for more than the ephemeralities of our physical, earthly existence.

The problem is that people seek to quench this void with money and the trappings of wealth, but all this does is leave the soul with a sense of emptiness. This is why the greedy never seem to assuage their greed. The ache can never be eased by seeking after more and more. The mystery of our greediness can be solved only by less concentration on materialistic, earthly pursuits and more concern about our human values and spiritual sides.

Since all human striving is in essence a striving after happiness, we can best find such peace by heeding several other great insights from centuries ago. Epicurus, the Roman philosopher, declared, "If thou wilt make a man happy, add not unto his riches, but take away from his desires."

And in *The Ethics of the Fathers*, the fifteen-hundred-year-old wisdom literature of the Jewish people, the question is asked, "Who is happy?"

The answer that is given is simple yet profound: "He who is satisfied with what he has."

This message of moderation is even more valid for our time.

ACKNOWLEDGMENTS

Although writing a book is largely a solitary effort, an author invariably finds helping hands—from typing and research assistance to editorial midwifery—that make book writing far from a lonely pursuit.

To thank those who have aided and abetted in the creation of this work, I would first like to cite my mother, Ida Goldberg, who was helpful in many ways during the book's long gestation period. She was an early reader of the manuscript as it emerged and was always encouraging, as she has been with all of my literary pursuits since I was eight years of age and discovered my father's typewriter in the basement of our home. For her words and acts of comfort and support throughout the writing of this book, I offer my heartfelt appreciation.

My children, to whom this book is dedicated, were also very encouraging throughout the writing process. Aviva, my oldest, and Seth, my youngest, were very interested and helpful, as was my son-in-law, Scott, who provided important feedback. I especially want to recognize the input of my son Stuart. As a successful vice president of a Wall Street firm even at his young age, he was intrigued with my research and with the way the book took shape and he offered many invaluable suggestions along the way. His insights proved to be a key factor in the finished work.

Others who helped me in various ways were my brother, Victor, who read much of the manuscript and provided me with excellent input and ideas, and Dr. Sheldon Glass, Dr. Arnold Blumberg, Ned Rubin, and

Robert Mead, who offered suggestions for use of material. For typing various parts of the work in progress or helping with aspects of the research, I thank Melissa Goldman, Michelle Hochberg, Sheila Jacoby, Kelly Putman, and John Stefancik.

I want to cite the work of this book's illustrator, Ray Driver, who once again showed what a fine artist he is. His caricatures have now enlivened three of my books, and they are all better for his creativity. He is a delight to work with, and his work is a delight to look at. I also thank my agent, Mitch Douglas, who was supportive of the concept of this work from the beginning and eagerly pursued its success.

I am very appreciative of the help of the librarians in my hometown of Baltimore who put up with my research requests, requests that literally came at all hours (the Enoch Pratt Free Library in Baltimore has a Night Owl service good until 11:45 P.M.; the service was very much used during the nights I worked on this manuscript).

Finally, I want to thank my editor, Andy Dutter, along with his assistant, Tom Darling, for their assistance throughout the more than three years that it took to bring this book from idea to published reality. I especially want to extend my appreciation to Andy for his unflagging enthusiasm, his deft way with an editor's pencil that didn't drive me daft, and his excellent suggestions for addition of material or changes that significantly improved the final work. In this regard, I also thank copyeditor Judy Steer for her efforts, which were invariably on-target.

Having thanked all these people, I still must point out that I alone am responsible for any lapses or errors in this book. Of course, that also means that, fittingly with a book on greed, I get to keep the proceeds. Samuel Johnson, the great eighteenth-century English author, once remarked that "no man but a blockhead ever wrote except for money." I am, I hope, not a blockhead, but I find there is much joy for an author in simply writing a book that others may come to read and savor. But let us also not overlook the joy there is for an author in creating a book that others want to buy. May this book bring much enjoyment to your life; may it bring me much with which to enjoy my life.

—M. HIRSH GOLDBERG
Baltimore, Maryland
January 11, 1994

INDEX

239

About the Author

M. Hirsh Goldberg is the author of four other books and more than 450 columns and articles in numerous magazines and newspapers. He has lectured widely in the United States and Canada, and has appeared on such national television programs as *The Joan Rivers Show* and *Good Morning America*.

Mr. Goldberg is a graduate of The Johns Hopkins University, with a bachelor's degree in English and a master's degree in teaching. A public relations executive accredited by the Public Relations Society of America, he was press secretary to the mayor of Baltimore at the age of twenty-four (he was then the youngest press secretary to a mayor of a major American city). He has also served as press secretary to the governor of Maryland.

A native of Baltimore, Maryland, Mr.Goldberg heads his own Maryland-based public relations agency, serving corporate and health care clients. He lives with his family in a suburb of Baltimore.